Mobilities of Self and Place

Mobilities of Self and Place

Politics of Wellbeing in an Age of Migration

Mahni Dugan

ROWMAN &
LITTLEFIELD
————INTERNATIONAL

London • New York

Published by Rowman & Littlefield International Ltd
6 Tinworth Street, London, SE11 5AL, UK
www.rowmaninternational.com

Rowman & Littlefield International Ltd.is an affiliate of Rowman & Littlefield
4501 Forbes Boulevard, Suite 200, Lanham, Maryland 20706, USA
With additional offices in Boulder, New York, Toronto (Canada), and Plymouth (UK)
www.rowman.com

British Library Cataloguing in Publication Data
A catalogue record for this book is available from the British Library

ISBN: HB 978-1-78661-160-4

Library of Congress Cataloging-in-Publication Data Available
ISBN: 978-1-78661-160-4 (cloth :)
ISBN: 978-1-5381-4805-1 (pbk :)
ISBN: 978-1-78661-161-1 (electronic)

∞™

To all the children
past, present, and future,
may your senses
of self and place
bring well-being
and opportunity to flourish
wherever you may be

Contents

Figures

All photographs prepared by Chris Holmes of Creolumen
Photography.
Graphic (2.2) prepared by Ella Hoban-Kelleher.

Acknowledgements

Connections with many people and places inspired me to write this book with its focus on contemporary migration, and as I bring the project to its conclusion I am mindful of its beginnings. As a child in the 1950s, growing up in the slums in inner-city Sydney, I experienced great kindness from migrants of the day, mostly Greek, Italian, and Maltese families seeking a better life in Australia, far from post-war Europe. They accepted me into their communities, fed me wonderfully tasty food, and cared for me when I needed that. Among other things, from them I learned early that my life is richer when I include people who are different than me. The opening of a detention centre for asylum seekers in Tasmania in 2011 and my subsequent involvement with refugees provided another significant thread. I am deeply grateful to the people I met both through those circumstances and in the years between who contributed to my learning, personally and professionally, and to my motivation to write this book.

My thanks go to Rowman & Littlefield International for enabling publication, and I am grateful to Gurdeep Mattu, Natalie Linh Bolderston, and the publishing team for their support and care in bringing the project to fruition. Elaine Stratford and Aidan Davison introduced me to the breadth and beauty of the discipline of human geography, and they were the first to encourage me to write this book. I am grateful, also, to the Institute for Study of Social Change at the University of Tasmania for funding early structuring of the project. I especially thank Elaine Stratford for taking time from her very full academic schedule and personal life to generously give me encouragement, information, guidance, and invaluable commentary on the drafts. Others to whom I am grateful for encouragement, reading, and suggestions are Millie Rooney, Phillipa Watson, James Parker, Sue Benner, Amelie Doran, and my stepmother, Joan Collins – herself an historian – who remembers how things were and cares that knowledge is passed on *and* that people *think* about it. I cannot thank enough Chris Holmes, of Creolumen Photography, for his generosity, expertise, and patience in preparing all of the photographs to illustrate the book. I thank Ella Hoban-Kelleher for translating my concept of a rhizomatic relationship between self and place into a diagram that works, and acknowledge her for grasping the idea so quickly. Acknowledgement is also due to Steve Street, who saved me from death by bibliography via an unstable relationship between Word and Endnote, and who has a magic touch when it comes to computers. Thanks also to the librarians and the document delivery service at the University of Tasmania – they make a difference that matters very much.

For his early recognition and encouragement for me to contribute through writing, I thank Stuart Hill, who is a founding father of the discipline of social ecology, and John Cameron and David Wright, both of whom were instrumental in having me bridge from lived experience to academia. This book could not have been written without the immeasurable contribution of all the authors cited and the many others whose work has provided foundation for my learning and understanding. I am indebted equally to them and to the people who have worked with me, individually and in groups, during the past forty years.

Most specifically, I thank the ten people who participated with me in a deep case study of the relationship of senses of self and place to well-being when migrating. Our conversations were personal, privileged, heartfelt, and evidence of how much each one of them also cares about the well-being of people in our world. They gave me permission to use their first names as well as their stories, so thank you, Carol, Carola, Connie, Julian, Jun, Kiros, Khadga, Nene, Shoukat, and Yukari.

And finally, thank you to my family and especially my husband, Geoff, for giving me the time and *place* to be and to express my *self.* Without you, I may not venture so far as to write a book that bridges from theory back into practice.

Part I

CONCEPTUAL FRAMES

At a time of migration crisis, some at the extreme right of politics sensation-alise suffering in order to justify tighter controls of borders and populations, and others claim that the crisis reveals a genuine human emergency. This situation raises deep moral issues and questions of human rights. Underlying this state of affairs are two fundamental assumptions: that human nature is flawed, and that people must stay in one place to achieve any kind of well-being. Contesting those beliefs, I explore human agency to think, to question, and to bring about change, personally and socially. I think about the complex relationality of senses of self and senses of place as central to discovery of how, in circumstances of contemporary migration, well-being may be engendered and provide opportunity for both people and place to flourish.

The number of topics that need to be addressed in relation to a politics of well-being in an age of migration is such that it begs the use of an approach developed recently by geographers John Horton and Peter Kraftl.[1] These two consider it urgent to reconcile autoethnographic accounts with readings of theory. To that end, they argue "for a move from *intersectional* to *extra-sectional* analyses that might retain intersectionality's critical and political purchase, whilst simultaneously folding social-material complexities and vitalities into its theorization". In a study of children's playgrounds they suggest that "social-scientific accounts habitually . . . foreground . . . *either* universalized, macrogeographical statements about play *or* microgeographi-cal particularities of play-itself", with the result that social-material *processes* are often "hidden in plain sight". Their argument can apply just as fully to accounts of any lived experience, and their approach is particularly relevant to this book as it draws both on insights and select theories from several disciplines, and narratives of people whose lived experience includes diverse migrations.

Part I sets the scene for the extrasectional work to come by critically outlining conceptual frames and theory related to mobility, place, self, and dynamics of the relationship of the self to itself. It explores how these factors are co-constituent of senses of self and place, and describes how prevailing meta-narratives promote alienation of people from self and place. A model of self-place relating indicates how senses of self and place are implicated in people's ability to migrate with well-being and agency. This first theoretical section concludes with a summary of the contemporary global situation of regular, refugee, and asylum-seeker migrants, and provides a brief history of Australia as background for narratives of lived experience that follow.

Introduction: Framing the Challenges

[As] the complexities and difficulties in the world increase . . . I am deeply convinced that these problems cannot be solved at all unless we boldly search for and revise our antiquated notions about the "nature of man" [*sic*].[2]

Human beings do not stay put; they never have. Wanderings and migrations of people have distributed and redistributed populations throughout history and even prehistory. Significant redistributions continue.[3]

Two decades into the twenty-first century, unprecedented levels of migration and displacement of people globally face us with profound moral as well as logistical challenges. Responses at international, national, and state levels have been woefully inadequate and failed to ensure the well-being of people and place. In 2015, media, political groups, and the United Nations Refugee Agency (UNHCR) variously declared a world migration crisis. Since then, tensions continue to rise and the tone of public debate has become openly aggressive.[4] Politically, reactions to migrants continue to polarise as conservative, nationalist, right-wing groups seek to tighten border controls and those on the more liberal left aim for greater inclusion and support of others. Refugees and asylum seekers attract most attention, but exigencies of migration also affect vaster numbers of regular migrants and people resident in places of origin, transit, and resettlement. Contemporary global migration – voluntary, of necessity, or coerced – challenges us to discover how we might engender well-being in these circumstances.

Much current literature and research focuses on extrinsic conditions and top-down politics: global and nation-state reactions and responses to migrants challenging borders, policies, ideologies, resources, and institutions. Such emphasis is obviously appropriate given the demand for change and improvement in the conditions many migrants face physically and in terms of basic human rights. Nevertheless, there is also a need for research and response in regard to *intrinsic* factors, beyond remedial work with trauma and mental ill-health, to focus on well-being rather than on illness. In this work, I address that challenge by investigating how people's internal states affect their well-being or lack of it, whatever the conditions, and by exploring how people can proactively change those states to increase well-being in diverse circumstances of migration.

When it comes to migration, there is no level-playing field. Some people are privileged, advantaged, and supported and others are marginalised, persecuted, and traumatised. Yet neither the extension of the rights or equalities for which many people advocate, nor provision of other extrinsic conditions *alone* is sufficient for well-being. This work asks: What is sufficient? Individually and collectively – what is it that people do – and can do – to change their own and others' experience from suffering to well-being, whether as migrants or as those already resident in places of transit and resettlement?

This book is about the agency of people – members of the general public – not all of whom are classed as citizens in the places where they live. It is concerned with the politics of everyday living: the relations between people and societies and the "production and distribution of power" among them.[5] Significantly constituting that politics are certain expression and manifestation of social, cultural, familial and – ultimately – individual assumptions, beliefs, narratives, and worldviews. Power produced and distributed from the top-down influences that politics. Forms and tools of governance that impact the politics of everyday living include law-making and law enforcement, the politics of ruling authorities and those who contest them, and diverse media that constantly moderate public thought. Here, I explore how common assumptions, beliefs, narratives, and worldviews of individuals and communities produce and distribute power from the bottom-up; how people's *senses of self and of place* contribute to the politics of everyday living and are significant in establishing the politics of well-being.

Considering processes by which people constitute their experiences through their beliefs, I examine some of the consequences of holding varying ideas as truths. Questions about human well-being ultimately bear on ontological questions about human nature. Two assumptions underlie – and fundamentally cause – much human suffering, beyond extrinsic conditions. The first – that *human nature is flawed* – is deeply embedded at the core of modern Western accounts of human nature; it is implicated in how people are valued and provides a foundation for people's senses of self. The second assumption – that *people must stay in one place to achieve any kind of well-being* – affects not only people's senses of place, but also their experiences of belonging and identity.

It is common to blame the flawed nature of human being for environmental, social, and individual problems. Some studies attribute environmental problems to alienation of people from place and social and individual problems to alienation of people from themselves.[6] I contend that *belief* that human nature is flawed is the deeper cause of alienation of people from self, from others, and from place that leads to those wider problems. Further, believing that there is something fundamentally wrong with people – including oneself – leads to other limiting ideas: for example, that some people are better or worse or of greater or lesser value than others, that some people are intrinsically good or bad, and that people who are different from oneself or one's culture are in some way threatening or dangerous. Such beliefs underlie situations of conflict, the problems and fears commonly associated with acts of migration, and principles underlying moral questions raised in regard to asylum seekers. How people are defined inevitably affects their behaviours and attitudes, as well as responses to them – as made obvious, for example, in racist reactions to migrants of different ethnic origins. Charles Taylor makes the point that such moral reaction assents to and affirms "a given ontology of the human":[7]

> Racists have to claim that certain of the crucial moral properties of human beings are genetically determined: that some races are less intelligent, less capable of high moral consciousness, and the like. The logic of the argument forces them to stake their claim on ground where they are empirically at their weakest. Differences in skin colour are undeniable. But all claims about innate cultural differences are unsustainable in the light of human history.[8]

Regarding the second assumption, is it true that well-being depends on people staying put? Does increasing migration mean that increasing numbers of people are destined for a rootless and alien existence of placelessness and anomie? Or is it possible to be both grounded in place and mobile – a question in which is embedded a series of other questions about how to conceptualise place, movement, and identity? What do these questions have to do with human rights – not just to life, but to quality of life? What rights do people have to move from place to place and to belong in place, show self-respect, and be accorded respect by others? What – beyond or even in spite of physical and other external conditions – provides opportunity for people to flourish? Taylor writes that to "talk of universal, natural, or human rights is to connect respect for human life and integrity with the notion of autonomy. It is to conceive people as active co-operators in establishing and ensuring the respect which is due them".[9] The issue is essentially one of agency, which depends both on rights accorded to people by governments or laws or other individuals or groups, *and* on people's senses of self. Perhaps the epitome of this latter dynamic is the remarkable story of the German Jewish psychiatrist Viktor Frankl (1905–1997). Frankl survived internment in Auschwitz concentration camp and went on to build a new life and to contribute to a positive understanding of human nature. In his words, "Everything can be taken from a man but one thing: the last of the human freedoms – to choose one's attitude in any given set of circumstances, to choose one's own way, [and further,] when we are no longer able to change a situation, we are challenged to change ourselves".[10]

As I see it, the challenge is not to change *who* or *what* we are, if that is even possible, but rather to change how we define ourselves – what we *think* who or what we are actually *is* – and to change what we do. What might be possible if we were to conceive differently of human being, that is, of the ontogenic process and potential of being human? I take as obvious that for both people and place to flourish, whether they are static or mobile, much needs to change in human behaviour. If we separate who we are – *being* – from our behaviour – *doing* – and presuppose that far from being flawed, human being is intrinsically wholesome, and conducive to well-being, what difference would that make to how we treat ourselves and each other?

So my intention here is to explore people's agency to *think* – to become aware of and change beliefs about themselves and others – and to change behaviour and the quality of their experience. Dynamics that are instrumental in the constitution of the self are relatively unconscious processes since we presuppose what we decided to believe at an earlier time, and also have absorbed many of those beliefs from our socio-cultural environment without question. And those beliefs are recursive – taking *as truth* that human being is flawed creates assumptions and practices that frame behaviour to confirm and perpetuate that there is something fundamentally wrong with self and others. The cost is that people are reduced to fit the belief. Here, I contest views that individual narratives are entirely culturally or socially determined and show that people *can* critique their assumptions and *do* have agency to change them. And further, when individuals change their own beliefs, they contribute to change and evolution of cultural and social narratives. I explore the intriguing interactions between and among narratives people embrace as reality and conditions they experience, and ask both how those contribute to their senses of self and of place, and what agency they have to change any of that. Three premises inform exploration of these dynamics:

> First, people's behaviours and experiences are bound up in self-validating ontological and epistemological beliefs.[11] For example, if people believe that their identities are tied to one place, relocation can threaten their sense of self. Often people experience themselves as displaced even years after migrating, and cling to the languages and customs of their places of origin unchanged from how they were when they left them.[12]

Second, ontological and epistemological beliefs and practices are woven into, and are at the core of narratives that establish what Michel Foucault called *conditions of truth*, and these determine how people know what they know, and what it is possible to know.[13] For example, if people believe that difference in others is a threat to themselves they are likely to maintain and assert their own ways, defend these against other customs, and believe that it is not possible to find value in different others. Such fear of difference can lead to "racist and xenophobic panics" that result in "ghetto-izing of immigrants".[14] Denmark's response to challenges of contemporary migration provides a chilling example: twenty-five residential areas are *official* ghettos, and the government is introducing a new set of laws "to regulate life in [those] low-income and heavily Muslim enclaves, saying that if families there do not willingly merge into the country's mainstream, they should be compelled".[15]

Third, problems that cannot be solved within the limits of the conditions of truth challenge the narratives underpinning them, and thus call into question the ontological and epistemological beliefs and practices at their core. Current challenges – specifically relating to mobility and migration – involve socio-political upheavals, ethnic cleansing and other abuses of human rights, definitions of citizenship, polarisation of disparate cultural and religious moralities and laws; racist, ethnic, cultural, and religious marginalisation; economic inequalities; and more personally, fears of loss, the erosion of ways of life, and other stresses of resettlement that lessen well-being and fuel fears of different others. In response, and with the hope of initiating positive change, my primary objective is to encourage people to question prevailing beliefs and assumptions underlying those challenging conditions. As Foucault came to argue, such questioning can lead people to free themselves from prescribed norms and old narratives.

In the course of working professionally over four decades enabling people to develop strategies for experiencing, maintaining, and enhancing their well-being, I came to understand two crucial keys: First, at the heart of human suffering are the negative meanings that people give to their own and others' experiences, which become part of their conscious and unconscious strategies and practices. Yet this suffering is not inevitable. Second, at the heart of well-being are other meanings people give to their own and others' experiences, and strategies and practices by which people value themselves, others and their worlds, and live in ways that affirm life.[16] These meanings, strategies, and practices form what Mitchell Dean calls *regimes of practice* – "the practices by which we endeavour to govern our own selves" – and they constitute the quality of intrinsic experience.[17]

People's regimes of practice are inextricably related to their experiences of migration and other mobilities, and to their senses of self and place. Recognition that self and place are interconnected has led to increasing multidisciplinary and interdisciplinary attention, but these multifaceted concepts are still often studied independently. However, as migration relates to and impacts upon people's senses *both* of place and of self, the extent of contemporary migration makes it compelling – even urgent – that we consider mobilities of these two senses together.

Mobilities denotes a field encompassing migration and the many ways in which it affects people and places. Such has been the extent of human movement in recent decades that John Urry called for a *new mobilities paradigm* in the social sciences to challenge the sedentarist focus he sees as implicitly underpinning most research.[18] Urry and Mimi Sheller claim that mobilities research valuably brings together a broad field covering a spectrum of human movement from the local to the global, and it also investigates the impacts of mobilities on people who stay in place; for instance, those providing services, raw materials, or other goods to more affluent places and people.[19] The plural form – mobilities – underscores the contingencies, multiplicities, and heterogeneity of this field that has grown significantly in the past decade across several disciplines and has attracted much recent attention from social theorists. Tim Cresswell, who defines mobility as "the entanglement of movement, representation, and practice", sees mobilities as inherently political; evidently, mobilities have implications for all.[20] Suffering and well-being are affected by people's freedom and ability to move or lack of it – to be pushed and pulled, sedentary, nomadic, or otherwise mobile in ways that are uni- or multidirectional, temporary or permanent, local or international. Mobilities are intimately associated with the ways in which place and self and senses of them are also mobile; that is, with how they are constituted, developed, modified, move, and change in varying conditions and over time.[21]

Given the complex relations between concepts of place and of nature, in this work I adopt a threefold understanding of *place*: first, the locations of geographical places; second, the attachments and meanings people have for places; and third, the "existential ground" from which human being emerges.[22] I understand *sense of place* as people's awareness of place in each of those ways. The state or quality of people's sense of place affects the quality of their experience and behaviour, including care for or neglect of places.

Among the widely contested definitions of *self*, I hold it as process – as *being*. I understand *identity* as the product of this process, at any given time. Thus, the self is always mobile – a work in progress – not a fixed thing. *Sense of self* I take to be awareness *of* oneself mediated by the meanings – and thus, identity or identities – one gives *to* oneself. If identity is taken to *be* the self, that is, if effect is mistaken for cause, then sense of self is limited to whatever is included in that identification, and flexibility of response is limited. However, if sense of self includes awareness of the processes of becoming that underlie identity, then the person experiences greater flexibility, more choices of response, and increased agency. Thus, the extent and meaning of a person's sense of self affects the quality of his or her experiences, sense of agency, and relationships with others, place, and movement.[23]

Recognising that both definitions and senses of self and place are infinitely mobile, I contend that dissonance arises when definitions are reified, and these senses are tied to specific locations – places – and to particular cultural and social representations of self – identities. Polarising those distinctions such that some people are identified as *Us* and the rest as some kind of threatening or lesser *Other* generates dilemmas of difference from commonplace racism to terrorism and violent conflict. Such disruptions are matters of the politics of everyday living – all too ordinary daily provocations and reflections of migration in today's world.

QUESTIONS OF RIGHTS, MORALS, AND ETHICS

In recent decades, the term *illegal* has been extensively used to identify people seeking asylum who arrive in a country without appropriate documentation. The 1951 United Nations Convention on Refugees and its 1967 Amendment define a refugee as

> a person who is outside his or her country of nationality or habitual residence, has a well-founded fear of being persecuted for reasons of race, religion, nationality, membership of a particular social group or political opinion; and is unable or unwilling to avail himself or herself of the protection of that country, or to return there, for fear of persecution.[24]

Although the United Nations High Commissioner for Refugees (UNHCR) insists that international law makes it entirely *legal* for individuals to seek refuge, national governments claiming and exercising *their* rights to control who can enter and who can stay in their territories generally declare that unauthorised asylum seekers are illegal refugees. Legality is conferred if people have applied for asylum and been deemed in need of refuge and protection, *prior to* entering a country. Others, arguably the most desperate, make hazardous journeys to plead for refuge and are classed as illegal entrants. The label – and stigma – of illegality has come into common use and is applied even to people who fail to reach any place where they might hope for sanctuary.

Writing in the aftermath of the Second World War, Hannah Arendt positions issues of rights as central to the dilemmas of asylum seekers.[25] The rights of *man* – proclaimed by the French and American revolutions – basically addressed rights of individuals within a nation-state. However, if people belonged to no nation then they had no rights. Arendt shows that although the rights of citizenship were defined as "inalienable", as soon as people were removed from the nation-state and lost their political status, "no authority was left to protect them and no institution was willing to guarantee them".[26] Arendt reflects that

> the great danger rising from the existence of people forced to live outside the common world is that they are thrown back, in the midst of civilization, on their natural givenness, on their mere differentiation. They lack that tremendous equalizing of differences which comes from being citizens of some common-wealth and yet, since they are no longer allowed to partake in human artifice, they begin to belong to the human race in much the same way as animals belong to a specific animal species. The paradox involved in the loss of human rights is that such loss coincides with the instant when a person becomes a human being in general – without a profession, without a citizenship, without an opinion, with-out a deed by which to identify and specify himself – and different in general, representing nothing but his own absolutely unique individuality which, deprived of expression within and action upon a common world, loses all significance.[27]

Although, since 1951, numbers of international laws and treaties based on the United Nations' Declaration of Human Rights have increased, and many states are signatories to them, some among them consistently breach the terms of these agreements, claiming primacy of national laws, and commitment to protection of refugees has declined.[28] Measures to minimise the refugee problem, which contravene international law, include *refoulement* – sending people back to the countries, and potentially life-threatening circumstances, from which they fled – imprisoning them in detention camps and simply refusing to let them in to places of safety.

It is common knowledge that uncounted numbers of people have died when pushed back into the desert from Libya, that thousands seeking asylum in the European Union have drowned in the Mediterranean, and far fewer but still too many en route to Australia, which now has one of the harshest border policies in the world. The Australian government has made *stop the boats* bringing asylum seekers to its shores into a mantra, but other sources refute its claims to have succeeded, and the United Nations has condemned the government's brutal imprisonment of asylum seekers in offshore detention centres. Such border policies are mooted in Australia, Europe, and elsewhere as a humanitarian response designed to save lives, but advocates for asylum seekers hold that this *glamour* conceals that the conception of contemporary migration as a "humanitarian crisis" is a contrivance: it is designed to weaken rights, promote border restrictions, justify military interventions, and mask a genuine "human emergency".[29]

Clearly, the global community is far from resolving the challenges of con-temporary migration and, as political theorist Chandran Kukasthas comments,

"It is hard to see how refugees will ever be given proper moral consideration. After all, the category of refugee was created by states not so much to enable us to fulfil our duties to the distressed and unfortunate as to make it easier for us to evade them".[30] In an interview in 1979 focused on the refugee crisis of his day, Michel Foucault says that such events are "an after-effect of the [colonial] past . . . [and] a foreshadowing of the future" that would continue to see forced migrations of populations involving millions unless the policies of states changed.[31] He contends that "No discussion on the general balance of power between countries of the world, and no argument about the political and economic difficulties that come with aid to refugees can justify states abandoning those human beings at the gates of death".[32]

It is increasingly obvious that we are facing both problems of logistics and deeply disturbing moral and ethical questions. If people have nowhere safe to live, then they are likely to die by violence, drowning, starvation, or disease.

Are national governments responsible for the deaths of asylum seekers when they refuse them entry to their territories? And by extension, are the citizens of those states culpable? Do we, instead, blame conditions in the asylum seekers' countries of origin or the individuals themselves for somehow not having the agency to avoid their circumstances? If we value human life, that is not morally defensible. But as Arendt clarifies, "It seems that a man who is nothing but a man [that is, when he has lost his citizen status] has lost the very qualities which make it possible for other people to treat him as a fellow-man".[33] Do we demonise people seeking asylum when, first we make them *not people,* and then, second, label them as illegal? Does that process shift responsibility for their deaths to them? And does that, then, become sufficient reason for denying them not just the right to flourish but to life itself?

Reporting the trial of Adolph Eichmann in 1961, Hannah Arendt identified genocide as a consequence of a failure to think. Considering not just Eichmann but, far more broadly, the Holocaust and other events of the Second World War and its aftermath, Arendt saw "a world in which true thinking was vanishing and, as a result, crimes against humanity became increasingly 'thinkable'. The degradation of thinking worked hand in hand with the systematic destruction of populations".[34] Considering events since that time – the many wars and on-going conflicts that have contributed to the extent of contemporary displacement and migrations of peoples, the extremes of fundamentalism playing out in terrorist events and in resurgence of nationalistic fear and fervour – I see a world in which Arendt's "true thinking" appears to glimmer and shine brightly for moments, but often seems only to flicker in a world where crimes against humanity are still "thinkable" and allowed to continue.

This book is an ambitious enterprise: I aim to unsettle certainties, to disrupt assumptions, to throw doubt on notions that some things are inevitable, to encourage questions that might open new possibilities, and to stimulate and engage in "true thinking". To that end, I position the moral and ethical and ontological questions raised here in the context of a broad inquiry into contemporary global migration. Using an *extrasectional* approach,[35] I engage both with theory – across several disciplines – and with practice, drawing upon the lived experiences of ten people whose diverse migrations and other mobilities provide a lens through which to consider the human condition. Movement from global to local, social to personal, intellectual to experiential offers a depth of understanding and personal engagement that I believe is critical to wider societal understanding of the phenomena and challenges of contemporary mobilities. Providing an overview that is missing from much current literature on migration, the scope of the work is indeed broad. Any of the various issues raised in the text could serve as the main focus of an entire book, and I hope that this work may stimulate further in-depth examination and research in at least several areas. To handle the breadth of material I have organised the work into four parts.

A MAP OF THE BOOK

I: Conceptual Frames

Part I provides the theoretic base to later examine and analyse lived experiences of migration. In the "Introduction: Framing the Challenges", recognising that current responses to unprecedented levels of migration and displacement of people globally are clearly inadequate in ensuring well-being of people and place, I contend that there is a need to explore what people can do themselves – individually and collectively – to engender greater well-being and opportunity to flourish. The situations within which refugees and asylum seekers are placed escalate this challenge and underscore the need to consider deep moral issues and questions of human rights. While it is obvious that the extent of people's suffering or well-being differs vastly in different circumstances, I contend that two fundamental assumptions underlie the current human condition – that human nature is flawed, and that people must stay in one place to achieve any kind of well-being. Contesting those beliefs, I explore human agency to think, to question, and to bring about change, personally and socially.

In chapter 1, "Mobilities of Place and Self", first I explore understandings of place and sense of place drawing on literature from philosophy, geography, social ecology, and place studies, and then I compare mobilities and sedentarism. Whatever may be the virtue of staying in one place, it is not always possible; noting this fact, I define strong and weak senses of place, and consider how that sensibility might affect people's relationships with different places. Second, I engage with literature from philosophy, sociology, social ecology, eco-psychology, and biology to investigate mobilities of self and sense of self. Although the delineation of what the self is may elude us, I describe how we know ourselves through our senses of self. Recognising that people derive their senses of self from the meanings implicit in the narratives they embody and perform, it is evident that people limit their experience of agency to what their narratives permit; and events such as migration challenge them to question long-held assumptions and to change those narratives.

In chapter 2, "Meta-Narratives and Agency", I acknowledge a dominant Western meta-narrative and consider dynamics of the "relationship of the self to itself" that make it possible to recognise when and how people constrain or free their agency. Discussing literature from political and historical sociology, philosophy, human geography, and history, I explore functions of beliefs, self-validating reduction, and semantic representations of self, others, and places. Defining strong and weak senses of self, I relate senses of self and place to qualities of experience in a rhizomatic model of self-place relations. The model shows how understanding factors of senses of self and place, and developing those sensibilities may help people to increase resilience and well-being.

Chapter 3, "All the World Is the Stage", sets the scene upon which lived experience of migration is played out in parts II and III. Distinction between mobilities and sedentarist opinions goes some way to explain the tensions implicit in contemporary migrations. A summary of migration over the past couple of centuries enables comparison with contemporary statistics that helps to delineate the scale of the problem. In some countries where regular and irregular migrations have contributed to a plurality of cultures and ethnicities, attempts have been made to assimilate disparate people, and other countries have aspired to multiculturalism. Now, however, deep rifts in the moral fabric of our times are revealed by a closer look at the escalation of irregular migration, reactions to it, and attempts of nation-states to tighten and control their borders and people within them. All this is background and provides the context necessary to locate the migrants whose narratives bring lived experience to following chapters. These people started life in different countries and most of them migrated to Australia, so I complete the chapter with a brief overview of that country – founded on migration, and exemplifying dilemmas of dealing with the challenges of contemporary migration that are faced by countries globally.

II: Lived Experience

Part II introduces a group of people – participants in a deep, qualitative case study – whose lived experience of migration and other mobilities is deployed throughout following chapters.

Although definition of a crisis lies in the sheer numbers of people migrating globally, the narratives shared with me by the participants show that understanding of these mobilities comes from the minutiae of the detail. These people have lived fascinatingly mobile lives and they represent a range of ethnic and cultural backgrounds as well as regular and irregular migrations. There is a vast difference in the scale of the severity of suffering experienced by these people, yet the difficulties they face – and which arise from their assumptions and beliefs about self and place – are essentially of the same character.

In chapter 4, "Regular Migrations", I introduce participants representative of regular migration from the 1950s to the present. Carol, a woman originally from Scotland, migrated as a child to Canada, and later as an adult to Australia. Carola, a German woman, came to Australia as a doctor and then applied to stay. Jun, a Japanese man, met his American wife, Connie, while studying in the United States. They lived in Australia for a time and then resettled in Japan. The stories of these people illustrate formation of senses of self in circumstances where basic rights and opportunities are taken for granted.

In chapter 5, "Irregular Migrations", four people exemplify experience of migration in the context of contemporary political dissent about people seeking asylum, onshore and offshore processing of their claims for refugee status, and the ignominy of detention centres. Kiros and his family fled Ethiopia and then survived for several years in Kenya before coming to Tasmania as refugees. Khadga lived in a refugee camp in Nepal for nineteen years before being accepted to migrate. Shoukat fled Afghanistan, then Pakistan, then came by boat to detention first on Christmas Island, and then on the mainland, finally resettling in Australia. Nene, homeless from infancy, came from a refugee camp in Sudan at the age of fourteen. Their stories illustrate a honing of senses of self through adversity.

Chapter 6, "Mobile Lives", traces the journeys taken by Julian, a man from England, and Yukari, a woman from Japan, demonstrating lives of high mobility and showing development of global senses of self. Julian has lived in various places in the Middle East, and India, has travelled extensively, and settled in Tasmania. Yukari, who lives for part of each year in Tokyo, Guatemala, and Denmark, continues to travel widely.

III: Challenges of Resettlement

In part III, I examine ways in which migration and other mobilities usher in changes to traditional ways of life, exacerbating uncertainties, and reshaping identities.[36] Such movements confront migrants and existing residents with a vast array of unknowns – unfamiliar people, changes to places, shifts in social, political, economic, and living conditions. Dealing with such unknowns raises significant tensions that affect people's senses of self and place, and their experience of suffering or well-being.

In chapter 7, "Settling in New Places", I consider both the deep attachment many migrants have to places elsewhere and the effects of place attachment on their ability to resettle, and I reflect on the moral and political implications of sedentarist ideas. Building on geographers' understandings of a range of senses of place, I find examples of multiple senses of place in the participants' narratives. Some have found that one place to call *home*, and others felt themselves to be *in between*. Although there are common themes, a distinct difference is revealed between the senses of place felt by irregular migrants and the other participants. I use the model of self–place relations to examine their experiences of changing places, and recount their views of what helps and what hinders when making home in a new place. It becomes evident that senses – both of place and of self – play significant roles in resettlement.

In chapter 8, "Dilemmas of Difference", I explore the difficult and stressful experiences often involved in processes of migration, whether people are new arrivals to a place, or already resident. Problems people undergo include their fears of difference and experiences of racism, ostracism, marginalisation, and other factors in the politics of recognition. Here, examples of limiting memes show up in expressed attitudes and beliefs and make it evident that the assumption that human being is flawed is central to these tribulations. Again, I draw upon the participants' narratives to illustrate these and other challenges, such as concerns about losing language – and the sense of self that goes with it – as well as learning a new language, finding opportunity to worship, and building community.

In chapter 9, "Identity and Belonging", I begin by considering what identity and belonging might mean. Issues affecting both relate to morality and power, inclusion and exclusion, citizenship and rights – and I ask: who has the authority to determine identity or belonging? The participants' narratives provide examples of agency and the lack of it in extreme situations. Often people come to develop a sense of self by identifying themselves with places, so belonging somewhere is critical to well-being, and the ability to belong is a resource. I explore different practices and perceptions of personhood, and strategies participants bring to making home in new places. Predictions that climate change will force migration of vast numbers of people emphasise the need for flexibility in relation to belonging and identity. I explore how the self produces identity and show that when sense of self includes distinction between identity and self, there is significant affect to well-being.

IV: Moving Forward

Throughout the book, I show that sense of self and sense of place deeply implicate the quality of people's experience and their assumption of agency. In part IV, I consider what might usefully be passed on from this learning to mitigate suffering and increase well-being in future. Reiterating profound moral questions arising from migration and what it reveals of the contemporary human condition, I look for ways forward.

In chapter 10, "Vital Sensibilities", I delve further into eco-psychology, social ecology, and philosophy to more deeply understand what weakens and what strengthens senses of self and place. People weaken these senses most when they dissociate from self as a consequence of unquestioningly accepting prevailing limited assumptions. Those I challenged at the beginning of the book – that *human nature is flawed,* and that *people must stay in one place to achieve any kind of well-being* – are fundamental to the common human condition. Freedom, according to Foucault and others, comes with questioning and explicitly recognising the sources of the beliefs and assumptions underlying these and other accepted truths. I draw examples from the participants' narratives of lived experience of sense of self and place, and their development of these sensibilities.

Finally, in chapter 11, I ask, *What Legacy Will We Leave?* Every day brings news of some atrocity, natural disaster, violence, famine, war, or other excess of social disruption somewhere on the planet. Politically, opinions continue to polarise. Far right conservatives and other fundamentalists are further tightening border and other controls in bids to contain and deflect disruption of their sovereign, neo-liberal, and other projects. The gulf between rich and poor has become unfathomable. Unprecedented numbers of people are on the move. Wildfires, floods, droughts, and other extreme climate events are growing in intensity, and compounding one upon another. Will we continue to hurtle along that trajectory? Many people are calling for alternatives to be considered, but young people – internationally – are demanding that governments take immediate action to mitigate climate change *now*.[37] The deep moral questions and issues of human rights I raise in this book are important to consider at this time. How different might our trajectories be if we were to conceive of the nature of human being as wholesome? What understanding of the relationship between senses of self and place might seed a world in which human life is valued, and people – truly thinking – would be free to come up with infinite ways for both people and place and all life to flourish. On both fronts – migration and climate change – this is a time of human emergency. If we truly think about it, might it become a time of human emergence?

NOTES

1. Horton and Kraftl, Rats, Assorted Shit and 'Racist Groundwater', 926–27.
2. Korzybski, xxiii.
3. Dahlman, Renwick, and Bergman, 179.
4. Ghorashi, Davis, and Smets, 381.

5. Cresswell, 'Politics', 21.

6. Castree; Cronon, 'Wilderness'; Davison; Fisher; Sattmann-Frese and Hill; Winter.

7. Taylor, *Sources of the Self,* 5.

8. Ibid., 7.

9. Ibid., 12.

10. Frankl, 75.

11. Bateson, *Ecology of Mind,* 1972.

12. Wendorf.

13. Bruner, Goodson.

14. Sandercock, 'Strangers Become Neighbours', 18, 23.

15. Ellen Barry and Martin Selsoe Sorensen, 'In Denmark, Harsh New Laws for Immigrant "Ghettos"', *New York Times*, July 1, 2018, accessed October 1, 2018, https://www.nytimes.com/2018/07/01/world/europe/denmark-immigrant-ghettos.html.

16. Brown, Buscaglia, Dugan, *Integrity*; Fisher; Sattmann-Frese and Hill, Seligman.

17. Dean, 13.

18. Urry, *Sociology Beyond Societies.*

19. Sheller and Urry, 'Mobilities Paradigm', 211; Urry, *Mobilities.*

20. Cresswell, 'Politics', 19.

21. Stratford, *Geographies, Mobilities, and Rhythms.*

22. Malpas, *Place*, 6.

23. Use of *their* and *they* with the singular person accounts for those whose gender is non-binary.

24. UNHCR, 'The 1951 Convention'.

25. Arendt, 'Perplexities'.

26. Ibid., 32.

27. Ibid., 43–44.

28. Kukasthas, 260.

29. Sciurba and Furri.

30. Kukasthas, 254.

31. de Montety. Elden, Uncollected Foucault.

32. de Montety.

33. Arendt, 'Perplexities', 41.

34. Judith Butler, 'Hannah Arendt's Challenge to Adolf Eichmann', *The Guardian*, August 29, 2011, accessed January 6, 2012, https://www.theguardian.com/commentis free/2011/aug/29/hannah-arendt-adolf-eichmann-banality-of-evil.

35. Horton and Kraftl, 'Rats'; Hopkins.

36. Elliott and Urry.

37. Sandra Laville, Matthew Taylor and Daniel Hurst, 'It's Our Time to Rise Up': Youth Climate Strikes Held in 100 Countries, *The Guardian*, March 16, 2019, accessed May 4, 2019, https://www.theguardian.com/environment/2019/mar/15/its-our-time-to-rise-up-youth-climate-strikes-held-in-100-countries.

Chapter 1

Mobilities of Place and Self

A clear distinction is often drawn between places and those travelling to such places. Places are seen as pushing or pulling people to visit. Places are presumed to be relatively fixed, given, and separate from those visiting. The new mobility paradigm argues against this ontology of distinct "places" and "people". Rather there is a complex relationality of places and persons connected through performances.[1]

PLACE AND SENSE OF PLACE

An understanding of place as a condition of existence explains that "the appearance of things – of objects, of self, and of others – is possible only within the all-embracing compass of place. It is, indeed, in and through place that the world presents itself".[2] Crucially, place is not "something encountered 'in' experience, but rather, place *is integral to the very structure and possibility of experience*".[3] This ontological understanding developed by Jeff Malpas significantly unsettles others' writing on sense of place. For example, in the 1970s and 1980s, Edward Relph and others such as Anne Buttimer, David Seamon, and Yi-Fu Tuan had taken the view that "places are fusions of physical attributes, activities and significance, aspects of the experience of the everyday world that can be explicated phenomenologically".[4] Twenty years later, reflecting on the elusiveness of place as a concept, Relph acknowledges that Malpas' enquiry and related work by Edward Casey turned such views "on their heads":

> Except in some very trivial senses, [place] is not a bit of space, nor another word for landscape or environment, it is not a figment of individual experience, nor a social construct, and it is certainly not susceptible to quantitative excavation.

It is, instead, the foundation of being both human and non-human; experience, actions and life itself begin and end in place.[5]

Following Malpas, Relph differentiates place and places, explaining sense of place as "the critical ontological awareness that existence is always placed and unavoidably engaged with the unities and differences of the world" and defining sense of *a* place as the synaesthetic faculty we use to identify and appreciate different properties of a place, that "combines seeing, hearing, smelling, and touching with memory, responsibility, emotions, anticipation and reflection".[6]

Malpas Natural beauty in places evokes sensory awareness, for example, see figure 1.1. to a quote from the novelist, Gertrude Stein.[7] On returning to her place of origin after many years abroad, Stein summed up her impression with the words: "There is no *there*, there". Malpas explains that the third "there" in Stein's utterance simply relates to location – a spot on a map, an address, a set of coordinates, a site. The middle "there" is about the significance of that locale, its history, and meanings given to it by different people according to their purposes or attachments, what it represents to them, their evaluations, and emotional responses. Those two usages of "there" designate places. The first "there" Malpas defines as the "existential ground" in which everything finds its being, and that determines human being and all that human can do. Furthermore, "Places occur in place". In this ontological way of thinking about place, Malpas defines "place as existential ground . . . a matrix . . . that nexus of elements that supports and enables things to be what they are . . . that nurtures, and sustains, and allows things to be able to come to presence . . . that supports, contains, and enables the complex interrelatedness of all".

If place is that existential ground, and places are various locales, environs, significances, attachments, and relationships arising from that matrix, how then might *sense of place* be understood? Can it occur only in relation to particular places – Relph's sense of *a* place? Or is it possible, as Relph suggests, to have an *ontological* sense of place – an awareness of place as a fundament of being – existentially as well as physically providing the ground on which we stand? Relph asserts that the "combination of sense of places and ontological sense of place . . . is an existential foundation for individual and communal well-being".[8] He further proposes that these senses of place – plus a related sense of the connections between many different places – are important when it comes to finding ways to cope with change.[9]

Generally, migration and mobilities literature does not address an ontological sense of place, and what goes begging as a result are these questions: What role does that ontological sense play? And is it possible to have a sense of place – in any place, at any time – that includes awareness of place as our existential ground? Relph's analysis suggests that it is, and that experience of

Figure 1.1.   Waterfall at Mt Field National Park, Tasmania.

these various senses of place might increase people's agency and well-being when migrating, and settling in new locations.

Lily DeMiglio and Alison Williams classify sense of place as "an umbrella concept that captures the essence of the relationships people form with places".[10] They suggest that sense of place encompasses emotional bonds; strongly felt values, meanings, and symbols; qualities of a place; continuously constructed socially and culturally shared meanings; and awareness of cultural, historical, and spatial context. Indeed, "Time, residential status, age, ethnicity and the characteristics of the place [influence and] mediate the relationship . . . and in turn, the sense of well-being derived from sense of place".[11] John Eyles sees sense of place as "an interactive relationship between daily experience of a (local) place and perceptions of one's place-in-the-world" and argues that this idea – which accounts for social position and material conditions – can be used to understand health and well-being.[12]

Evidently, as well as the capacity of place to provide the essentials for physical existence such as water, food, and shelter and for social opportunities such as work, education, and lifestyle variations, place is significant to people in terms of more symbolic and relational dimensions of human existence such as identity, belonging, and well-being. Exploring notions of *home*,

David Morley writes that "it is still common to think of cultures as depending on and being rooted in places".[13] In considering "stable patterns of interaction of the same people doing the same things, over and over again, in the same places", Morley sees that "place comes to act as a generator of cultural belongingness, so that the geographical boundaries round a community also come to carry a symbolic charge in separating out those who belong from those who do not".[14] There is considerable agreement that sense of place is firmly linked to places of origin, and that it can be difficult to develop in new locations.[15] Holding sense of place as connected to people's relatively unconscious "state of rootedness", Yi-Fu Tuan explains that "people identify themselves" with the place they feel is home for them and for their ancestors.[16] When people are displaced or migrate to foreign territory alienation from place can result.

Alienation from place refers to people's various experiences of *placelessness* and of being separate, disembedded, or dissociated from, or not belonging to whatever place they are in. Relph defines "an alienation from people and places, homelessness, a sense of the unreality of the world, and of not belonging" as "existential outsideness".[17] In everyday experience feelings of alienation from place range from discomfort to being out-of-place in a location, to struggling with a hostile environment. Alienation from place affects people's well-being and is evident in disregard of places – for example, when people fail to pay attention to the place they are in, litter, pollute, or otherwise despoil their environments. When people are alienated from place both lack well-being.[18]

Mobilities are also held to cause alienation of people from place. Tim Cresswell writes that some authors consider that mobilities involve "the absence of commitment and attachment and involvement – a lack of significance – [and are] antithetical to moral worlds".[19] Such sedentarist views hold that redress of that alienation can only occur when people stay in one place. Some, such as Freya Mathews, suggest developing a healthy sense of place within cities. She recommends this: "if you possibly can, find a place of residence that you can occupy indefinitely, and commit to it".[20] Mathews insists both that only by being in one place over time can people be accepted *by* place, and that place "can never receive the casual or expedient sojourner or stranger in such familiar fashion".[21] In similar vein, for Peter Cock staying in one place is a normative *good*, and the idea that "we can be separated from country and community, wander from place to place, and still be whole, powerful people [is a] false myth of individualistic humanism".[22] However, people can and do experience alienation from place even when living in one place, particularly in cities.[23] In contrast, while Relph recognises that rootedness "is generally considered to be positive, something that contributes to well-being and quality of life because knowing and being known somewhere provide security and dependability", he also writes that "concomitants of narrow place experience are parochialism, exclusion, and a tendency to reject unfamiliar differences".[24]

Whatever may be the virtue of staying in one place, it is not always possible. Indeed, the capacity to stay put is "at least partly a function of one's privilege [and] power in the world".[25] On one hand, mobility might be considered a privilege of the wealthy, along with recognition that vast numbers of people living local lives are poor. On the other hand, being able to stay in one place is an unattainable luxury for many others, whether they move voluntarily or are forced to move from place to place in search of work or accommodation, or as attested by the numbers experiencing migration and homelessness following political and social upheaval or extreme climatic events.[26] In the context of global mobilities, Val Plumwood sees place attachment as a casualty of "dominant market cultures which commodify land and place" and of labour markets that usually want "individual workers who have few or portable attachments".[27] She claims that the dissociation permeating the culture of the global economy problematises even the concept of "a singular homeplace" or "our place".[28] Plumwood recognises both the itinerant nature of many people's lives, and the concurrent dwelling-in-place of others, many of whom she sees as remaining largely unaware of, or ignoring the mobilities, interconnections, and dependencies that make their lifestyles possible.

John Cameron emphasises the point that place is not "the mere passive recipient" of whatever people want to do upon it, but rather is "an active participant in a very physical sense".[29] Cameron describes sense of place as "the relationship between people and the local setting for their experience and activity"[30] and points out that sense of a place includes "a growing sense of what the place demands of us in our attitudes and actions".[31] Such understandings are particularly relevant to how people relocating might regard, experience, and treat places of resettlement. For instance: What is the climate? Is it similar to or different from their places of origin, or transit? Do people find it easy or difficult to live in these places new to them? Are these places hard to maintain, or accommodating? Is there a need to conserve water, or is it abundant? And in these times of climate change, are there earthquakes, wildfires, floods? Do people feel supported, or uplifted by a place? Do they find a place depressing, and feel they have to endure it? Do they despoil the environment, exploit it, simply disregard it, or take care of it? Advocates of ecopsychology, social ecology, and related disciplines assert that if people have a strong sense of place, they will care for it.[32]

Although people sometimes speak of a collective sense of a place, Cameron stresses that *sense of* implies individual experience, not just a commonly held idea, description, or categorisation.[33] Even though family, community, and collective society are formative of and central to the meanings a person holds for a place, one's own sense of place can only occur as an internal experience. At the same time, Cameron emphasises that it is important to be clear whose sense of place is discussed, "the danger being that one person's or culture's interpretation of the qualities of a place can be imposed on others as if it had externally-derived authority".[34] There is wide support for the need always to respect other people's understandings of places, but such respect is particularly important when places are held to have sacred significance, and in places that have been colonised – Australia's history in relation to its indigenous, Aboriginal and Torres Strait Islander peoples is a well-documented (and deplorable) example of disregard.[35] The overarching point here is this: whatever happens in place affects people and thus influences relationships between long-term residents and immigrants in any locale. Respect – or lack of it – for other's sense of place can profoundly impact people's actions, from simple caring for or trashing a place, to changing places by developing them, exploiting environmental resources, marketing them as desirable tourist destinations, or despoiling them through warfare and other forms of conflict.

Many who write about place idealise natural places, and exhort people to experience sense of place as some sort of good feeling available through connection with those natural places. At times, commentators conflate those idealised perspectives with various normative opinions that can become political. Others imply that sense of place is somehow opposite to alienation from place, in which is embedded an assumption that awareness, or sense of place is always a positive and desirable experience. Intrinsically, a person's capability to sense place is a benign process of experiencing and relating to place. In that context, sense of place is neither negative nor positive.

The capability to sense place provides the potential for people to be aware of place, for instance, in the ways distinguished by Malpas and Relph. People may also become aware of characteristics of a place, or something happening there that they might experience, or interpret, as being either negative or positive. As to whether having such awareness is desirable, it is understandable that people might (unconsciously, or by choice) dissociate from place – that is, shut off their sense of place – in unpleasant conditions. Yet, I argue that to have a strong or acute sense of place supports well-being both of people and place. In positive conditions, that acute sense enables people more fully to enjoy a place, and encourages them to behave in ways that are likely to maintain positive, mutual relationships with it. In negative conditions, an acute sense of place provides opportunity for people to detect what is wrong, or unsafe, and to act appropriately. It is obviously useful for refugees to be aware of both negative and positive senses of place.[36] That an acute sense of place is of value aligns with notions such as Joanna Macy's that if ever we felt the pain of the world we would do something about it.[37] It also fits William Cronon's assertion that by continuing to bifurcate human and other nature we "evade responsibility for the lives we actually lead".[38]

Much of the work I have cited relates to sense of *a* place, and, predominantly, that is what I have found in place literature. There is little about the ontological sense of place discussed earlier. At the same time, some authors write of authentic and inauthentic senses of place and others of weak and strong senses of place, and as if inauthentic or weak senses of place are somehow illegitimate.[39] I deploy the terms *strong* and *weak* in regard to sense of place very differently – without value judgements. To clarify, I consider sense of place as a continuum from dissociation to acute awareness of place and of relationship with it. We are always inseparably connected with place as our existential ground. Physiologically we are in relationship with and react or respond to place all the time, but often we are only conscious of that when changes reach certain thresholds, for example when it becomes light or dark, or when temperature changes to an extent where we feel hot or cold, or when we come upon some unusual or distinctive feature of place. Sense of place that includes a cognitive as well as sensory awareness – a sensibility of relationship with place – is rhizomatic, with flows of awareness and nodes that have no single cause but rather may be intersections of a multiplicity of connections with the whole.[40] A dissociated – weak – sense of place might be described as experience of self as disengaged from place, relatively unaware of it, and insensitive to it. An acute or associated – strong – sense of place might be described as experience of self in place – that is, aware of and sensitive to the place one is in – deeply aware of relationship with particular places, of the interconnections of those places with others, and even more fundamentally, of an ontological sense of place as the existential ground of being.

SELF AND SENSE OF SELF

There are views, particularly among eco-psychologists and social ecologists, that for any change to occur in human relationships with place, people need to address their relationship with themselves. Writers such as Stuart Hill, Andy Fisher, and Werner Sattmann-Frese consider it crucial to overcome views that the health and well-being of place, people, and other living beings can be separated, and assert that addressing the human condition is a first step to well-being of people and place.[41]

As Malpas writes, human beings appear not to begin life with any sensory or abstracted awareness of self as separate, but experience "being already involved . . . already part of a meaningful whole".[42] Extensive research into the development of human neurology shows that it is only later that "we begin to separate out a sense of ourselves and sense of things as they are apart from us".[43] To separate awareness of self from whom or whatever else is other enables people to function autonomously, to distinguish difference, and relate to those others. But separation is not the same as alienation. To be alienated from whom or whatever is other is to be indifferent or hostile to the other; this, in turn, implies that differences – or even a lack of sameness or familiarity – at some time have been given meaning that results in alienation. So further questions arise: How are self and other defined? How do we know what we know about them? What meanings are implied in those definitions, or identifications that alienate people from others, from place, and from themselves? And from where, and when do those meanings come? These questions are particularly significant in regard to people's ability to adjust to other people and places in an era of high mobility. To address them, we need both to explore understandings of self and sense of self, and to consider how what the self is held to mean contributes to a narrative of self, an ontology and epistemology that becomes reductive and self-validating. Then, we can begin to perceive how the content of that narrative influences personal relationships with – and thus senses of – self, others, and place.

Dictionaries provide a range of meanings for the word *self*, but in common define it as inferring a particular person or thing as distinct from any other person or thing. This meaning is in a class altogether different from academic attempts to define what a generic self is – or to determine if it even exists. The common definition more readily fits the cry I have heard on countless occasions in the course of my professional life, when people say, "I want to know myself" or "I want to find myself". It seems this apparent lack of self-knowing, or search for self, is a fairly widespread, modern human condition, at least in the Western, or Western-influenced world – in my experience, this same lament has shown up consistently in Canada, the United States, Japan, New Zealand, Europe, and Australia. As one example, a fifty-year-old Japanese woman declared: "All my life I've been someone's daughter, someone's wife, someone's mother. I want to know who *I* am".

Scholars have written extensively about the challenges of defining the self. The literature is characterised by wide disciplinary diversity and deep intellectual disagreement. At one end of a spectrum, authors refer to the self as an object or thing, isolated and separate from what else is; and at the other, as a process participating in its environment, and indivisibly part of the whole.[44] Academic responses to the question of what a self is, collated by Shaun Gallagher and Jonathan Shear, include assertions that: "there is no self . . . the idea is a logical, psychological, or grammatical fiction . . . the sense of self is properly understood and defined in terms of brain processes . . . it is merely a constructed sociological locus, or the center of personal and public narratives, or . . . it belongs in an ineffable category all its own".[45]

Humberto Maturana and Francisco Varela present a radical view of "the biological roots of knowledge" showing that consciousness – including self-consciousness – arises from complexity.[46] In another version of that dynamic, Antonio Damasio also considers self as *process* and not a bounded *thing*.[47] In Damasio's explanation, the self evolves as new layers of neural processes give rise to further layers of mental processing; the "self-as-knower grounded on the [process of] self-as-object".[48]

In seeking to define the self, there is difficulty in arriving at any kind of consensus; between and within cultures, notions of self vary. Charles Taylor has observed that "the very idea that we have or are 'a self', that human agency is essentially defined as 'the self', is a linguistic reflection of our modern understanding", and that, even in the Western world, it was not always so.[49] Clifford Geertz has commented that "the Western conception of a person . . . is . . . a rather peculiar idea within the context of the World's cultures".[50] Nevertheless, correlations are sometimes drawn between understandings of self from vastly different sources. For example, Peter Riviere reflects on a concept of self "based on a mind created through interaction with its environment" that has been developed by neuroscience, and is also found in the cosmology of a Western Amazon indigenous people.[51] The contested status of the self remains open; an "intractable problem", as Gallagher and Shear conceive it.[52] Or, in Hannah Arendt's wonderful terms, the self is an "unanswerable" question.[53] For Arendt, "It is highly unlikely that we, who can know, determine, and define the natural essences of all things surrounding us, which we are not, should ever be able to do the same for ourselves – this would be like jumping over our own shadows".[54]

Although delineation of what the self is may elude us, we *know* ourselves through a *sense of self*. To examine the use of the word *sense* I draw on a number of contemporary dictionaries and one of etymology. These categorise the senses as both physical (visual, auditory, kinaesthetic, olfactory, gustatory, tactile, and proprioceptive) and abstract (including intellect, mind, spirit, and occult senses). For example, in these sources responsibility, morality, shame, and delight are considered to be abstract senses. *Sense* is said to refer variously to capability to be aware, to awareness or knowing of something, to the meaning attributed to that something, and to evaluations that might be applied to what is known, and even to the one who is sensing. Thus, the phrase *sense of self* refers to the capability to be aware of the self, to awareness or knowing of the self, to the meaning attributed to the self, and to evaluations that might be applied both to what is known of the self, and to the self who is making sense of all that.

I understand *sense of self* in three ways: first, as the capacity to be self-aware; second, as the content at any point in time of what of oneself one is aware; and third, as a description or narrative of one's idea or knowing of oneself. In both the second and third ways, sense of self is apprehended through the lens of meaning and evaluation one applies to oneself. Whatever the self may actually be, what any self may be held to mean is of primary significance – the meaning one gives to oneself governs regimes of practice – contextualising behaviour, limitation, possibility, and the quality of personal experience. Further, parameters for relationships are set by the meanings one gives to others – and to places – as well as to oneself.

So, from where does the meaning of oneself come? Is it given? Does it come with the territory – from particular genetics, physicality, or capability; or the location of the self in particular physical environments, cultural traditions, or economic, political, religious, or other social conditions? Is it a question of nature, or nurture – is it inherent, or is it learned? Is it fixed in place? Or does it move? Does it imply fixed qualities, or characteristics? Or do they change? Because what we think something means indicates what we believe about it – that is, what we think is true – these questions might be phrased in terms of beliefs as well as of meaning. How do people attribute meaning and acquire or develop beliefs? For Gregory Bateson,

> [a person's] beliefs about what sort of world it is will determine how he sees it and acts within it, and his ways of perceiving and acting will determine his beliefs about its nature. The living man is thus bound within a net of epistemological and ontological premises which – regardless of ultimate truth or falsity – become partially self-validating for him.[55]

In turn, Michel Foucault's stated objective in more than twenty-five years of study was "to sketch out a history of the different ways in our culture that humans develop knowledge about themselves".[56] He set out to show "how the subject constituted itself" through *epistemes* encapsulated in what he called "games of truth" and "practices of power".[57] In his words, truth is "a thing of this world", produced within societies or institutions as a way of establishing and maintaining power.[58] Foucault conceived the notion of epistemes as periods of history organised around specific worldviews.[59] The "organising principles" or truths that constitute epistemes determine "how we make sense of things, what we can know, and what we say"; they are "more or less unconscious" and they are "the grounds on which we base everything, so we more or less take them for granted".[60] As Mitchell Dean explains: "It is a matter not of the representations of individual mind or consciousness, but of the bodies of knowledge, belief and opinion in which we are immersed".[61] Richard Bawden writes that epistemes encompass the sets of beliefs and assumptions "to which we subscribe (essentially tacitly)" and which find expression in all that we do.[62] For Bawden, "Epistemes represent the particular systems of valuing and values, knowing and knowledge, emotioning and emotions, believing and beliefs that we bring to bear on our everyday activities".[63]

The historic aspect of epistemes introduces the temporal dimension that is central to *narrative*.[64] A concept more readily graspable than episteme, narrative also encapsulates sets of beliefs and assumptions specific to societies, cultures and individuals over time.[65] The terms *grand* or *master* or *meta-narrative* "are sometimes applied to culturally assumed truths with a long history".[66] Narrative is involved in the making of meaning in everyday life, and can serve as an heuristic device with which to examine how people give meaning to themselves and others.[67] Narratives seamlessly integrate meaningful pasts with meaningful futures, and make sense of the present socially, culturally, and personally.

In relation to sense of self, Taylor writes that "self-understanding necessarily has temporal depth and incorporates narrative".[68] John McLeod holds that we are "born into the story of our family and community and the story of who we are".[69] From infancy, we absorb whatever cultural, social, familial narratives prevail in what Joseph Chilton Pearce describes as "a spontaneous, imitative learning below the limen of our awareness".[70] An individual's embodiment of a narrative occurs through interaction within the world, influenced by language and other cultural artefacts, relationships with people and environments, actions, practices, education, religion, politics, media, and more.[71] It is a cognitive process, in that it has deeply to do with knowing, but it is far less an intellectual process than a visceral one, occurring in practice. It is not just that we are handed a set, or sets, of ideas and practices; rather, we grow up immersed in the context of them, model them from the demonstration of others around us, learn, rehearse, improvise, and replicate them in our everyday practice. For example, see figure 1.2.

We stabilise views of the world, along with ways of seeing, feeling, and knowing what we know; and hold as fact sets of beliefs and assumptions of what is true and what is false, and of meaning. Thereafter, unless the underlying premises are questioned, we live and act as if those beliefs are not representations of reality but reality itself. Those beliefs admit of certain possibilities, but exclude others from the field of reality, locking out whatever does not make sense in terms of the narrative within which we have learnt to operate. Narratives and practices are co-constitutive and reinforce or substantiate those sets of beliefs, and further influence behaviour, and govern experience. Thus, those sets of beliefs become self-validating. We come to believe the assumptions embedded in a narrative because we participate in the world it makes possible.

Of course, there are many truths by which people live and countless narratives to encompass and explain those truths that are differentiated by culture, nation, religion, ethnicity, social status, wealth, poverty, and more. For example, at a bush place in the Bay of Islands area of New Zealand, a Maori elder introduced me to "older brother" rock, "brother" tree, and to several

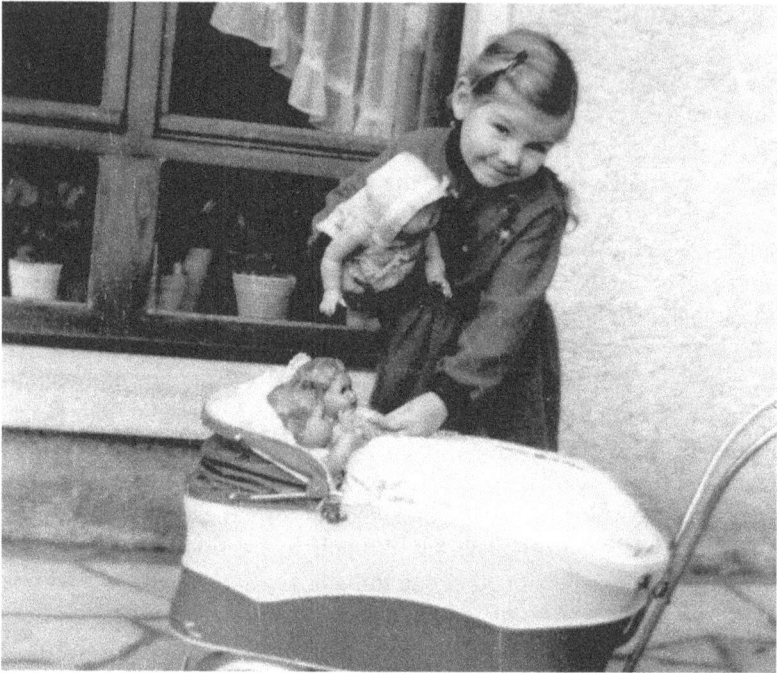

Figure 1.2. Carola – who later became a pediatrician – playing with her dolls when she was five years old. Carola grew up in a very old German town, where the end of the Plague in the fourteenth century is still celebrated every year.

other samples of flora he named as relatives. In response to my comment that I was used to such terms being applied only to people, he gave me a considering glance and said: "These *bro* were here long before us. We come from them, not them from us. They look after us and we learn from them". In Japan, when I asked a woman about her belief in reincarnation, her eyebrows flew up and she said, "But I grew up with this", amazed that I should even comment on what she so fully took for granted.

Whatever the variations of the content of narratives, formation of those stories – from personal to worldviews – is always a relational process; and any sense of self can only occur in a context of inextricable placement within, and in distinction of self from, what else surrounds it. In this respect, Guy Widdershoven writes that the meaning of "personal identity is dependent on a mutual relation between lived experience . . . and stories [and that] . . . experience elicits the story, and the story articulates and thereby modifies experience".[72] To the extent that beliefs become self-validating, each narrative creates its own evidence and justification, and establishes its own conditions of truth. In this way, a narrative is a collective, social phenomenon. And yet, whatever beliefs may commonly be held, to whatever extent people's understandings may align, no two people have exactly the same beliefs. In spite of commonalities, each person filters, modifies, and represents experience uniquely, with the result that each person holds an individual – and mobile – version of any collective or grand narrative.

As a child grows up, culturally and socially reiterated and reified assumptions about human nature become personalised. This process of development from birth through childhood and adolescence to adulthood has been studied and documented by many theorists and practitioners, particularly in the *psy* disciplines. An exemplar is Jean Piaget, whose work provides a basis for much Western understanding.[73] More radical is Stanislav Grof, who reports that people learn even in the womb.[74] These thinkers and many others – notably Damasio and Pearce – correlate developmental stages, expressed conceptually and behaviourally, with stages in the unfolding of neurological development.[75]

Morris Massey describes three major developmental periods: the imprint period, up to the age of seven, within which we are like sponges, absorbing everything around us, mostly without challenging it; the modelling period, from the age of eight to thirteen, when we copy others' ways of doing things, trying things on to see how they feel, no longer just blindly accepting, but checking things out for ourselves; and the socialisation period, from fourteen to twenty-one, when we are doing our best to work out the stance we will take as adults – a time of contradictions, when we are largely influenced by our peers, yet developing as individuals, and looking for something beyond what we learned and experienced as children.[76]

At the heart of any person's beliefs is a complex identification and meaning of his or her individual self in relation to the world. Compared with a social or cultural, grand or meta-narrative of what a self is generically; this is a uniquely personal narrative of self. Jacquelynne Eccles distinguishes between personal and social or collective types of identity because she believes that not all aspects of personal identity are grounded in social roles: personal aspects of identity "serve the psychological function of making one feel unique", and collective aspects of identity "serve to strengthen one's ties to highly valued social groups and relationships".[77] The balance of personal and collective aspects varies from culture to culture, for example, individualism is showcased in the United States, whereas in Japan, traditionally, there is a more collective base for identity, and, in common with other eastern cultures, "a view of the self as interdependent".[78] Unless a person thinks about and challenges their uniquely personal narrative of self, it governs the nature and quality of their experience and behaviour – how they feel and act in the world. Thus, a person's narrative of self is fundamental to presuppositions about their nature, and the nature of others and, indeed, to all of life.

Of course, growth and change are experienced within the parameters of the conditions of truth – including narratives of self – to which we hold. As Taylor writes, "My sense of myself is of a being who is growing and becoming".[79] In that process of becoming the self is continually being modified, changing, and unfolding. But to what extent is that process determined by externalities, and what agency do people have? To assert that individual narratives are entirely culturally or socially determined would be to say that individuals have agency only within the parameters of those stories. In this regard, Geoff Danaher and his colleagues write that Foucault began his early work with the idea that:

> people are not free agents who make their own meanings and control their lives; rather, they have their lives, thoughts and activities "scripted" for them by social forces and institutions . . . In his later work, however, Foucault considers the ways in which people – what he calls "subjects" – are active in "crafting" or negotiating their identity.[80]

Danaher and his colleagues consider Foucault's view that we cannot "escape the regulatory institutions and discourses in which we are produced", and emphasise the point that by identifying them, and our "practices of the self", we can "reinvent ourselves".[81] In Foucault's words, "The critique of what we are is at one and the same time the historical analysis of the limits imposed on us and an experiment with the possibility of going beyond them".[82] This critical ontology, he writes,

> consists in seeing on what type of assumptions, of familiar notions, of established, unexamined ways of thinking the accepted practices are based . . . uncovering that thought and trying to change it: showing that things are not as obvious as people believe, making it so that what is taken for granted is no longer taken for granted. To do criticism is to make harder those acts which are now too easy . . . as soon as people begin to have trouble thinking things the way they have been thought, transformation becomes at the same time very urgent, very difficult, and entirely possible.[83]

Related concepts underlie Jack Mezirow's development of *transformative learning*; an approach that encourages critical reflection to challenge presuppositions of meaning.[84] In similar vein, Carolyn Merchant writes that we internalise meta-narratives as "ideology . . . a story told by people in power"; but she also holds that "by rewriting the story, we can begin to challenge the structures of power".[85] In these politics of self, people do have choice and can change their personal narratives by becoming aware of and questioning the assumptions underlying the conditions of truth.

However, when we are not aware of the sets of beliefs and assumptions upon which a narrative is based, we see only the story. In this respect,

Vladimir Dimitrov points out that when we are not aware that a narrative is only a story we risk becoming captive to it.[86] Narrative theorists and therapists also claim that we have choice, and that both stories and experience can be transformed.[87] As Jerome Bruner states, "We constantly construct and reconstruct our selves to meet the needs of the situations we encounter, and we do so with the guidance of our memories of the past and our hopes and fears for the future".[88] Ivor Goodson explains that there are strategies and resources within narratives of self "to flexibly respond to the transitions and critical events which comprise our lives and equip us to actively develop courses of action and learning strategies".[89] In accord with Dimitrov, Bruner says that for some people "the life story involves an early narrative closure, that is, that the range of choices as to how to live and story a life is *closed* at an early stage".[90] In Goodson's view, this closure "is important in not only showing the somewhat deterministic nature of a scripted life, but also . . . the way in which other possibilities are neither imagined nor subsequently experienced".[91] Nevertheless, he asserts that people can bring about change through what he calls the work of *re-selfing* that is an aim of narrative therapy.

People limit their experience of agency to what their narratives permit if they never question their assumptions or ask how they know what they know. Yet, events can challenge them to question long-held assumptions.[92] The challenges may be deeply personal, perhaps to do with changes in health, close relationships, disappointments, or achievements. People question their certainties when they are confronted by the exigencies and crises of social, global, and environmental changes. Migration and other mobilities constitute events that significantly challenge people to question their assumptions. In later chapters, the case study narratives provide examples of such events and questioning.

It is clear from the foregoing both that people derive their senses of self from the meanings implicit in the narratives they embody and perform, and that they do have agency. Thus, it might be said that people *make* their worlds – albeit in processes of more or less unconscious absorption of what is presented to them – and sometimes never realise the part they play in constituting themselves according to or in response or reaction to myriad external influences.

NOTES

1. Sheller and Urry, 214.
2. Malpas, Place, 15.
3. Ibid., 31–32, original emphasis.
4. Relph, 'Senses of Place', 35.
5. Ibid., 36.
6. Ibid.

7. Presentation at the University of Tasmania by Jeff Malpas, 2010.

8. Relph, 'Senses', 38.

9. Ibid.

10. DeMiglio and Williams, 20–21.

11. Ibid., 23.

12. Ibid., quoting Eyles, 26.

13. Morley, 212.

14. Ibid.

15. Bhugra and Gupta, Migration; Kobayashi, Preston, and Murnaghan; Pallasmaa; Relph, Placelessness; Tuan.

16. Tuan, 194.

17. Relph, 'Senses', 51.

18. Albrecht et al.; Keith and Pile; Malpas, Place; Morley; Relph, Placelessness; Tuan.

19. Cresswell, On the Move, 31.

20. Mathews, 'Becoming Native', 199.

21. Mathews, Reinhabiting Reality, 55.

22. Cock, 95.

23. Urry, Mobilities, 2007.

24. Relph, 'Senses', 37.

25. Plumwood, 'Shadow Places'.

26. Massey, 'Global Sense'; Bissell, 'Thinking Habits'.

27. Plumwood, Feminism.

28. Ibid.

29. Cameron, 6.

30. Ibid., 3.

31. Ibid., 6.

32. Fisher, Hill, Naess, Wheeler, Winter.

33. Cameron, 2–3.

34. Cameron, quoting Seddon, 3.

35. Cock, Kanahele, Read, Woodford.

36. Hiruy.

37. Macy.

38. Cronon, 'Wilderness', 81.

39. DeMiglio and Williams, Relph, Placelessness.

40. Bissell, 'Thinking'; Cockayne, Ruez, and Secor; Di Masso et al.

41. Hill, Fisher, Sattmann-Frese and Hill.

42. Malpas, Heidegger, 52.

43. Ibid.

44. Abram; Hillman; Madell; Maturana; Naess; Russell; Seigel; Strawson; Taylor, Sources.

45. Gallagher and Shear, x, xi.

46. Maturana and Varela, 254.

47. Damasio, Self.

48. Ibid., 10.

49. Taylor, Sources, 177.

50. Pile and Thrift, quoting Geertz, 15.
51. Riviere, 87.
52. Gallagher and Shear.
53. Arendt, Human Condition, 10.
54. Ibid.
55. Bateson, Ecology of Mind, 314.
56. Foucault, 'Technologies', 17–18.
57. Foucault et al., 'Ethics', 33.
58. Foucault, 'Truth and Power', 131.
59. Danaher, Schirato, and Webb, 15.
60. Ibid., 17.
61. Dean, 16.
62. Bawden, 52–54.
63. Ibid., 54.
64. Schiff, 39.
65. Bruner, Chase, Crossley, Goodson, Payne.
66. Payne, 21.
67. Bruner, Josselson, Josselson and Lieblich, Payne.
68. Taylor, Sources, 50.
69. McLeod, 22.
70. Pearce, 25.
71. Bawden, Dean, Fell, Giddens and Sutton, Rose, Taylor, Sources.
72. Widdershoven, 9.
73. Piaget.
74. Grof.
75. Damasio, Descartes, Feeling, Self; Pearce, Magical Child, Religion and Spirit.
76. Massey, Morris.
77. Eccles, 78–79.
78. Kan, Karasawa, and Kitayama, 303.
79. Taylor, Sources, 50.
80. Danaher, Schirato, and Webb, 116–17.
81. Ibid., 131.
82. Foucault, 'Enlightenment', 56.
83. Foucault 'Important to Think', 172.
84. Mezirow.
85. Merchant, 157.
86. Dimitrov.
87. Bruner 2003, Crossley 2002, Dimitrov 2003, Goodson 2013, Josselson, Schiff 2012.
88. Bruner, 64.
89. Goodson, 63.
90. Bruner, original emphasis, 76.
91. Goodson, original emphasis, 79.
92. Ibid., 97.

Chapter 2

Meta-Narratives and Agency

> Stories can be "located", which means they can be seen as the social constructions they are, located in time and space, social history and social geography. Our stories and storylines need to be understood, not just as personal constructions but as expressions of particular historical and cultural opportunities.[1]

To more deeply understand how people *make* their worlds we need to read their individual narratives against a backdrop of the historical context – the meta-narratives – and the contemporary politics of self from which they emerge. In addition, to recognise when and how people constrain or free their agency, we need to consider dynamics of the relationships people have with themselves, and with place.

According to Ivor Goodson, meta-narratives are "genealogies of context [that] privilege certain storylines".[2] See figure 2.1. Correspondences in the histories of many peoples seem to indicate that some beliefs – or versions of them – are common across diverse cultures, even though origins and explanations of those assumptions may vary greatly from one to another. For instance, people have long warred against, colonised, and enslaved others, and depended on hierarchical structures of race, class, caste, or other systems to justify and enforce beliefs that some people are superior to others. In Western thinking, such beliefs can be traced to underlying and interrelated concepts that separate human being from nature and assume that human being is flawed.[3]

In Richard Tarnas's summary, the development of Western thinking has produced a "profound sense of ontological and epistemological separation between self and world . . . [ensuring] the construction of a disenchanted and alienating world view".[4] Premised on the idea that self-alienation emerged

historically and dialectically with world alienation, the ontological conception of human being as flawed is central to this alienating perspective. In
Western thought, such assumptions persist in individualistic notions of the
self that Charles Taylor describes as "a function of a historically limited mode
of self-interpretation".[5] Val Plumwood writes that such belief is generated
by conceiving of the self as human virtue striving to remain above a "lower,
baser" animal nature.[6] In consequence, Mary Clark considers that the modern
notion of the self prompts deeply reductive and negative assumptions "that
profoundly affect both our understanding of human nature and the way we
treat the world that supports us".[7]

Critical to understanding the human condition, according to Taylor, is the
emergence and historical embedding in Western thinking of "the stance of
disengagement towards oneself".[8] Taylor traces this dynamic particularly
through Descartes and Hobbes, and explains it as "radical reflexivity" – a process in which we stand back from experience, "withdraw from it, reconstrue it
objectively, and then learn to draw defensible conclusions from it".[9] In other
words, we create a split between the rational, objective observer (thinking,
consciousness, the mind) and the rest of the self (emotions, sensory awareness, intuition, body, soul, and spirit). This "unprecedentedly radical form of
self-objectification" allows us to change our habits, and gives us "the possibility to remake ourselves in a more rational and advantageous fashion".[10]
Given an entrenched self-understanding of human nature as flawed, the
stance of disengagement provides a way to *better* ourselves. The act of disengagement, locating the sense of *I* as the rational, objective observer, creates
the self as something that the *I* has – a possession – and leads to alienation
from the self; "Man [*sic*] as an observer is becoming completely alienated
from himself as a being".[11]

Disengagement also underpins modern projects of individualism at one
and the same time by recognising the freedom inherent in people's ability to
reform themselves and placing responsibility upon the individual to do that
in accord with prevailing moral and ideological determinants.[12] According to
Michel Foucault and others, the Socratic counsel to "take care of yourself"
was intended to enable an individual to be of service and to fulfil his obliga-
tions to his community.[13] Individualism in its modern form implies that all a
person's actions take place for the benefit of that individual, not for society
as a whole.

Critique of the modern dynamics of individualism and other aspects of
the contemporary Western meta-narrative intensified after the Second World
War; a period which saw many people involved in gender, sexuality, and
other civil rights activism; and the emergence of green, environmental,
human potential, and other counter-cultural movements. These movements
rapidly grew in popularity in the 1960s and 1970s; they represent many and

sometimes conflicting views and also advance alternatives to prevailing narratives.[14] Certain advocates propose theories and practices intended to emancipate people and bring about well-being; and to challenge many tenets of the Western meta-narrative. However, as Mitchell Dean points out, what often goes unnoticed is that many of these movements and their critiques have been appropriated and "remapped" in service of particular agenda:[15] Individualism has been cultivated so that the more people have yearned for well-being and happiness, the more they have been encouraged to believe that achievement of that is up to them – nothing to do with any responsibility of the state, or anyone else. "Where the political and cultural movements sought a utopian vision of the emancipated self . . . the neoliberal critiques of the welfare state sought to redeploy the 'free subject' as a technical instrument in the achievement of governmental purposes and objectives".[16] In other words, people are urged to become *self-empowered* and responsible for their own welfare, concurrent with government moves to reduce health and other social services and well-being is increasingly equated with consumerism in pursuance of neoliberal economic agenda.

In Taylor's critique, the modern project of individualism results in loss of moral orientation – a confusion focused on "what it is right to do rather than what it is good to be".[17] In later work, he describes individualism as "a centring on the self and a concomitant shutting out, or even unawareness, of the greater issues or concerns that transcend the self, be they religious, political, historical".[18] Such projects of individualism engender indifference to the needs of others and promote competition at the expense of cooperation, thus achieving greater control of the workforce and the economy. This instrumentalist arrogation further entrenches prevailing Western meta-narratives and translates much of the counter-cultural drive for liberation into modernity's highly critiqued empowerment of the atomistic individual. Appropriating key themes and reducing the meanings of key concepts to *truths* that then are employed to shore up the status quo defuses the potency of alternative movements.[19] Hence, Peter Doran concludes: "a strategic silencing of alternative ways of seeing the world and the human being has been one of the major achievements of unfettered capitalism – a strategic silencing that effectively patrols what can and cannot be contemplated in the course of current global environmental diplomacy".[20]

Ironically, the success of this arrogation, and of modernity's project of individualism, rests on the presupposition that there is something fundamentally wrong with people. People still do contemplate alternative explanations, and influential writers from the natural sciences, the humanities, the social sciences, and others explore the need for human reunion with nature, often presenting their well-being as "inextricably bound".[21] There is increasing interest at grassroots levels in alternative understandings of life and of ways to achieve well-being of people and place, and this interest is influencing personal, social, and environmental activities. Yet, anomalies remain – even the persistent use of language naming human and nature as distinct entities perpetuates the divide. Despite the development of successive explanations for the human condition, and in spite of successive revisions and refinements to each, the fundamental assumption that the self is flawed persists. This tendency is particularly pronounced when negative judgements of behaviour are conflated with definitions of human nature, as, for instance, Zygmunt Bauman does (albeit unwittingly) in his condemnation of people who espouse individualism – if they are not bad, they must at least be stupid![22] In other examples, Mitchell Thomashow writes that environmentalist objectives are often framed as moral choices implying that "something is wrong with the way people live their lives".[23] Still other views, generated by environmentalist and human potential theorists, expect that an expanded or transformed ecological self – evolved beyond our current state – will naturally identify with and care for place. Until we so evolve, the message is clear: humanity remains flawed.

My point is this: Who or what people are – their allegedly flawed human nature – is held as causal of conditions and events. That assumption makes it easy to control people, even to direct their conduct to fit instrumental prescriptions, as exhumed, discerned, and revealed by Foucault, and as elaborated by others cited. As Nikolas Rose writes, "While our culture of the self accords humans all sorts of capacities and endows all sorts of rights and privileges, it also divides, imposes burdens, and thrives upon the anxieties and disappointments generated by its own promises"[24] – and thus reveals a contemporary politics of self. Critics and proponents of alternatives limit their efficacy and perpetuate the dominant, Western meta-narrative so long as they fail to question the central assumption that human being is flawed.

WHAT AGENCY DO PEOPLE HAVE?

In Erich Fromm's terms, "Man can deceive himself about his real self-interest if he is ignorant of his self and its real needs".[25] For so long as the dominant Western meta-narrative persists, it presages ongoing conflicts and social unrest and anticipates that people will continue to generate myriad problems on the basis of *disdain* for others, or fears of differences in people, and of unfamiliar places. Other, more wholesome understanding of human nature can help people to handle migration and other mobilities with well-being of people and place, and could generate different conditions. The increasing scale and intensity of displacement, forced migrations, and relocations of huge numbers of people makes more urgent the need for further research. Several of Foucault's works are useful in this regard.

Figure 2.1. **We co-constitute our disparate worlds according to the meta-narratives prevailing in different places.**

Foucault's early work refers to the "games of truth [and] practices of power" involved in how people constitute themselves on the basis of knowledge which forms a meta-narrative, and is held socially, culturally, and politically.[26] Acknowledging that people actively constitute themselves, Foucault explains that "these practices [of the self] are nevertheless not something invented by the individual himself. They are models that he finds in his culture and are proposed, suggested, imposed upon him by his culture, his society, and his social group".[27] In later work, Foucault explores the "relationship of the self to itself" and intends his "concept of 'governmentality' to cover the whole range of practices that constitute, define, organize, and instrumentalize the strategies that individuals in their freedom can use in dealing with each other".[28] He comes to believe that "the concept of governmentality makes it possible to bring out the freedom of the subject and its relationship to others".[29]

Understanding the dynamics of the "relationship of the self to itself" – instrumental in people's constitution of themselves – makes it possible to recognise when and how people constrain or free their agency. First, is the dynamic of *belief*. According to Foucault's understanding that truth is produced as a way of establishing and maintaining power, and to Gregory Bateson's explanation that whatever a person believes to be true becomes self-validating; we become, experience, and behave in ways that validate what we presuppose to be true. This process is generally unconscious – since what we presuppose is something decided at an earlier time – and often absorbed from our socio-cultural environment without question. And the process is recursive – taking as truth that human being is flawed creates assumptions and practices that frame behaviour to confirm and perpetuate that there is something fundamentally wrong with self and others. Anthony Weston defines this process as one of *self-validating reduction*, which occurs in a cycle of "disvaluing" – through reductive beliefs or prejudices – and of "devaluing", which he frames as the resultant "actual reduction – the real-world destruction, defacement, devastation".[30] The cost of this second dynamic is that people are reduced to fit the belief. As Weston explains:

> A small "reduction" of another person or class of people – say, the exclusion of some discriminated-against class of persons from certain activities or places – disempowers or isolates them to the point that further exclusions and reductions become natural. Then the original disvaluation – the prejudice, the slander – becomes easier to sustain. Counter evidence is harder to come by, and people are progressively blinded to what remains. Then exclusion and reduction only deepen and worsen, until the combination of desperation and anger on the part of the discriminated-against class and distance and fear on the other side makes the situation volatile, undiscussable, and in the end lethal.[31]

This understanding of self-validating reduction is particularly pertinent to any discussion about the challenges of migration and other mobilities, and about the politics of self. For instance, race riots – such as those in Sydney in 2005 between local white youth and middle eastern young men – can readily be traced to a "disvaluing" and subsequent "devaluing" of immigrants, particularly of Muslim background, in the period leading up to that event.[32] As well as reductive beliefs people hold about others because of differences – for instance, of culture, ethnicity, or religion – some disvaluing assumptions are held about people in general. For example, commonly held beliefs prescribe that human beings are naturally aggressive, that there will always be war, and that people are naturally competitive in the struggle for survival of the fittest. Evidence of those beliefs is certainly present in much human behaviour, and in practices that perpetuate the human/nature and other dualisms Val Plumwood describes as pervading the dominant Western meta-narrative.[33] But of course, evidence is not destiny.

The third dynamic strongly affecting the relationship of the self to the self might be described as reification of the process of self-validating reduction. It is the internal process by which Alfred Korzybski explains we produce *maps* of experience.[34] In this description, a person processes information from outside the self through neurological filters that delete, generalise, and distort – that is, give meaning to – the incoming information.[35] Those neurological filters are benign – neither negative nor positive – but the result might be either. The action of filtering occurs as incoming information passes through a person's senses, thoughts, feelings, attitudes, past decisions, memories, beliefs, and values, and transforms the incoming information into an internal representation. In Korzybski's terms, those internal representations combine to form a person's *map of self*, as well as maps of others, and of the world. Those internal representations affect people's internal states, and their behaviour, which can be understood as a response or reaction more directly to their own maps than to what is actually out there in the world. Thus, this dynamic has important implications in regard to people's relationships with themselves, others, and places. Understanding this process can help people to mitigate the challenges of migration and other mobilities.

To amplify: People's semantic representations – their maps – often render themselves and others as being of greater and lesser worth. They will tend to react to others according to those evaluations, rather than by getting to know what people are actually like. This dynamic equally applies to place. People's maps significantly influence their ability to cope with differences of culture and place, a situation faced both by immigrants and people in host countries. As well as colouring their reactions to difference in others, people's maps directly affect their ability to adjust to changes in their circumstances, and to settle in new places.

The fourth dynamic of the relationship of the self to itself is *sensibility*, which is variously defined as the capacity for – or being open to – feeling, consciousness, appreciation, and responsiveness sensorially, mentally, emotionally, and spiritually. Anthony Elliott and John Urry write that the capacity to engage in new experience is closely tied to this openness.[36] Sensibility is moderated by the degree to which we are associated with or dissociated from the self, or anything else. The ability to associate and to dissociate is a function that interacts dynamically with beliefs, maps, and correspondent self-validating reductions.

Taylor's "stance of disengagement towards oneself", discussed above, is a form of dissociation from the self that provides a way by which it is possible to reform and remake ourselves. This capacity corresponds with elements of Foucault's thoughts about governmentality, and his ideas that we can free ourselves from the confines and dictates of conditions of truth by revealing and challenging the assumptions upon which they are based. However, there are two aspects to such reflexivity that are critical to sense of self. First, for the duration of dissociation – standing back to observe the self – *sense* of self is reduced; thus, disengagement from oneself for critique and review needs to be followed by re-engagement. Second, the extent of that critique determines the degree of freedom possible. If the concept of flawed human being is not brought to light and challenged, then freedom is limited to developing and *bettering* the good, and *controlling* what is held as flawed, within whatever may be the conditions of truth held by an individual or in any culture. This limited notion of freedom is essential to instrumentalist projects of individualism, consumerism, and technologies of citizenship and not less to marginalising projects – for example, of regulating immigration according to ethnicity or race.[37] And it is this limited notion of freedom that maintains people's conduct of their own conduct – their regimes of practice – in line with the agenda of those projects and keeps individual narratives relatively closed.

People tend to associate with what they value, and to dissociate from what they judge to be flawed; this is obvious in any segregation of people, for instance on the basis of racial, ethnic, or gender differences that are evaluated as inequalities. In similar fashion, people tend to dissociate from what they disvalue in themselves, for instance, emotions they judge to be negative; and in the process they desensitise themselves.[38] People associate with their identification, or map of themselves. Importantly, Korzybski writes, "A map is not the territory it represents, but, if correct, it has a similar structure to the territory, which accounts for its usefulness".[39] When people assume that their map of themselves fully encompasses who they are, then they function as if the map *is* the territory – that is, as if their whole self is fully encompassed in the beliefs and representations of the map. This then becomes a self-validating reduction – a reduced map of self – that, over time, is less and less similar to the potential of the self as a whole. Association with identity in this way is a significant dissociation from self, a state of being Korzybski claims is delusional and eventually produces insanity.[40] In everyday experience, dissociation from self reduces sensibility, and thus limits people's ability to be aware of and respond to the conditions of their existence. Understanding this dynamic can assist people to cope with challenges of migration and other mobilities, and to generate increased well-being.

These dynamics of the relationship of the self to itself are fundamental to peoples' senses of self and have strong bearing upon the strength or weakness of those senses and how they relate to their senses of place. How I deploy the terms *strong* and *weak* in regard to sense of self – as in regard to sense of place – is very different to common value-laden definitions of those terms. I consider sense of self also as a continuum from dissociation and alienation from self to association and relationship with self. A dissociated – weak – sense of self might thus be described as experience of association and identification with a reduced map of self, disengaged from the process of the self as a whole, relatively unaware of it, and insensitive to it. An associated – strong – sense of self could be described as an holistic experience of self, that is, engaged with a wholeness of self that is more than the sum of its parts, and always in process of becoming. In these terms, a strong sense of self is characterised by openness, awareness, and sensibility.

RELATING SENSES OF SELF AND PLACE
AND QUALITIES OF EXPERIENCE

The philosophical concept of a rhizome aptly describes the relationship of sense of self and sense of place as they are always connected in a multiplicity of ways that give rise to varying qualities of experience.[41] Recognising this connectivity led me to develop a model of self-place relations (figure 2.2) I apply as a framework for understanding the dynamics of these interactions. For this model I am indebted to literature from a wide range of disciplines, as well as research in the field of migration, and close to forty years of personal and professional development work with people from many ethnic and cultural backgrounds. The state or quality of a person's sense of self relates to his or her capacity to be open to sensory awareness of place – a sensibility extending beyond cognitive perception into modes of embodiment that enable people, wherever they are, to develop sense of place. In turn, sense of place provides a foundation from which people can realise and develop their senses of self. Thus these senses modify each other, they are inseparably relational, intersectional, and rhizomatic. The quality of this relationship is critical to people's well-being, whether they stay in one place or move many times; it underpins their ability to adjust to transitions, relate to different others, and care for changed environments.

Although studies of human consciousness are approached from many perspectives, I am not aware of any method that has been developed for measurement of the strength or weakness of these sensibilities. They are individually experienced and subjectively described, yet it is possible to recognise and validate them in people's experience, and to observe and assess how they correspond with people's behaviour. For the model, I take varying qualities of people's experience and modes of behaviour as expressions of an infinite array of intersectional nexuses or *nodal moments* of the rhizomatic relationship of their senses of self and place.

As the number of possible nodal moments is infinite, for this work I have selected four nodes to represent distinctive intersections of the varying intensities of strength and weakness of senses of self and place that may occur at different times during a person's life course. This suffices to allow for some useful distinctions to be made about how the strength or weakness of people's senses of self and place affects their experience and modes of behaviour – it is not intended to be used to categorise who they are. I use the model primarily in part two to clarify and add nuance to the stories of case study participants. As their narratives testify, each has experience that can be positioned at more than one node in the model at different times in their lives. To attempt to label people according to any nexus would be to conflate experience with identity, and thus be reductive and limiting. In line with principles of narrative inquiry,

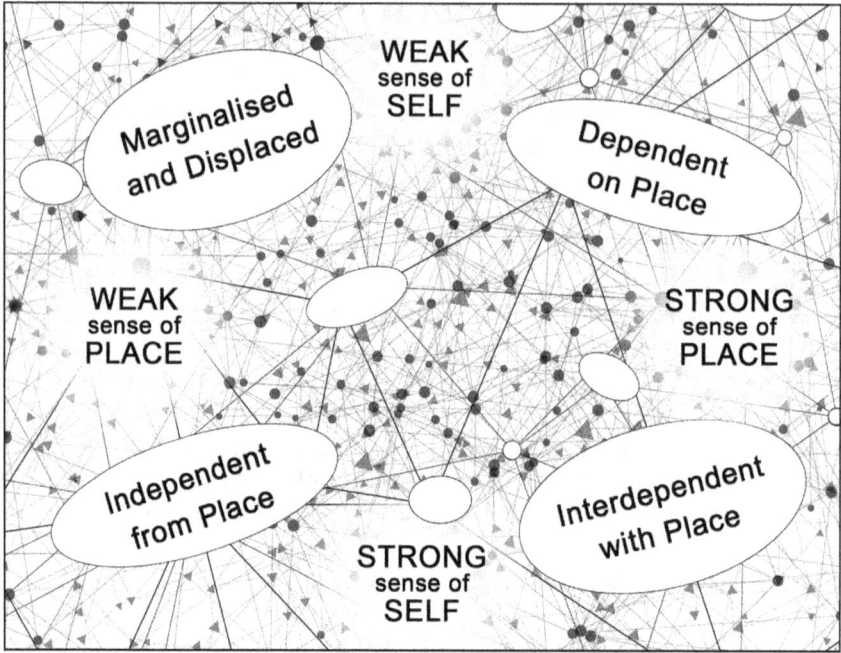

Figure 2.2. The rhizomatic relationship of senses of self and place.

the model is useful, rather, to draw out patterns over a person's life course, or meaningful interpretations of inner and outer experiences at any stage, rather than bare data. A brief introductory description follows of what each node represents.

MARGINALISED *AND* DISPLACED

The interaction of a weak sense of place and a weak sense of self results in people's experience of being *marginalised and displaced*. Identity is often based on experience of powerlessness, struggle, poverty, and a need for environmental justice. People who are placeless and homeless are likely to relate their experience to this node. Capable of heroism, they are directed or governed by survival needs. Senses of place and self are likely to be weakened if a person is displaced, homeless, or living in intolerable conditions – for example, in a place where there is danger, disease, lack of water, food, sanitation, medical services – and with limited or no human or civil rights. Sense of self may also be weakened by lack of social recognition, racism, ghettoisation, persecution, torture, trauma, and ethnic cleansing. Sense of self may be weakened if there is little or no opportunity for education, employment, or possibility of improving on prevailing conditions. Such conditions position the people experiencing them as being without value or worth and demonstrate that some people are believed to be better or worse than others, with those who are marginalised also subordinated. A weakened sense of self can leave people feeling helpless, hopeless, and worthless, learned states that undermine people's senses of self and agency.[42]

It is understandable that people shut down their sensitivity and dissociate their awareness as much as possible from intolerable experience, and thus also limit their sense of place. It can also occur that people in these situations seek refuge, solace, and conviction in structures that provide relief and support, such as religion, and in so doing affirm and strengthen a sense of self that transcends psychology. In relation to social groups, people experiencing marginalisation and displacement are likely to be polarised with others experiencing dependence on place, for example in situations where the local people depend on place and feel that their livelihood is threatened by the arrival of refugees.

DEPENDENT *ON* PLACE

The *dependent on place* nexus expresses the relationship between a strong sense of place and a weak sense of self. Identity is often based on and there can be strong identification with location, ethnicity, history, culture, religion, nationalism, or environmentalism. Experience of being at home is conflated with being in *my* place. At this node, people can be sacrificial, and they are directed or governed by their environment, for example, by local issues to do with water, soil, markets, and climate. Dependence on place may include sedentarism, which can lead to problematical senses of place, and to intolerance and fear of different others. It can also express as attachment to a particular place through physical interaction with it and meanings attributed to it. A strong sense of place indicates stability, and awareness of orientation in place, of one's place in the world, which can support a person's sense of self-worth. Thus, a strong sense of place can provide opportunity for strengthening of sense of self and can be a path to interdependence with place.

The dependence on place node involves a weak sense of self – based on some variant of the underlying assumption that human being is flawed – and might manifest in two main ways. First, taking the idea that some people are better than others, people identifying themselves with a particular culture-religion-ethnicity in a particular place are inclined to see as inferior anyone from a different culture-religion-ethnicity or place. Within one place, people maintaining its singularity are more likely to be valued above anyone who questions it or seeks to change it. Difference is thus perceived as threatening. Sense of place is enhanced by engagement with and a love of place and land and other-than-human nature. Sense of self might include assumptions that people who cared for place and other-than-human nature are more or less worthy, and people who despoil those things are more or less lacking in value. Ownership of and rights in a place are important, as also are having boundaries and keeping others out. In relation to social groups, experience of dependence on place is likely to polarise with experience of independence from place. Such polarisation can be observed between developers and environmentalists, for example in conflicts over logging or preservation of forests, mining opposed to farming, and global or corporate versus local control of agricultural and other resources.

INDEPENDENT *FROM* PLACE

This node brings together a strong sense of self with a weak sense of place. Identity is based on control of nature, achievements, and possessions. As they experience separation from place, people seek to control and change, to take from, use, exploit, and manipulate places and other people. A weak sense of place at this nexus indicates a lack of deep connection with place, little sense of being supported by place, and a concomitant lack of respect for place that often results in an instrumentalist relationship with it. Actions aligned with the *independent from place* nexus show less concern for community and cooperation than is common at the other three nodes. People may gain and maintain independence from place through their achievements and possession of material wealth; the project of individualism is engineered, and individualistic expressions of the self prevail. Here, a context of individualistic competition produces a need for strong identification of and assertion of the self through comparison with others, which can be at their expense, or one's own. If sense of self is based primarily on identity defined in terms of achievement, its strength depends on achieving more, having more, and being valued more highly than others, which can lead to high levels of stress and breakdown. With a strong sense of self that is based on a more integrated and holistic valuing of self, people are likely to be less competitive, and to recognise when they have achieved and amassed enough to provide for their needs and wants. At this node, when self is not reduced merely to identity, a strong sense of self can lead to greater openness to others and to place, and to altruism; and, thus, can be a path to interdependence with place.

INTERDEPENDENT *WITH* PLACE

At this node, a strong sense of place combines with a strong sense of self. Identity is based on autonomy, capability, and mutuality; people experience being at home anywhere, and being able to engage effectively with change. There is a strong sense of agency and a sustainable relationship with the environment. A strong sense of place includes an awareness of the relational quality of self and place – that is, experiencing place as the ground for being – as well as openness to receiving from and responding to place. With a strong sense of self and of place, experience of belonging is not so much attached to any particular place but has more to do with people being at home with themselves wherever they are. A strong sense of self is often indicated by an absence of self-absorption, which also results in far more openness to others and to places, and a willingness to take risks to develop excellence rather than defending any particular position. A way of describing this state is that there is neither attachment to a particular place, nor to a particular identification of self. Instead there is mutuality and awareness of a strongly fluid and mobile relationship between self and place, neither of which is fixed. As in all of the nodal moments, the degree of strength of these senses will affect the quality of people's experience and expression of their capabilities. So long as the assumption that human being is flawed underlies people's sense of self – and, thus, their evaluation of others – the potential of this node cannot fully be realised. Movement towards, and experience and expression of, this node is evident in some of the case study participants' narratives and is discussed in later chapters.

Designed to provoke thinking and questioning, this model is not intended to be prescriptive. It offers a representation of types of experience that – like a map – can assist in appreciating and negotiating the territory. It thus serves as a tool that can add another piece to *extrasectional* understanding of how factors of identity, sense of self and sense of place contribute to the quality of people's experiences, including migration and relocation. The model can thus be used to provide clarity about what might help people to increase resilience and well-being. I apply the model principally in chapter seven in relation to examples of lived experience of settling in new places.

Whatever may be the strength or weakness of people's senses of place and of self as represented by the model, the capability to experience those senses is inherent in human being. What we do with that capability, however, is affected by and dependent upon a myriad of factors, not least of which are the beliefs and worldviews that we embody, what we presuppose to be true.

The alienation of people from other life, from place, and from self – expressed in behaviours including consumerism, competition, aggression, devaluing of human and other life, disregard for and exploitation of all nature – is evidence that the assumption that humanity is flawed still is a central tenet of a dominant Western meta-narrative. If, even as we recognise the need for alternative ideas – including an expanded, relational sense of self in place, and a respect for all human and other life – we continue to dichot-omise, and to disvalue and devalue people and the rest of nature, then we still validate, reinforce, and perpetuate a meta-narrative that produces alienation with all its concomitant ills.

Undeniably, the challenges of contemporary migration make it imperative for us to question the assumptions fundamental to prevailing meta-narratives, and to think of alternatives to many of them. In line with Foucault, my aim is "not [to] deduce from the form of what we are what it is impossible for us to do and to know; but [to] separate out, from the contingency that has made us what we are, the possibility of no longer being, doing, or thinking what we are, do, or think".[43]

To throw light on further aspects of "the contingency that has made us what we are", in the next chapter I broaden enquiry into historical contexts of contemporary migration. I use this narrative theory approach to locate stories illustrating the lived experiences of migration that are documented in following parts of the book.[44] The stories are drawn from a deep, qualitative case study conducted with a group of ten people – the *participants* in this inquiry – whose narratives are grouped in three categories of mobilities: (i) regular migration, (ii) irregular migration, and (iii) mobile lifestyles. Their countries of origin and transition include England, Scotland, Germany, Canada, the United States, Japan, Ethiopia, Sudan, Kenya, India, Nepal, Pakistan, Denmark, and Guatemala. All but one of the participants relocated in Australia, at least for a time. As conditions in that country provide the context for many of their experiences of resettlement, I include here a brief background of the contemporary Australian situation. It serves to illustrate some of the complexity of issues that challenge immigrants, existing residents, and present-day policy-makers, not only in Australia, but globally.

NOTES

1. Goodson, 5–6.
2. Ibid., 5.
3. Arendt, Portable; Buttimer; Clark; Plumwood, Feminism; Tarnas.
4. Tarnas, 431.
5. Taylor, Sources, 111.
6. Plumwood, Feminism, 71.
7. Clark, 2.
8. Taylor, Sources, 177.
9. Ibid., 163.
10. Ibid., 170, 171.
11. Havel, 234.
12. Cruikshank, Dean, Doran, Reith, Rose, Winter.
13. Keck, quoting Foucault, 108; Roof, discussing Emerson and Nietzsche's views on the ethics of individualism in pedagogy, 168.

14. Capra; Drengson, Devall, and Schroll; Roszak, Unfinished Animal; Russell, Global Brain; Ryback; Sheldrake, Rebirth of Nature; Thomashow, 1995.

15. Dean, 154–55.

16. Ibid.

17. Taylor, Sources, 3.

18. Taylor, Ethics of Authenticity, 14.

19. Cruikshank, Dean, Doran, Reith.

20. Doran, 43.

21. Davison, 1286.

22. Bauman.

23. Thomashow, 145.

24. Rose, 3.

25. Naess, 6.

26. Foucault, 'Enlightenment', 33.

27. Ibid., 34.

28. Ibid., 41.

29. Ibid.

30. Weston, 47–48.

31. Ibid.

32. Perera.

33. Plumwood, Feminism.

34. Korzybski, 58.

35. Woodsmall.

36. Elliott and Urry, 40.

37. Cruikshank, Dean, Doran, Reith, Rose, Winter.

38. Damasio, Feeling, Self; Fisher; Macy; Winter.

39. Korzybyski, 58.

40. Ibid., 11, 15.

41. Cabrera and Roland; Hopkins; Høstaker; building on the concept of the rhizome as a representation of the structure of knowledge first proposed by Gilles Deleuze and Felix Guattari in *A Thousand Plateaus* (1980).

42. Seligman.

43. Foucault, 'Enlightenment', 54.

44. Goodson.

Chapter 3

All the World Is the Stage

> It is no exaggeration to claim that the modern system of immigration controls, so much a part of the present political landscape in liberal democracies, was born of racism – of hostility to those perceived as inferior races. While political communities of all shapes and sizes always have taken measures (often ineffectual) to exclude unwanted outsiders, and to expel unwanted insiders, the kinds of state centralized, bureaucratized forms of immigration restriction that we know today were inventions of the late nineteenth and early twentieth centuries.[1]

A mobilities approach allows for recognition that, in all their diverse forms, migrations are not isolated incidents. Take as one example – a scenario probable even as I write – people afloat in a leaky boat, risking life to seek asylum somewhere. Each one is a nexus in an apparently infinite field of relationships; at the centre of connections that span causal conditions of conflict or strife, and which motivated those people to risk safety and life to flee from their places of origin; that extend outwards both spatially (here, there, between) and temporally (past, present, future). Consider other connections of personal relationships with community and to friends and families left behind; to people dead and living; to those praying that each traveller's journey might offer new hope for a safe and decent life; and to others who would wish them ill. Consider connections to places of origin, transition, and destination, in which are entangled the possibilities of asylum, refuge, resettlement, and freedom; or detention behind razor wire – with loss of rights and identity, trauma, and even death.

In short, migrations are intricately connected with movement and change in politics, economies, social structures, and governance – that is, forms of the conduct of conduct – from the personal to the local to the global.[2] This complex connectivity is at the heart of emerging interdisciplinary studies of mobilities.[3] Peter Adey describes mobility as both a relational concept and a process deeply involved in how we address the world and make sense of it, and implicated in how we engage with other people and places.[4] Adey sees mobilities as "surely as important to us as the conceptions and debates that surround notions of space, time and power".[5]

Any mobility always involves other mobility; because to be mobile is to be capable of moving or of being moved, and because movement can only occur in relation to something other, any movement invokes mobilities. What is at stake is not whether things do or do not move but rather the frames or perspectives we use to determine what those mobilities mean. There are altogether different implications and responsibilities involved, for example, if we take any individual's migration to be an act in isolation, or recognise it as indivisibly connected in a network of mobilities of which we are part.

John Urry's *mobilities turn* reflects a shift in thinking from perceiving the world as a collection of separate people and places, capable of acting in isolation, to conceiving of it as a fluid, global network.[6] Seeds of that shift are evident in earlier discourse, for instance, in David Harvey's "reactionary response" to globalism and mobilities in the 1990s, and Doreen Massey's critique of Harvey's views.[7] Although this exchange took place within the discipline of human geography, it has wider relevance. Adey points out that Harvey's aim is to seek fixity, stability, boundedness, and permanence for places, with concurrent desires to "hold off suspicious migrants" and to sustain economic flows.[8] On the other hand, he says, Massey encourages us to look beyond ideas that "the 'real' meanings of places can only be found in fixity and rootedness" or that such views are just a reaction to globalisation.[9] In Massey's opinion, views such as Harvey's emphasise "the insecurity and unsettling impact" of effects of global mobility, and "the feeling of vulnerability which it can produce".[10] She argues that there are "serious inadequacies" in responses to notions of mobility that link ideas of security with fixity, and that these can result in uncertainty about places and promote "problematical sense[s] of place from reactionary nationalisms, to competitive localisms, to introverted obsessions with 'heritage' ".[11] Massey considers, therefore, that we need "to think through what might be an adequately progressive sense of place" that looks beyond local details to grasp their connections to global patterns and processes.[12]

Making an appeal for the new mobilities approach, Urry argues that traditional sociology – based on the study of society – is "outmoded in an increasingly borderless world".[13] Calling for researchers to let go of sedentarist views, Urry advocates a mobilities perspective that engages "with the flows of people within, but especially beyond, the territory of each society".[14] Although Urry holds that globalisation "fractures" the metaphor of society as made up of bounded regional clusters, he insists that globalisation should not be seen as competing with, or as replacing, those societal clusters with a global economy and culture. Rather, he sees a need to replace "the metaphor of society as region with the metaphor of the global conceived of as network and as fluid".[15] His views have not gone unchallenged. Writing in 2001, Adrian Favell predicted that Urry's project was unlikely to last, and that globalisation and international migration were "fashionable topics . . . the academic publishing world has gone crazy about".[16] Claiming that "Urry proceeds to sweep away practically every recognizable feature of twentieth-century sociological thought", Favell makes a scathing attack on Urry's 'globaloney' as "a spectacularly ambitious manifesto . . . of off-the-wall ideas", parading "the usual philosophical heroes – Heidegger, Derrida, Deleuze/ Guattari, Rorty, Virilio – alongside a number of other social theorists to whom he owes a good deal".[17]

Notwithstanding Favell's comments, which are unseemly at best and certainly poor in their predictive accuracy, the ongoing debate about the relative merits of mobilities and sedentarist viewpoints highlight at least two things. First, "dislocation, displacement, disjuncture, and dialogism [are] . . . widespread conditions of migrant subjectivity". Second, "the complex interrelation between travelling and dwelling" remains.[18] Mimi Sheller and Urry claim that a mobilities view "is not simply an assertion of the novelty of mobility in the world today", but aims to shift research from a sedentarist approach to one that goes beyond examination of social processes in spatially fixed settings.[19] Arguing that all places are tied into networks of connections elsewhere, they seek to explore the "complex relationality" of people and places, rather than treating them as distinct entities.[20] Contributing to this debate, Tim Cresswell holds that sedentarist views position mobility as "an alternative to place, boundedness, foundations, and stability", but he relates mobility to power.[21] Cresswell points out that mobility is often portrayed "as a threat, a disorder in the system, a thing to control", and he cautions that, for mobile people, consequences of a sedentarist metaphysics are severe:[22] "Thinking of the world as rooted and bounded is reflected in language and social practice. Such thoughts actively territorialize identities in property, in region, in nation – in place. They simultaneously produce discourse and practice that treats mobility and displacement as pathological".[23]

In Cresswell's view, proponents of sedentarism see place in ideal terms, "as a moral world, as an insurer of authentic existence, and as a center of meaning for people", and often assume mobility is a dysfunction.[24] He argues that much social research is informed by "a very strong moral geography that marginalizes mobility ontologically, epistemologically, and normatively".[25] As an example, in the field of architecture, Juhani Pallasmaa states unequivocally that as "fundamentally biological, cultural and historical beings [humans are] bound to space and place".[26] Deploring the frequency with which many people move from house to house, or even have "a novel life style without a home altogether", he calls this "an existential nomadism . . . life itself in constant transition without roots and domicile".[27] Pallasmaa asserts that "increasing mobility, detachment and speed must have dramatic consequences for our consciousness, our sense of belonging and responsibility, and our ethical responses".[28] In the field of comparative religion, Peter Nynäs considers that there is "an intrinsic relationship" between place and a sense of being a moral subject.[29] However, rather than holding that such relationship depends on any single place, he views it as contingent, for example, on whether or not people find the rules of a place familiar.

The mobilities turn is a shift in thinking from a place-based perspective and way of filtering the world to one of movement and fluidity, from boundary to connectivity, defence to linkage. The discussion is politically significant, not least in relation to migrations of all kinds. Cresswell writes that "a term such as refugee [used to label] people without a place who need to be regulated . . . highlights the entanglement of mobility with meaning and power".[30] Roland Dannreuther examines the politics and perception of migration as a challenge to the security of nation-states.[31] He points out that it can "appear particularly hypocritical that the developed countries preach the doctrine of economic liberalization and globalization while setting up strong and seemingly impenetrable borders to forestall the free movement of people", especially when globalisation increases economic inequalities.

Migration is stressful, even perilous, for many people, particularly – but not only – under conditions of hardship, forced relocation, or persecution.[32] In the process, place and environment also suffer neglect, exploitation, and damage. Other people seem to find it possible to adjust to movement and change in ways that draw on and engender well-being. Clearly, then, migration need not be harmful to relationships with people and place. Yet, it is obvious that contemporary mobilities often have a disassembling effect, unsettling certainties, and presenting people with novel views of themselves and their worlds.

REGULAR MIGRATION

Migration broadly means movement of people from one country, region, or place to settle in another; it encompasses moves made voluntarily and others coerced or forced. Some people migrate within the requirements of national and subnational border regulations – regular migration – and others move outside those parameters and fall into various categories of irregular migration. There is no clear agreement as to what the term *irregular* actually covers, but commonly it includes labour migrants, refugees, and asylum seekers.

Migration is not new. What is new is the unprecedented extent and volume of that movement, which has been described as "an inevitable consequence of globalisation".[33] That might account for much migration, but wars and other extreme social disruptions and violence certainly contribute more, and numbers of climate refugees are also rapidly increasing. Available figures are not precise because there are too many variables in reporting and collection of data for real accuracy, and migrations emanating from non-Western regions are often not included. Nevertheless, the UNHCR estimates that there were one billion migrants in the world in 2018–258 million international migrants and 763 million internal migrants – one in seven of the world's population. These figures represent people living in countries or areas other than their places of birth – migrant *stock* – as well as those currently migrating – migrant *flow*. The rate of regular migration has increased rapidly in recent times, with current flows at about five million per year.

Some comparison can be made with migrations of relatively large numbers of Europeans over the past two hundred years.[34] Between 1846 and 1890, around seventeen million people left Europe for the New World, but migration peaked around the turn of the century, with twenty-seven million people leaving Europe between 1891 and 1920. The rate tapered off with the First World War and the Great Depression, and was effectively stopped again by the advent of the Second World War. Over the whole period, from 1846 to 1939, about fifty-one million people left Europe.

At the end of the Second World War, around fifteen million people moved from one country to another within Europe, with relatively small numbers migrating elsewhere. Migration commentator Peter Stalker writes that even though many Europeans were "tempted to emigrate during the austerity years of the 1950s . . . few European governments were keen to encourage emigration, since the war had cost 7.8 million lives", and people were needed to rebuild economies.[35] Nevertheless, migration continued. For example, there was a strong revival of emigration from the United Kingdom in the 1950s and 1960s. Although numbers dropped significantly after 1964, more than seven million people migrated from the United Kingdom to non-European destinations between 1951 and 1998.[36] The United Kingdom is listed as the major source of emigrants, then Italy, the Netherlands, and the Federal Republic of Germany; and the main destinations as Australia, Canada, and the United States, then South America and Israel, see figure 3.1.

According to Stalker, the tide turned when reconstruction in Europe led to an economic boom and Germany, France, and the United Kingdom needed labour. Workers were recruited at first from among those displaced during the war, then from other European countries, and then from each country's colonial ties, with net immigration for Western Europe during this period – until 1973 – reaching about ten million. Since then, migration has become steadily

Figure 3.1. Left: Brothers about to migrate from a small town in northern Germany after the Second World War. Right: the Australian Minister for Immigration welcoming children who arrived on the migrant ship *General Black*, when it reached Melbourne from Europe, in 1950. The two boys are at the front right.

more difficult, as governments have "effectively closed the doors to further labour immigration", migration policies generally have been tightened, and much of the debate about migration has turned to refugees, and *illegal* immigrants – the asylum seekers.[37]

Although some countries have maintained a relatively stable social base, in many others a consequence of migrations of people, worldwide, is a plurality of cultures and ethnicities. Among attempts to integrate or assimilate disparate groups, contemporary multiculturalism emerged in Western countries along three main trajectories. First, philosophically it is a vehicle for replacing older forms of ethnic and racial hierarchy and exclusion with new relations of democratic citizenship, inspired, and grounded in human-rights ideals.[38] Second, politically it is a means of controlling ethnic (and economic and political) diversity.[39] Third, in practice it is the everyday experience of people living in places with mixed populations of diverse ethnicities, cultures, and countries of origin. According to Will Kymlicka, multiculturalism arose from decisions in liberal-democratic states from the 1970s to mid-1990s "to develop more multicultural forms of citizenship in relation to immigrant groups".[40] Kymlicka states that the trend of these policies was towards "increased recognition and accommodation of diversity . . . and involved a rejection of earlier ideas of unitary and homogeneous nationhood".[41] Pointing out that there have been many past multicultural societies, Tariq Modood sees contemporary multiculturalism as "the political accommodation of minorities formed by immigration to western countries from outside the prosperous West".[42]

In recent years, political leaders in various countries have declared that policies of multiculturalism have failed.[43] These claims are also then critiqued on grounds that the focus on failed multiculturalism obscures other issues – such as border and security controls, pressures of intensified immigration, anxieties about terrorism, and economic crises – that generate reactions to cultural diversity, and moves to preserve strong national identities. In this light, Kymlicka argues that there is "significant, if not yet conclusive, evidence" of progress towards the goals of multiculturalism, and it "should remain a salient option in the toolkit of democracies".[44] Modood writes that multiculturalism is timely and necessary, but needs a theory that "does not have an anti-immigrant bias".[45] In his view, ideology confused with policy obscures what occurs and needs to be addressed in practice.

Australia and Canada are two countries where multiculturalism is identified as having been relatively successful, albeit in somewhat different forms, and yet in both jurisdictions it is undercut by recent policy changes.[46] Notably, both countries also have unresolved cultural and citizenship issues in regard to Indigenous populations being placed outside conversations about multiculturalism.[47] Multiculturalism is problematic, complex, and varies in different places – and is under threat by extreme right and fundamentalist reactions, especially to levels of irregular migration deemed to present a humanitarian crisis.

IRREGULAR MIGRATION

The UNHCR's emergency list in 2018 shows *millions* of "persons of concern" worldwide – "the highest levels of displacement of people on record" – with an unprecedented 68.5 million people forced from their homes, 25.4 millions of those being refugees of whom over half are under the age of eighteen, more than three million asylum seekers, and "an estimated ten million stateless people who have been denied a nationality and access to basic rights such as education, healthcare, employment and freedom of movement". Numbers vary according to conditions current at any time but the figures show a rapid increase in the rate of displacement of people from about two and a half million a year between 2012 and 2014 to about five million a year by 2018 – about the same as contemporary rates of regular migration. At this rate, *one person is forcibly displaced every two seconds* as a result of conflict or persecution.

Words such as *crisis* and *emergency* fail to convey the enormity of this situation. High on the list are 5.6 million people who have fled from Syria, and 6.6 million internally displaced by its civil war that has now been going on for longer than the Second World War. Involving Russia, the United Kingdom, and the United States, it is a political conflict that has become a human tragedy.[48]

The Rohingya situation provides another example of conflict escalating the scale of irregular immigration. One of the ethnic minority groups in Myanmar (previously called Burma), the Rohingya Muslim people have lived in that predominantly Buddhist country for generations, many of them pushed back and forth between Pakistan and Myanmar at times of political conflict, especially during and in the aftermath of the Second World War. Many of the Rohingya came to the country during the period of British rule (1824–1948), and the Myanmar government contends, therefore, that they are illegal immigrants. The government of Myanmar denies the Rohingya citizenship, excluded them from the 2014 census, and refuses to recognise them as a people. Long described by the United Nations as one of the world's most persecuted minorities, the Rohingya people have been fleeing alleged abuses by Myanmar security forces for years. In August 2017, Rohingya ARSA militants are alleged to have retaliated with deadly attacks on more than thirty Myanmar police posts.[49] In the month that followed, government military troops, backed by local Buddhist mobs, burned 288 Rohingya villages, killing 6,700 Rohingya, including at least 730 children under the age of five, and raping and enslaving women and girls. The Myanmar government puts the number of dead at 400, and claims that "clearance operations" against the militants ended weeks before observers saw any end of violence. Of the approximately one million Rohingya people estimated to be living in Myanmar prior to August 2017, close to 700,000 had fled to neighbouring Bangladesh by early 2018. As they joined over 200,000 others who had fled previous waves of violence, the situation escalated into what the United Nations describes as a "textbook example of ethnic cleansing".

In addition to wars, political conflicts, genocide, persecution, and terror, irregular migration is motivated by famine, natural disasters, poverty, and land being rendered untenable by environmental impacts of armed conflict, and climate change; and it includes seasonal workers and labour migrants. Not all such conditions qualify people for refugee status as defined in the 1951 United Nations Convention on Refugees and its 1967 Amendment. This definition leaves out "those compelled by deficiencies in the local social, economic, or environmental context".[50] Environmentalist Norman Myers estimates that over coming decades, the number of environmental refugees alone could range from fifty up to two hundred million people, when global warming takes hold.[51] Environmental catastrophes, such as the earthquake and tsunami in Indonesia in 2018, floods, landslides, wildfires, and famine increase levels of migration – both regular and irregular – and these are also attributed to results of economic and development policies worldwide.[52]

Political philosopher Sarah Fine holds that "gross economic, social, and political inequalities between the Global South and North" – a legacy of colonialism – impel people to migrate.[53] There is also an increasing number of *gender* refugees – people who identify themselves as gay, lesbian, bisexual, and transsexual.[54] All such categories fall outside the United Nations definition of refugees, but even without them current numbers who fit the definition, worldwide, challenge the capacity – and willingness – of receiving nations to respond.[55]

Many millions of refugees and asylum seekers have been, and are still provided with minimal protection, shelter, and humanitarian aid in camps built to be temporary, but in use for many years. Most of them are in sub-Saharan Africa, the Middle East, and Asia, with a small number in Europe.[56] In 2012, the estimated number of people in these camps was about twenty million. More recently, numbers are far higher but difficult to estimate with violence escalating in Syria and other places. Dadaab, established more than twenty years ago in north-eastern Kenya, hosts more than half a million people including about ten thousand third-generation refugees born in the camp.[57] Until recently, Dadaab was considered to be the world's largest camp, but the plight of the Rohingya people has increased the number of refugees at a camp in Bangladesh to about one million.[58]

In 2019, figures show a small percentage of Syrian refugees in camps, and Turkey hosts close to three and a half million registered Syrian refugees. For more than a million in Lebanon, life is a daily struggle with most below the poverty line. Without formal refugee camps, Syrians are strewn throughout urban and rural communities in more than two thousand locations.[59]

International protection for asylum seekers and refugees begins with admission to a country of asylum and registration and documentation by national authorities or the UNHCR: "Registration and identification of refugees is key . . . [it] facilitates access to basic assistance and protection . . . [it can] protect against refoulement (forced return), arbitrary arrest and detention; it helps keeps families together and assists in reuniting separated children with their families".[60] However, far-right conservatism has led to growing nationalism, and national governments have used a "crisis narrative" to make it possible to prevent registration, and to exclude, or return refugees.[61] Coupled with "faltering international cooperation", this move has profoundly undermined the global response, and has significant consequences:

> An erosion of refugee rights and a deterioration of the overall protective environment in many parts of the world – including border closures and refoulement . . . restrictive or discriminatory immigration and asylum measures, limitations on access to asylum procedures, the pursuit of "off-shore" processing arrangements, indefinite detention in appalling conditions, and other deterrent measures.[62]

According to international law, asylum claims should be processed in the country where they are filed; however, until recently, the European Union has devolved responsibility for processing and determining refugee status to the country of first entrance. In practice, this policy has meant that asylum seekers are regularly sent back from other European Union countries to Italy and Greece, which are often the first countries of entrance, and also to Libya, which is held to be "both a receiving migration area . . . and a transit region functioning as a bridge between Europe and Africa for maritime irregular migration".[63] Agreements between the European Union, Italy, and Libya in 2008 required Libya to implement restrictive migration policies and border controls with dire consequences – "Most of those intercepted at sea, and readmitted by the Italian government to Libya have been subjected to ill treatment and detention, removed from Libya to neighbouring countries, or left stranded in the desert".[64]

At early stages of what increasingly was labelled as a migration crisis, refugees fleeing ongoing conflicts – for example in Syria, Afghanistan, and Iraq – were initially welcomed in at least some European Union countries; but responses changed as the number of refugees seeking to enter Europe steadily rose until it peaked at over one million in 2015. Restrictive migration policies were instituted, often characterised by building razor wire border fences and border closures along the Balkan corridor through Turkey, Greece, the former Yugoslav Republic of Macedonia to Serbia, Hungary, Croatia, Slovenia, Austria, Germany, and beyond.[65] An accord reached at a 2018 European Union summit provides for other European Union countries to alleviate some of the burden on Italy, and also Greece, but media reports say that details remain unclear, and such measures would be voluntary.[66] The lack of safe alternatives pushes people into the hands of smugglers and makes the journeys more dangerous:

> This movement towards Europe continues to take a devastating toll on human life. Since the beginning of 2017, over 2,700 people are believed to have died or gone missing while crossing the Mediterranean Sea to reach Europe, with reports of many others perishing en route. These risks do not end once in Europe. Those moving onwards irregularly have reported numerous types of abuse, including being pushed back across borders.[67]

To manage migration, European Union countries began to develop instruments that "appear to fall outside the scope of legislative processes, and . . . democratic scrutiny" in an expedient approach that risks undermining the European Union's stated values.[68] Response to the crisis has evolved to conflate humanitarian aims to rescue people and save lives with military objectives to combat people-smuggling and control borders and movements of people:[69]

[This military-humanitarian approach] escalated into warfare within a humanitarian framework whereby EU military forces are deployed against the entire business of migrant travel across the EU. In other words, a military-humanitarian frontier where the military deployment becomes more specific while the humanitarian framework becomes increasingly diffuse.[70]

Political commentator Daniel Trilling points out that such policy has "a deadly price": he contends that the most extreme of the far-right politicians in the European Union "are trying to use the issue of migration to push a vision of the nation based on ethnic privilege and defined in opposition to racialised outsiders, be they Muslims, or unspecified dark-skinned 'migrants' or indeed Roma".[71] He also suggests that such policy puts to the test "the founding myth of the EU, that it exists to ensure that the horrors of the twentieth century are never repeated".[72] Others write that these policies specifically make use of humanitarian reasoning to recommence militarised border controls, to criminalise migratory movement, and to disempower the right to asylum.[73] Further, the rhetoric places European Union citizens and institutions as "spectators who have no involvement":

The escalating number of deaths at the borders can thus be considered as a mere "collateral effect" of such conflicts. As a result, migrants who die during the journey are displayed as images for collective mourning, deaths without any responsibility; the only subject singled out for blame is the smuggler.[74]

Overall, national governments have used a crisis narrative to control populations, and it is evident that refusal of entry to asylum seekers is based more on ideology than capacity, particularly with the significant rise of extreme right-wing opinion in the European Union, the United Kingdom, the United States, Australia, and other first world countries. Such far-right conservatism is influencing government policies, not only to tighten borders but also to restrict and control existing immigrant groups. Urry confirms that much political organisation "presumes a citizenship of stasis" – in other words, that rights and responsibilities apply to people with long-term membership in bounded territories.[75] Notably, however, length of residence does not necessarily translate into rights or citizenship: Ethiopian migrant workers in Norway, for example, claiming a right to citizenship on the basis of their long-term work and relationships with local communities still faced deportation.[76] France deports thousands of Roma immigrants each year.[77] Punitive new laws introduced by the government in Denmark in 2018 force Muslim immigrants to assimilate and merge into Danish culture:[78]

Starting at the age of 1, "ghetto children" must be separated from their families for at least 25 hours a week, not including nap time, for mandatory instruction in "Danish values", including the traditions of Christmas and Easter, and Danish language. Noncompliance could result in a stoppage of welfare payments. Other Danish citizens are free to choose whether to enrol children in preschool up to the age of six.[79]

Such clearly racist policy and action is strongly reminiscent of Nazi Germany, not only during but in the lead-up to the Second World War. Contemporary discourse on the ethics of migration points out that although "so-called liberal democratic states today would deny that their immigration policies directly discriminate on racial and ethnic grounds, and discrimination of that sort is widely condemned as unacceptable", clear examples of such invidious practice are easy to find.[80]

To a large extent, the Australian response to migration, and in particular to refugees and asylum seekers, reflects and aligns with policy changes in the United Kingdom, the European Union, and the United States. In Australia, in recent years, the treatment of asylum seekers has become a political football, centred on grievous detention of asylum seekers in contravention of international law to which the Australian government is a signatory.[81] Detention of people of all ages – without any charge being laid against them, and for indefinite periods that can amount to many years – is justified on the basis that it functions as a deterrent to others who may attempt such migration, and because of worldwide fears for security, particularly since the events of 9/11 in the United States, and strident rhetoric that it is essential to protect the borders against terrorists. As Sarah Fine notes, the "equivalence between terrorism and refugees is a false one, reactions to immigration are racist".[82] Further, as many advocates reiterate, rather than perpetrating terrorism, asylum seekers are people in flight from it.

THE CASE OF AUSTRALIA – FOUNDED ON MIGRATION

In 1788, Britain claimed the land that was to become Australia and settled parts of it as a penal colony from what is now New South Wales.[83] There was no treaty with the Indigenous Aboriginal inhabitants, whose forebears are understood to have migrated to the continent by boats or land bridges from at least 40,000 to 60,000 years ago. In 1889, British courts declared the land *terra nullius*, because it was "practically unoccupied" – a decision repeated in 1979 by the High Court of Australia because, it judged, prior to British colonisation, Australia was a territory which, "by European standards, had no civilised inhabitants or settled law".[84] It was only in 1992, more than two hundred years after colonisation, that the High Court of Australia decided the doctrine of *terra nullius* should not have been applied.[85] There is evidence of earlier "discovery" of *Terra Australis* by Dutch and Spanish explorers, of trade between Aborigines and Chinese and Macassan sailors, and of significant contact between Aboriginals and French explorers prior to Britain claiming the country.[86]

Since British occupation, Australia's history shows that the colonies and nation – federated in 1901 – were successively founded on migration, and attitudes towards migrants have changed dramatically over the years. The first arrivals were transported convicts and their guards. A small number of voluntary migrants, also principally from Britain and Ireland, gradually followed, and settled in six colonies. The discovery of gold in 1850 attracted great numbers of people from Britain, Ireland, Continental Europe, China, the United States, New Zealand, and the South Pacific:

> Australia never again saw such a rush of new immigrants. . . . By the time of Federation in 1901 [when the Commonwealth of Australia, with the reigning British sovereign as head of state, was constituted from the six colonies of New South Wales, Victoria, Tasmania, South Australia, Queensland, and Western Australia], the total population was close to four million, of whom one in four was born overseas.[87] [The Aboriginal population was not counted!]

The first legislation passed by the new Commonwealth was the Immigration Restriction Act 1901, commonly known as underpinning the infamous White Australia Policy, which aimed to create a "white" nation, and persisted until 1973.[88] Despite comparatively large numbers of Chinese residents, this policy effectively banned Asian immigration for the next fifty years. Assisted passages gave priority to the British and Irish; and Pacific Island labourers who worked in the Queensland sugar industry were deported.[89]

With the outbreak of the First World War, in 1914, migration almost ceased; some migrants considered acceptable prior to that time were reclassified as "enemy aliens" and about seven thousand people born in Germany, the Austro-Hungarian Empire, Bulgaria, and Turkey were interned. From the end of the war, in 1918, assisted and sponsored migration schemes were revived, then stopped again with the start of the Great Depression, in 1929. James Jupp writes that an important consequence was that "immigrants formed a lower proportion of the population between 1930 and 1950 than ever before or since . . . and those born and brought up in that period were living in an Australia becoming steadily more provincial and inward looking".[90] By the start of the Second World War, in 1939, Australia was "small in numbers, British in origins, 99 per cent white, provincial, homogeneous and psychologically dependent on the British Empire".[91] During the Second World War, once again, certain nationalities were classed as enemy aliens – Germans,

Italians, and Japanese among them. Again, most were interned, as was a large group of Jewish refugees who arrived in 1940.

After the war, in response to the near invasion of Australia by the Japanese, migration policy changed. Under the slogan of "populate or perish", the government set out to attract about seventy thousand immigrants a year.[92] The government offered ex-service personnel free passage, and others paid their own way, including increasing numbers of people from southern and eastern Europe, and from among the Jewish diaspora, many of them refugees from the ruins of Hitler's Europe. Although the Australian government sought a majority of Anglo-Celtic immigrants, it agreed to accept twelve thousand refugees a year from among some eleven million people who had survived the Nazi labour and concentration camps – including Poles, Yugoslavs, Latvians, Ukrainians, Hungarians, and Jews. When much of the flow of migration slowed after about seven years, and with a view to continuing to boost the population, the Australian government negotiated migration agreements with its counterparts in countries including the Netherlands, Italy, Austria, Belgium, West Germany, Greece, Spain, the United States, Switzerland, Denmark, Norway, Sweden, and Finland; and was second only to Israel in the proportion of migrants accepted in the decade or so following the end of the war in 1945.

From the 1950s, the White Australia Policy began to weaken as migrants were sourced from a wider range of countries. During this period of the Long Boom,[93] it was common to hear Australians refer to "Mother England", and many still called England "home", but understandings of what it meant to be an Australian were beginning to change with a new sense of nationalism. Australia's relationship with Britain was challenged (in the lead up to its entry into the European Economic Community in 1973); Australia's alignment with the United States increased in political and military terms – and was typified by engagements in the Korean War (1950–1953) and the Vietnam War (1962–1973). The Australian economy also began to diversify, deindustrialise, modernise, and restructure; and became more integrated into the Asian region and the global economy.[94]

In 1967, a referendum "gave official recognition to the existence of Aborigines as a distinct group of people".[95] Some people feared that the nature of Australian society could be changed through indiscriminate immigration levels and composition that might tip the balance "to one of non-Anglo dominance".[96] Fear of loss of national identity, racist behaviour, and other discriminatory practices were still prevalent. In that climate, until the 1970s, immigration policy was one of *assimilation*, aiming to have people abandon their previous culture and language, learn English, and become *new* Australians. In 1973, Gough Whitlam's Labor government declared Australia a multicultural society, and, according to amendments to the Australian

Citizenship Act 1948, all migrants were to be accorded equal treatment.[97] Introduction of that multicultural policy aimed for "social cohesion" – to have immigrants integrate, rather than assimilate.[98]

In 1975, a new round of asylum seekers – newly dubbed *boat people* – began to arrive in Australia. Over the next thirty years, more than 25,000 people arrived, initially from Vietnam, Cambodia, Laos, Burma, China, and later, East Timor, and the Middle East. In spite of criticism by the United Nations and Amnesty International, since 1992, all, including children, are subject to mandatory detention while their claims of refugee status are assessed. By 2006, many other immigrants had come from China, South Africa, and India, as also refugees from countries previously unrepresented, the fastest growing groups from Sudan, then Afghanistan, and Iraq.

Critics describe a weakening of policy favouring multiculturalism from the 1990s. Alper and Hurriyet Babacan attribute that weakening to economic rationalist agendas, failure to tackle deep-seated racism, and the neoliberal policy agendas of successive Commonwealth governments.[99] They note that the formal status of multiculturalism was diminished by the closure of many of its supporting organisations, such as the Office of Multicultural Affairs and by severe cuts in funding to the Human Rights and Equal Opportunity Commission, the Aboriginal and Torres Strait Islander Commission, and the multicultural and multilingual public radio and television broadcaster, SBS.

Following the events of 9/11 in the United States in 2001 and the ensuing Iraq War, in which Australia participated, harsh asylum and counter-terrorism policies in Australia made conditions increasingly unwelcoming for refugees, asylum seekers, and particular categories of migrants. However, the tightening of Australia's borders was well in train *before* that iconic event. In August 2001, the Norwegian freighter *Tampa* rescued four hundred and thirty-eight Afghan asylum seekers en route to Australia in a sinking boat; in response, the Australian government sent a navy vessel with SAS counter-terrorism troops to refuse entry into Australian waters. Australia's then Prime Minister, John Howard, claimed that on 6 October that asylum seekers threw their children overboard from another boat in an attempt to force acceptance of them. This claim was later proved to be untrue, but Howard's manipulation stirred nationalist isolationism, stepped up criticism of multiculturalism, and built on the hysteria following 9/11 to support re-election of his conservative government:

Australia's 2001 Howard government decided that the primary function of its refugee policy was not to provide humanitarian assistance and relieve the suffering of refugees fleeing far off war-torn countries but to protect its nation's borders against unwanted migrants. No evident policy goal of deterring human rights violations was apparent. Quite the reverse: Australia's ad hoc policy

towards arriving boat people, reflected in the handling of the Tampa affair
and the hastily prepared Pacific Solution, indicated a policy of national self-
interest above all other concerns and election politics pursued in the name of
sovereignty.[100]

The extent of isolationist reaction was brought into focus by racial rioting at
Sydney's Cronulla Beach, in 2005. In a powerful critique, Suvendrini Perera
points to a history of racist attitudes leading up to the riots, and claims that
media-fuelled fear over "the war on terrorism" heightened racist hysteria; for
instance: "Women wearing hijab or burqa are subjected to a spectrum of violence from physical assault to the suspicion of concealing bombs under their
burqas and accusations of 'confronting' the sensibilities of Anglo-Australia
by their mere presence in public places".[101] In accord with several other
authors, Babacan and Babacan assert that:

> the Howard government . . . deliberately and persistently negatively portrayed
> Arabs and Muslims as the "other" with the effect of demonising and dehumanis-
> ing them [as part of] a deliberate attempt to create a unique and homogeneous
> national identity . . . new forms of patriotism that have emerged are racialised
> and draw boundaries of inclusion and exclusion. Who is an Australian, what are
> Australian values, and what is "un-Australian" have been re-defined resulting
> in the marginalisation, criminalisation and exclusion of the "voiceless other".[102]

Farida Fozdar and Brian Spittles write that a key aspect of the Australian
government's retreat from multiculturalism was further modification of citizenship eligibility requirements, in 2007, which "served to re-direct the Australian imagination away from a nascent 'multicultural' identity, back to one
redolent of the times of the 'White Australia Policy', confidently celebrating
connections with an Anglo-Saxon heritage, the European Enlightenment,
and Judeo-Christian roots".[103] In this regard, David Nolan and his colleagues
argue that media discourses contribute to integrationist agendas challenging
multiculturalism, perform a role that shapes government policy, and "define
how different groups experience rights".[104] They cite numerous studies in
Canada, the United Kingdom, and Australia that demonstrate how refugee
groups and asylum seekers are frequently portrayed in a negative and problematic manner; represented as an immigration "crisis; a threat to the security
of the nation and an 'embodiment of danger'; constructed as a homogeneous
group, sharing similar characteristics, backgrounds, motivations and economic status" and with terms such as *refugee, asylum seeker, boat people,*
and *illegal immigrant* used interchangeably.[105] Summarising this backlash
against, and retreat from multiculturalism since the mid-1990s, Kymlicka
writes that it is "partly driven by fears among the majority group that the

accommodation of diversity has 'gone too far' and is threatening their way of life . . . [a fear often expressed in] the rise of nativist and populist right-wing political movements".[106]

In 2012, the UNHCR issued new guidelines on detention of asylum seekers, affirming that "seeking asylum is not a criminal act, and that indefinite and mandatory forms of detention are prohibited under international law". Successive Australian governments have attracted censure and concern from the UNHCR for "unlawful and increasingly harsh and punitive treatment of asylum seekers arriving by boat".[107] Asylum seekers arriving in Australian waters by boat are detained off shore in appalling conditions on Nauru, Christmas Island, Manus Island, and in Papua New Guinea; and the Australian Navy was used to *push back* boats, forcing other asylum seekers into fully enclosed, lifeboat capsules and towing them out of Australian waters until the government claimed that there were no more.[108] According to Pauline Maillet and her colleagues,

> The strategic entanglements of legality and geography were always part of Howard's design to deflect, deter and exclude. These have been carried forward in subsequent extensions of the excised territory and additional "solutions" implemented by Australia in the years since. The result has been a fairly continuous series of policies enacted by diverse political parties to mediate access to asylum and exclude, including interception, excision and detention on islands.[109]

In spite of government attempts to stop all scrutiny of its offshore detention centres, the United Nations, Médecins Sans Frontières, and others condemned the poor conditions and reported the seriously deteriorating health of people detained on Nauru and Manus Island. These reports led to increasing social pressure which culminated in December 2018 with the Parliamentary Upper House (the Senate) voting to pass a bill that would see evacuation of asylum seekers on medical grounds. By dint of delaying the vote, the incumbent right-wing government avoided dealing with the bill in the Lower House (the House of Representatives) until February 2019, when the law was finally passed with some amendments.[110] Within days of this historic defeat, the government ramped up rhetoric about the risks of the boats starting up again and the potential that these asylum seekers could be terrorists – although the government's own figures show that almost all of the people who have had their claims assessed are found to be refugees, and many are stateless.[111] Subsequently, the incumbent Prime Minister, Scott Morrison, announced reopening of the Christmas Island Detention Centre and that medical evacuees would go there from Nauru and Manus, not to Australia. Media report that his rhetoric, which includes allegations about "numerous alleged criminals on

Nauru and Manus", is "ferocious, full of exaggeration and scaremongering"; that it is an attack on the opposition party in the lead up to an election, and that it is a "risky gamble".[112]

At the height of the detention era, the total number of men, women, and children incarcerated was just over two thousand five hundred; by the time of the medical evacuation legislation only a few hundred people were left including sick children; and the cost of this project has been estimated at more than $5 billion.[113]

Notwithstanding the volatility, ambiguity, and uncertainty that typifies Australian migration policy, and setting aside for a moment the added complexity of government approaches to asylum, Jan Pakulski describes Australian multiculturalism as a success.[114] He considers that racism, conflict, and other related concerns are at a comparatively low level in Australia, and argues that their expression is symptomatic of a need for more action to fulfil the goals of multiculturalism (see figure 3.2). This view is shared by Val Colic-Peisker, Will Kymlicka, Mark Lopez, Tariq Modood, Maree Pardy and Julian Lee, and others whose arguments support a return to multiculturalist settlement policies with a human-rights base.[115] Kymlicka cautions that "It is precisely when immigrants are perceived as illegitimate, illiberal, and burdensome that multiculturalism may be most needed".[116]

Figure 3.2.   People from many lands enjoying a multicultural festival in Adelaide, 2019. Courtesy of Creolumen Photography.

Statistics from Australia's 2016 Census of Population and Housing show that "Australia's multicultural landscape is as diverse as ever".[117] Over three hundred ancestries were separately identified in the census, and this finding certainly indicates cultural and ethnic diversity. A closer examination of census figures, however, reveals some facts that bear both on the current and contested status of multiculturalism, and on the lived experience of immigrants. Twenty-eight per cent of the population (people referred to as first generation Australians) were born overseas – roughly the same as the 'one in four' at the time of Federation in 1901 – and a further twenty per cent (second generation Australians) are people born in Australia but with at least one parent born overseas. Whatever the mix of ethnicity, close to half the population is composed of people with a brief Australian ancestry, or none at all. Yet, despite including three hundred ancestries, the population still retains a high proportion of people of Anglo-Celtic origin – in this most recent census, English 36.1 per cent, Australian 33.5 per cent, Irish 11 per cent, and Scottish 9.3 per cent accounted for 89.9 per cent of people. A further six of the leading ten ancestries reflected a European heritage. The two remaining ancestries in the top ten were Chinese 5.6 per cent and Indian 4.6 per cent. Figures given for the *Islamic* population – a religious rather than racial distinction – made up only 2.6 per cent of the total population. The breakdown has, perhaps, not changed greatly since James Jupp wrote in 2007 that,

> while the major cities have large Chinese, Italian, Greek, Vietnamese, Muslim and South Asian districts . . . rural and provincial Australia are still not multi-cultural in any meaningful sense. This shift in the ethnic character of the cities is one reason for constant questioning of the national identity by those who still believe all Australians are essentially alike. They are not and cannot be.[118]

Notably, Jupp and others fail to make the distinction that *Muslim* refers to a *religion*, not an ethnicity or nationality – a conflation that indicates that this type of confusing and problematic elision or slippage in use of language occurs more broadly than just in media discourses, and thus, insidiously, also influences opinion. Nevertheless, Jupp's point is that

> ethnic diversity based on a multiplicity of origins, is unlikely to dramatically challenge the established attitudes and practices of the core population derived from the British Isles over the past two centuries. Australia is not the most multicultural country in the world, as politicians often proclaim. It remains part of the English-speaking world, influenced mainly from Britain and the United States.[119]

At the same time, multiculturalism *is* an everyday fact of life throughout Australia – albeit to varying degrees; every day, "people from different backgrounds mix together, whether by design or necessity, in our multicultural neighbourhoods and cities".[120] Pardy and Lee write that their research with ethnic groups, immigrants, refugees, and related communities and organisations shows that

> a multicultural reality is not something to be accepted, rejected or debated. [It] emerges in places where people live with cultural plurality as an inevitable consequence of a globalised world, where mundane, everyday bodily engagement with cultural difference is not negotiable. Coming across, bumping into and sharing space, often involuntarily, with people from a range of cultural and ethnic backgrounds, is how people live in many parts of multicultural Australia [and is] a social fact of everyday existence.[121]

The people whose stories appear in following chapters face, and contribute to, that multicultural reality every day, and it is background to their experiences of resettlement.

NOTES

1. Oberman.
2. Dean; Foucault, 'Truth and Power'; Foucault et al.; Rose.
3. Sheller and Urry.
4. Peter Adey, 19.
5. Ibid., 31.
6. Urry, 2007.
7. Adey, 74–76.
8. Ibid.
9. Ibid., 75.
10. Massey.
11. Ibid.
12. Ibid.
13. Urry, Sociology.
14. Ibid., 3.
15. Ibid., 33.
16. Favell, 389.
17. Ibid., 391.
18. Sheller and Urry, 211.
19. Ibid., 208–9.
20. Ibid., 209, 214.
21. Cresswell, 1–2.
22. Ibid., 26.
23. Ibid., 27.
24. Ibid., 30.
25. Ibid., 32.
26. Pallasmaa, 144.

27. Ibid.
28. Ibid.
29. Nynäs, 169.
30. Cresswell, On the Move, 264.
31. Dannreuther, 106–107.
32. Bhugra and Gupta, *Migration.*
33. Bhugra and Gupta, 'Globalisation', 56.
34. Stalker.
35. Ibid.
36. Hatton.
37. Ibid.
38. Kymlicka.
39. Pakulski and Markowski.
40. Kymlicka, 1.
41. Ibid., 3.
42. Modood, 5.
43. Metz et al.
44. Kymlicka, 14, 22.
45. Modood, 33.
46. Metz et al.; Collins; 'Multiculturalism'; Kymlicka; Pakulski.
47. Kowal, Dunn et al.
48. UNHCR, *UNHCR* Emergencies at 27 September 2018.
49. Rohingya Refugee Crisis, *Medecins Sans Frontieres*, March 9, 2018, accessed June 6, 2018, https://www.msf.org/rohingya-refugee-crisis.
50. Bates, 467; Farbotko et al.
51. Stratford et al.; Myers, 609.
52. Bhugra and Gupta, Migration.
53. Fine, 131.
54. UNHCR guidelines (2002) provide for international protection in regard to gender-related persecution, but there is no means of enforcing them.
55. International Organisation for Migration (IOM). *International Migration Report*, 2018.
56. Ibid.
57. Ibid.
58. Myanmar, Rohingya, What You Need to Know about the Crisis. *BBC News*, April 28, 2018, accessed August 25, 2018, https://www.bbc.com/news/world-asia-41566561.
59. UNHCR, *Syria Emergency*, 2018.
60. . Ibid.
61. Slominski,102.
62. Grandi, 184. Mountz.
63. Tucci, 25.
64. Ibid., 31.
65. Arsenijevic et al.
66. Jon Henley, EU Migration Deal, *The Guardian*, June 29, 2018, accessed July 10, 2018, https://www.theguardian.com/world/2018/jun/29/eu-summit-migration-deal-key-points.

67. UNHCR, *UNHCR* Emergencies at 27 September 2018.

68. Cardwell.

69. Sciurba, 766.

70. Garelli et al., 665–67.

71. Daniel Trilling, The Irrational Fear of Migrants, *The Guardian*, June 28, 2018, accessed July 10, 2018, https://www.theguardian.com/commentisfree/2018/jun/28/migrants-europe-eu-italy-matteo-salvini

72. Trilling, Lights in the Distance.

73. Cardwell, Garelli, Sciurba, Slominski.

74. Sciurba, 767.

75. Urry, Mobilities, 188.

76. Bendixsen.

77. France's Unwanted Roma, *BBC News Magazine*, February 13, 2014, accessed July 10, 2018, https://www.bbc.com/news/magazine-25419423

78. Ellen Barry and Martin Selsoe Sorensen, In Denmark, Harsh New Laws for Immigrant 'Ghettos', *New York Times*, July 1, 2018, accessed October 1, 2018, https://www.nytimes.com/2018/07/01/world/europe/denmark-immigrant-ghettos.html

79. Ibid.

80. Fine, 132; Oberman, 130.

81. International Organisation for Migration (IOM) *International Migration Report*, 2018.

82. Sarah Fine, Keeping Them Out, interview by David Rutledge, Philosopher's Zone, ABC Radio National, September 2, 2018, accessed September 9, 2018, https://www.abc.net.au/radionational/programs/philosopherszone/keeping-them-out/10169906.

83. Sources for this summary of Australia's migration history include Austin, Babacan and Babacan, Bennett, Commonwealth of Australia National Native Title Tribunal (2013), Curthoys et al., Lopez, Mann, McMaster and Austin, Perkins and Langton, Walsh, Webber and Fernandes.

84. National Native Title Tribunal, 2013.

85. Ibid.

86. Bennett, Woodford.

87. Ibid.

88. Fine, 136; Oberman, 130.

89. Walsh, 47.

90. Jupp, 66.

91. Ibid., 67.

92. Babacan and Babacan, 26.

93. The Long Boom began at the end of the Second World War in 1945 and ended in 1973, the longest period of consistent economic growth in world history. It was a time of low unemployment, greater choice of consumer goods, and optimism about the future. Keith, Suter, 'The Long Boom'. http://www.globaldirections.com/Articles/Business/TheLongBoom.pdf.

94. Babacan and Babacan, 26.

95. McMaster and Austin, 54.

96. Ibid., 54–55.

97. Lopez.

98. Pakulski, 26.

99. Babacan and Babacan.

100. Fox, 372–73.

101. Perera, 142–48.

102. Babacan and Babacan, 31.

103. Fozdar and Spittles, 496.

104. Nolan et al., 659.

105. Ibid., 659–60.

106. Kymlicka, 3.

107. Emily Howie, HRLC Statement at the 25th Session of the UN Human Rights Council, UNHCR, March 21, 2014, accessed April 15, 2014, http://hrlc.org.au/australias-punitive-asylum-seeker-polices-set-for-more-scrutiny-at-un/.

108. Power.

109. Maillet et al.

110. Senate Passes Controversial Refugee Evacuation Bill, *ABC,* February 13, 2019, accessed 18 February 2019. https://www.abc.net.au/news/2019-02-13/senate-passes-controversial-refugee-evacuation-bill/10806196.

111. Janet Phillips, Asylum Seekers and Refugees: What Are the Facts? March 2, 2015, and Elibritt Karlsen, Australia's Offshore Processing of Asylum Seekers in Nauru and PNG: A Quick Guide to Statistics and Resources, December 19, 2016, both edited by Australian Government Parliamentary Services.

112. Katherine Murphy, Coalition to Reopen Christmas Island Detention Centre as Senate Passes Refugee Transfer Bill, *The Guardian*, February 13, 2019, accessed February 18, 2019, https://www.theguardian.com/australia-news/2019/feb/13/coalition-to-reopen-christmas-island-detention-centre-as-senate-passes-refugee-transfer-bill.

113. Refugee Council of Australia, 2019.

114. Pakulski, 24.

115. Colic-Peisker, Kymlicka, Lopez, Modood, Pardy and Lee, Metz et al.

116. Kymlicka, 24.

117. Australians are among the most residentially mobile populations in the world, with about 40 per cent of people moving house within each five-year census period; see Graeme Hugo, Helen Feist, and George Tan, *Australian Population*.

118. Jupp, 70.

119. Ibid.

120. Wise, 917.

121. Pardy and Lee, 300; Kamp et al., for findings of a survey of Australians' views of cultural diversity.

Part II

LIVED EXPERIENCE

In part II, I introduce ten people – participants in a deep, qualitative case study – who share their lived experiences and diverse histories in three chapters: regular migrations, irregular migrations, and mobile lives. Although the experiences of the irregular migrants are significantly different from those of the others, their narratives are more than a counterfoil for the others and show that some essential challenges are comparable and that there are patterns in their resilience and regimes of practice that bring about well-being.

Quoting directly from transcripts of our conversations, I present these narratives without *tidying* the participants' English. As far as possible, I think it important to provide opportunity for these people to speak in their own voices. All chose to share their stories in the hope that they would help others and they gave permission for me to use their names. Their stories powerfully bear witness to some of the challenges people suffer and the wonderful resilience and determination with which they meet them.

At the same time, these chapters utilise the *extrasectional* interweaving of theory and lived experience to reveal social-material processes. Introducing the participants, I focus on the early parts of their lives, which might be considered formative of their senses of self and of place. Then, as their stories unfold, it is possible to track how they come to understand themselves, how they build regimes of practice, and how they shape their senses of self and place through their mobilities. Their narratives gesture to the conditions of truth that provide context for their diverse beliefs and show how these people negotiate their worlds – how they be and do and think and feel in and into the world – and thus reveal various insights that have a broader salience.

Chapter 4

Regular Migrations

> My grandmother found her sense of belonging in her devotion to her family and her religion. Her children, now living in exile, find their sense of belonging in common memories, culture and the language they share with others from Iran. Her grandchildren left Iran before they could form any lasting memories of their own, yet our dark features and slight accents set us apart from the locals in our new country. We exist at the peripheral edges of both cultures and at times struggle with our identity and sense of belonging. We celebrate our New Year, do our best to follow the proper etiquette, attempt to follow our mothers' recipes, and do our best to pass on our culture to our children.[1]

Various *push, pull,* and *networking* factors influence voluntary migrants. People move away from religious and political persecution, and from limited, negative, even life-threatening conditions in their places of origin. They are attracted to places elsewhere that they perceive to be safer, freer, healthier, and offering greater opportunities, particularly for employment and education. They move because at some level they may think that their lives could be, or should be better – a notion that perhaps reflects some deeper faith that they are not flawed but actually deserve to flourish. They also move to be closer to family and others of similar ethnicity, religion, other association, or persuasion.

The primary motivations for contemporary regular migration probably have not varied much in type from earlier times; but globalisation of most careers, job markets, and cultural identities is quite novel, and migration is significantly different in scale. Modern technology has also hastened the time it takes for many journeys to new locations and provides modes of communication that allow people, far more easily and rapidly than in the past, to stay in contact with those left behind. It is a far cry from the days of sail and steamships that, for example, could take as long as six months to make the journey from Europe to Australia. Nevertheless, migration continues to be a challenging and significant event in people's lives, and can arouse varied emotions from grief and loss, excitement and expectations, to hopes and fears. Carol, the first to be introduced of the participants exemplifying regular migration, *did* migrate by boat, back in the 1950s, from Scotland to Canada.

CAROL

Dunbarton, where Carol was born in 1951, is a town on the north bank of the River Clyde, on the west coast of Scotland. Built on the site of the capital of the ancient kingdom of Alclud, the town is dominated by Dunbarton Castle, which has the longest recorded history of any stronghold in Scotland. The economy was severely depressed from 1922, and despite brief war-time prosperity the town returned to depression after it was bombed during the Second World War.[2] When Carol was five years old, her family migrated to Canada, away from Scotland's post-war sense of hopelessness and poverty. Carol feels that poverty defined them. Her father was from the Vale in Balloch, next to Loch Lomond, and one of a generation of boys called Jelly Piecers – a piece being a sandwich – because they grew up on little else than bread and jam. Beginning her story, Carol says,

> It's all going to sound terribly Monty Pythonesque – like, "You think *you* were poor, *we* were poorer!" But I suppose it was that my dad would come home and there would be no food, so he had to go out and find it. I think he was very much shaped by the need to *make do*.

Carol's father's family came from Glasgow and played in the music halls. They were Protestants, so when Carol's grandfather, John, married Mary Duffy, an Irish Catholic mill girl, there was a lot of tension. "Later on, my grandmother went back to being Catholic, once John died. She had, I don't know how many pregnancies, it was up to ten, but my father was the only survivor". Only one other sibling grew to adulthood, and he died at El Alamein in the Second World War. From their marriage, Carol's father and mother lived with Grandmother Mary in a tiny, two-bedroom, council house in the Vale, and in time their two daughters also shared that cramped space:

> My granny didn't like my mother's Protestant ways, and I think it was incredibly difficult for my mother. One time she shut the door when she was feeding me, and Granny said, "I won't have closed doors in my house!" There was an unholy row and my mother grabbed me, and my sister, Alice, and stormed back

to Dunbarton, a two-hour walk. This is post war. Dunbarton was bombed so a lot of it was gone. There was a housing shortage, people lining up everywhere. I don't know how they got a place – it was an old tenement with stone steps. It had one bedroom, a tiny living room, with a little fireplace and a little kitchen bench; everything was in it, and one toilet outside. Women peed in the sink because you get desperate waiting for that single toilet! My mother got down on her knees and she thanked God for that place.

With the couple and two children sharing one bedroom, the house was a temporary refuge, and it would take years in the housing queues to get another, so Carol's parents decided to emigrate:

Dad was the kind of guy that I think was always trying to make a solution out of a locational change, rather than a material change, and he wanted to go to Australia; but my mother didn't because it was too far away, and she thought she'd never get back again. Canada seemed more of a go. The irony was that she never came back anyway. My dad put a knapsack on his back and went to Canada – I don't know how he did it, perhaps he jumped ship – but his idea was that if he got out there he would find a job and a place to stay, and he would bring us over.

Mum went to work at the West Clocks factory, and we lived with my Protestant Nanna, in another council house; better, because it had an internal toilet, and a living room, and separate kitchen, but I've been back there and it just cracks me up, the size of it, it was so small. But it was a far more *Protestant* place than down in the Vale. The Catholic-Protestant thing was huge. Bigger Protestant kids threw stones at Catholic kids, and bigger Catholic kids threw stones at Protestant kids.

Nanna was severe. Every day had its own tasks; Mondays were washing days, and so on. Every week, all the furniture was moved out and everything washed, all the walls washed, everything. The stones outside that little council house had to be chalked to make them white. It rained in Scotland, and they would be chalked over and over again; but she knew how to run a place, and she ran it that way, and she was a wonderful bigot – I mean she would say, after she finished cleaning, "That's a bit more Protestant looking". I thought, then, that *Protestant* meant *clean*.

After many months of waiting, Carol's mother and the girls sailed for Canada. Carol remembers a lone piper lamenting the departure of the emigrants as the ship pulled away: "many a heart will break in twa, will ye no come back again?" Her mother was dreadfully seasick for the whole voyage. Carol recalls that even while they were still on the ship, she and Alice felt that their parents were not equipped to forge this new life, and that they would "have to navigate this space ourselves". Seven-year-old Alice showed five-year-old Carol how to fly: "When the ship goes up, crouch down, and when it starts to go down, jump up in the air, and when you jump up you stay up, until the ship comes back up".

Figure 4.1.   Carol, now living in the Blue Mountains, west of Sydney.

They arrived in Montreal in April, and it was hot. "People have an idea of Canada as a cold place, but it can be hot as hell, and there we were in our woollen kilts!" Carol's father took them by train to the first of many places they rented in Toronto, a basement containing a furnace that serviced the whole building. Carol said that other people, including other immigrants, lived in bungalows, or apartments – the basement was what her father could afford, but it set the family apart as *odd*. Describing how strange they felt, Carol says that Canada had become an affluent place by 1956, but to the family, the impoverished world of post-war Scotland was *reality*, a place where "to have even a treacle scone was a treasure". Canada, where they saw a supermarket for the first time, "was unreal, beyond our comprehension". Whatever the cause, Carol's mother was unable to cope and developed agoraphobia:

Mother always turned up for school things, education was so important, but she couldn't deal with shopping, or much else. When *my* mother was a little girl, *her* mother died of TB [tuberculosis], and she was sent to an orphanage. Lots of people moved away from Scotland, but *we* carried poverty with us – like TB – it was like we always had a nagging cough, and it was like we couldn't get beyond that. My mum wasn't making it in Canada, and that meant Alice and I had to figure it out. We felt materially poorer than other people, and shamed on that level, but we felt better than them with loftier thoughts . . . a kind of reverse pride.

It was a very different world. In Scotland, the school provided uniforms – everything was provided – you just went to school. In Canada, we had to provide it all. "You're not going to school in party dresses", my mother said. In Scotland we had a slate. We didn't have pencils, even in the house. How I lusted after a box of coloured pencils. I shamed my mother by asking, so she turned on me. I began to figure it out, got very creative. I pinched other people's pencils. I took money in other girls' houses, and got what I needed for school.

Carol says that she and Alice felt uncomfortable in their new environment – it was brighter and flatter than the mists and mountains of Scotland – so they escaped to a local ravine, which mimicked the landscape from where they came:

It was just down the back of the flats and round the corner and down. We claimed that ravine; we named all the different parts. There was a little bit that went up like a meadow; we called that Sunshine Land. We built a tree house and we had big adventures down there. I thought of stories that I loved – one of my favourites was *The Snow Queen* and the girl that I loved in that was the little Lapland girl, because she had a knife and she was dressed in furs and she was tough, and I wanted to be like her, or like *Pocahontas*.[3] We'd go there and we'd stage these big stories – we created a story world in the ravine.

Carol survived her experiences of migrating to Canada from Scotland in part by escaping into fantasy. Her real life continued to be turbulent and included having a baby and giving it up for adoption when she was seventeen, marrying an Australian man while still a university undergraduate, moving to Australia with him, moving back to Canada when the marriage failed, then back to Australia again to be with her children. Alongside many moves within Australia, while working and raising children during her second marriage, Carol completed a PhD and now works as a communications consultant, writes books, and is a mentor for other authors (see figure 4.1). Later, I elaborate upon this very condensed summary of Carol's adulthood, and those of the other participants, with quotes from their narratives to illustrate part three: challenges of resettlement.

CAROLA

Born in 1957, in Florsheim, West Germany, Carola grew up there and describes it as "a really, really old town . . . with an old wall and watchtowers" dating back about fifteen hundred years. A small, sleepy, country town of fields and vineyards, where her father's family goes back for at least a hundred years, it is a place where "most everyone knew everyone else". Overall, her story is of a mostly happy childhood, nurtured and peaceful. Although Germany was still recovering from the Second World War, Carola says "all that" was remote from the little town. There was not much talk of the war in Florsheim, but, with hindsight, Carola is sure its impact on people continued, and gave her mother's demeanour as an example:

> I've never been nurtured by my mother, not in memory. If there's something negative or depressive, that's what she would focus on, and she still does that. My father was much older than her, but he loved having kids, he was the one playing with us. She was never really affectionate and close. With my mother, I would just always be careful.

As a child, Carola knew that her mother and father met during the war, when both worked in an outpost transport factory in Danzig, in Poland. As the Russians moved in, they were evacuated and fled on foot, ending up in a prisoner-of-war camp in the English zone, in northern Germany. When released, they returned to their homes, her father to Florsheim and her mother to a small village near Potsdam, in East Germany, and they did not meet again for many years. However, it was only recently that her mother told Carola about those journeys.

As an adult, Carola sees her mother's wartime experience as a possible explanation for her later behaviour. Her mother's twenty-second birthday occurred while she was fleeing Danzig, "stuck somewhere on the road in a long track of people". Again, upon her mother's release from the prison camp she mostly walked to get to her home, by then in the Russian zone. "It was before the Wall,[4] but there was still a zone where it was very difficult to get through; there were guides to take people through the forests, often they had to hide. There is a three-day period that is completely blacked out for my mother. She was still a very young woman".

Carola's mother had a brother, who lived at some distance, and her mother's parents lived in East Germany until Carola was about eight.[5] From then "they lived with us until they died, which was very difficult". Carola says that, as a child she felt her mother's coldness was balanced by the nurturing she received from others. The third of five children, she felt a strong sense of belonging to an extended family on her father's side, with lots of people, including many children and the "most loving and nurturing" family of her father's first wife, who died soon after the end of the war. Carola's father's side of the family was "very charitable Catholic, very supportive, doing things in the community"; her mother was Protestant and taught theology to the town's small Protestant community. The children went with their father and the rest of the family to the Catholic Church. "That's a big part of growing up in Florsheim; there's a lot of tradition around it. One of the highlights of the year is when we celebrate the end of the *Pestilence*.[6] It's an absolute holiday, with a big Catholic procession through town, very big, and everyone goes to it".

Florsheim was Carola's world until she was fifteen, providing sport, music, youth groups, social events, church, and school:

> It is not isolated, but you had very little to do with other places even if they were only ten minutes away. Only then did my horizon actually extend beyond the place where I grew up. [To complete high school, Carola had to go further afield, a twenty-minute cycle ride] out of the town, over the bridge crossing the Mein River, and into the next town. We grew up on bikes – in snow, in hail, in sunshine, everything – that's what's normal, and that's mobility, too, and independence.

That independence supported her well when she left home at nineteen to study medicine in the industrial area of Bochum, 250 kilometres north – her first major move. Rapidly widening her horizons, Carola says the following years were "an intense time of exploring and making friends – lots of late night discussions, free spirited and free thinking – Who are we? How do we live together? How do we communicate? How do we relate?" While completing orthodox medical training, Carola also studied psychology, social work, and alternative therapies in company with a tight-knit, student group of friends.

Altogether, she lived in Bochum for ten years, six studying, then working as a paediatrician at the university's children's hospital, and at another in Dortmund. She travelled to the United States and Australia for practical experience, and on a later holiday in Australia decided to apply to work at Camperdown Children's Hospital, in Sydney. "It just happened to be a time when it was difficult to have enough trainees for the jobs, because really only then can they take people from overseas . . . they had met me – that helped – they knew my English was good. So I got offered a position and I packed my bags and came".

Arriving in Sydney, Carola remembers, "I had this very strong experience of coming home. That was incredible. It was only the third time I had been in the country". After two years, Carola says she felt clearly, "my roots are shifting", so she applied to stay (see figure 4.2). Once she achieved resident status, her medical qualifications would no longer be accepted, even though she had already worked at Camperdown for one year, for a second year in paediatrics at Royal North Shore Hospital, and had been offered a senior position in neonatology, as a Fellow. Her decision to live permanently in Australia meant that first she had to apply for immigration and then do the Australian Medical Council exams. In the meantime, she could no longer work as a doctor. "It was huge. The way I dealt with it was one step at a time, because otherwise it would have been overwhelming".

Figure 4.2.   Carola, at the beach in Sydney in the 1990s, soon after arriving in Australia.

Two decades later, Carola became – and still is – Head of Paediatrics at Royal North Shore Hospital in Sydney. Married to an Australian citizen of Turkish origin, she has stepchildren and stepgrandchildren, a teenage son, and many relatives whom she visits regularly in Germany and Turkey. Passionate about caring for children, she continues to explore – contributing to the evolution of medical and social paradigms from disease-focused and remedial approaches towards eliciting and sustaining health.

JUN

Jun was born in 1973, in Sakado, Japan – a town upgraded to city status a few years later. Allied military occupation of Japan after the Second World War had ended about twenty years earlier, but there was a strong U.S. military-based presence. Jun says he grew up in a Japan that was still very traditional, but with a foreign overlay and modern technology. An only child, his parents both worked full-time – his father as a salesman for a pharmaceutical company and his mother as a secretary. Outside school and until he started high school Jun was mostly cared for by his aunt, whose daughters were "like big sisters". He remembers that when he was seven or eight years old, his aunt was cooking in her kitchen, and he asked, "Can I call you my mother?" and she said something like, "Oh, that would be nice but I think you need to ask your mother about that". Jun says he remembers being confused, because "I spent so much time at my aunt's house, and she was taking care of me".

Jun's strongest memories of growing up are to do with his schooling, which is understandable in light of his description, particularly of junior high school: classes were held for almost seven hours a day, six days a week, then there was sport for a couple of hours in the afternoons – Jun did *kendo* – and four nights each week there was *juku* – cram school – until after nine o'clock: "I would get home around 10 o'clock and have dinner, my parents have already eaten, so I was eating by myself at the table, as my parents were watching TV. So, I would eat and take a bath and then it's time to go to bed at eleven. Yeah, that was a typical, everyday life".

Jun spoke in detail of the assessment system used to rank students, and said that although he is not a competitive person, he always knew his standard deviation from the average, identified on a bell curve. "Every student is forced to be aware of where they are. In Japan, getting into high school is a big deal, you have to take a test to get into the best possible high school that you can, so that you can move on to best possible university. I knew that I could get into a good high school if I just kept trying. So, I think that's what I did, I just kept trying".

Jun's entry to a prestigious high school pleased his parents; they relaxed their vigilance, expecting the school to keep him performing well. However, the public school Jun attended expected students to be self-motivated, and Jun's grades began to slide. His parents did not know because "they didn't even take the school report card". Jun loved music, and from his first year in high school started to teach himself piano – "I wasn't interested in studying at all, so I would go to the music classroom and teach myself how to play". Excited that he was doing something that no one was telling him to do, something for himself, he practised every day, and eventually got an electric piano at home, "a very cheap, small one, but I loved it".

At seventeen, in his senior year at high school, Jun's father asked him what university he wanted to go to. Jun says that when he named a university of music, his father "became furious, because he was expecting something normal like – I don't know, science, or economics – something ordinary". Jun says he did not understand his father's reaction, because "maybe for the first time . . . I'm trying to make my own life, becoming more of an adult . . . thinking for myself", but his parents did not approve:

> It is my father who does the talking. When he talks, he can be scary, he is a man and he is my father, so when he yelled at me for having stupid dream, I was very scared and affected by it . . . shaking . . . scared and nervous . . . so I think my

dream was crushed by my parents, and I was forced to think that I should go to a regular university, whatever that means.

Failing entrance exams for four "regular" universities, Jun went for a year to a full-time *cram* school, available because "many Japanese students are in the same situation". From there, glad to be away from his parents, he went to university in Yokohama, and studied international business. In his final year, Jun decided to go to the United States to live, and to study English. He explains that this was a choice his parents could accept because, in Japan, English is recognised as a language of international currency – in technology, the sciences, economics, and politics – and thus, "studying English is a great thing – it is *the* international language".

One year into his studies at a university in Washington State, Jun met Connie, and they quickly became close. Connie had already arranged to go to Japan to teach English. For Jun, this was a dilemma:

> I didn't want to go back to Japan because that meant having to deal with my parents, and having to worry about what job I maybe could get; and I was enjoying this life in a foreign country, doing whatever I wanted to do, so I didn't want to go back. But I didn't want to lose her either, so it was kind of a tough decision. I asked Connie if it was okay for us to live in Japan for two years, but come back to the US after that.

Connie agreed, so they went to Japan, working and living together in Utsunomiya. In 1999, they were married "just a paper thing . . . at Sakado City Hall". Jun thinks that in modern Japan, "Japan's tradition of not mixing bloods or ethnicities is going away quickly, and international marriages are becoming more and more common". Before he and Connie returned to the United States in 2000, they had a more formal and elaborate wedding ceremony, mostly, Jun says, to please his mother.

CONNIE

Born in Seattle in the United States, in 1967, Connie is uncertain just what her ethnic background is – unlike the three other participants introduced thus far. The United States, built initially on colonialism and slavery, has seen continuous mass immigration since the first half of the nineteenth century. Connie's parents were both born in the United States, but Connie does not know from where or when the first of her ancestors migrated to that country, just that there were several American-born generations from the late 1800s, and Irish, Scottish, and German are part of her ethnic background. Her father's adoptive parents were Norwegian and what her great-grandma called "Yankee-German-Dutch".

Although Connie grew up in western Washington and stayed there until she was in her early twenties, she says she never felt that any place she lived in was "really home". Her parents divorced when she was about three years old, and from then on, Connie and her younger sister moved about during both school and vacation times, sometimes living with their mother, their paternal grandparents, or their father. "The place that felt the best was the grandparents' house, but they weren't our parents, and when we would do things with other kids, or go places, *they* had parents, but always we were with grandparents. They peppered our growing up with Scandinavian foods, Christmas traditions, religious ideas, and strong work ethics". Connie describes her grandparents as "mellow". Retired, they lived in a small country town in a farming area, quiet, and slow paced:

> My grandmother was very loving and warm. She was baking cookies or she was down at the church helping organise something, and it was very regular, very routine. It was the same every time – we slept in the same place, we had our toothbrushes there, we had the same tree to climb in – the tree was always there. We knew what the deal was, and we just folded into it. It goes way back before my memory starts, so we were just part of that, and that felt good. We knew what the expectations on us were, and everything was regular.

The girls found the routine comfortable and felt they belonged. Connie says they were very much loved, but "we were the *grand*children, not the children". She recalls that she always wished she could have the same feeling of being at home when living with her mother, but "it just wasn't there":

> My mother was seventeen when I was born, and at seventeen, I think, actually she was more like maybe thirteen, or fourteen. She just didn't really know *how* to be a mom, and I don't think she ever . . . I don't think she *wanted* to be a mom, and so, how was it living with my mom? She had a lot of issues, you know . . . personal emotional issues, and I think she didn't know how to not be selfish, or somehow part of her never came out of the teenage years, or something. I have always felt *loved* by my mother, but not *cared for*, or taken care of, she just doesn't have it to give. I heard an expression one time: "you can't expect your cat to bark", and I thought, "yeah, that's my mom". I guess that's how, in my mind, I think about my mom. My mom had three children, and she and my step-dad had just really some rough patches. There were periods of time when there was a lot of drinking happening, and my mom not being around, she would be gone all day, or she wouldn't come home until late at night, or something, and so it wasn't regular and reliable, and it wasn't predictable.

Connie's mother and stepfather lived in suburban Seattle, moving house from time to time, but always within walking distance of her stepfather's business. Connie describes the places as "lower socio-economic", but says that in the 1970s and early 1980s in the United States there was not such a gap between rich and poor as she sees now. They lived a couple of neighbourhoods away from government housing projects:

> We had tons of what – we called them boat people – people from Laos, you know, they were all coming in the 70s, and they were sort of tucking into these pockets, and we were maybe a mile away, is all. As a kid – I always thought, I wish we could live in a house that *looked* better, or I wish the front yard of our house looked a little more *normal*. I think here [in Australia] people would call us, like, *bogans*.[7] I heard the word *bogan* here a lot of times, and probably that's what our house always looked like, and I mean, inside the house, my mother was not a house-proud, sort of housekeeping, homemaker person. She never was. But I always wished for it, and I always *wanted* it, and I don't know if it's because we always had it with my grandparents.

Connie reflects that the phrase "well, if things had been normal" often comes up in conversations with her sister about those days, "but I don't really know, because in the neighbours' house – what looks normal – you don't know what's happening in the neighbours' house either". To Connie, the houses "never felt homey. They could have felt homey, but my mom, her heart wasn't there, somehow":

> Each time we moved it was to a *better* place, so although I didn't think about it while I was growing up, it's obvious now that my stepdad was moving us forward. So, each time the rent went up because we were moving into a better place. Each time we moved was on a better street, and a better looking house, with a better looking yard, but after – it wasn't long before it was looking like the crappy last one we lived in, you know, because my mom wasn't *doing* anything.

In her early twenties, Connie moved away to college in eastern Washington State – still in the state where she was born. Working to support herself, it took her six years to complete a two-year university entrance degree. Then, with a student loan to pay for university and living expenses, Connie was "so happy!" She saw university as "a big jump-off point", which would take her to live in other countries – a ticket to freedom from her family background and to discover herself, rather than being obliged to fulfil anyone else's expectations:

> I knew that this was like the gateway to the rest of my life. I really thought, right, I've been doing things and I've been busy, but now, this is where my dream takes off. I wanted to just check things out . . . not to dig my roots in anywhere right away at all; and not having anyone, any person, lay anything heavy on me, that I would have to stay, or I would have to – I wanted to be free to make my own choices and my own life, and go – yeah, I wanted to *just see:* "Where will I go? Where will I land? Where will I be?"

However, Connie met and fell in love with Jun. She did go to Japan and taught English there for two years, but at the end of that time, after she and Jun married they returned to the United States. Back in Washington, "the US was having a small recession, so a job was hard to find", and the couple lived with Connie's grandmother in Seattle for a year. Work took them to New Orleans for a further year, where they had a baby; then to Oregon State for a couple of years, and a second baby, then back to western Washington.

Limited employment opportunities, economic factors, and a growing disillusionment with social conditions and politics in the United States led Jun and Connie to emigrate. They carefully compared conditions and immigration requirements in Canada, New Zealand, and Australia, and at the beginning of 2011 relocated to Tasmania, an island state at the southernmost part of Australia. Their visas were based on Jun's enrolment in a postgraduate course at the University of Tasmania, which they chose so he could qualify for a profession on the list of those acceptable for immigration at the time. During the two years the family lived in Hobart, that category was dropped from the list, and they failed to meet immigration requirements. Neither Jun nor Connie wanted to return to the United States, which they felt had become too difficult, economically, and politically. With two sons now at school, they felt it was time to settle down, so at the beginning of 2013, they returned to Japan. Jun planned to work as a teacher and to compose music, and Connie to continue enjoying being a full-time mother, fulfilling their hopes for a new and good life in Hokkaido.

FORMING SENSES OF SELF

In this introduction to some of the experiences and histories of migration shared with me by Carol, Carola, Jun, and Connie, I have provided only a sketch of the wider social and cultural narratives within which their personal narratives of self developed. Details from their childhoods capture elements of what may have been formative of their senses of self. Closer reading and analysis of their stories can illuminate how the sense of self they each developed in those early years affected their ability to cope with challenges of migration.

Noting significant differences of origin and experience between participants several points of correspondence nevertheless emerge. Each felt that they needed to look after themselves when they were growing up, that they were left to their own devices much of the time, and that they developed resilience as a response to challenging relationships with their parents. It is interesting to consider this outcome in light of Hara Estroff Marano's claims that parental overinvolvement hinders a child's development socially, emotionally, and neurologically.[8] Her study of children and adolescents in the United States concludes that overprotection of children produces psychological breakdown and – as the book's title states – *A Nation of Wimps*. Marano writes, "What's significant about these [overprotected] kids . . . is that they commonly lack a fierce internal struggle toward a deeper state of authenticity".[9]

Carol, Carola, and Connie all decided early in life that their mothers could not cope and thus could not be depended upon. On the surface, Carola's childhood appears comfortable, happy, safe, and protected, yet from her earliest memories she felt:

> Emotionally I needed to support my mother. From that, for a start, I got that I'm strong enough to do that – even though it should be the other way round – so I think that's a lot of where this comes from; that I feel I can look after myself and that, from whenever, I was able even to support the person who should have nurtured me.

At the age of six, Connie realised, "I can't count on my mom, so I'm going to have to take matters into my own hands. I can't trust my mother's perception of how the world is, I need to think things through for myself". Carol – growing up in straitened circumstances, with an ailing mother, in a culture she experienced as alien – saw self-reliance as essential for survival. In Jun's case, it was not that his parents were unable to cope; more that they were effectively absent, so he learned to look after himself, and to think for himself, although it would be years before he would free himself of fear of his father.

The desire to be free from his parents' expectations led Jun to enrol in a university far from home, and then to travel to the United States for further study. For the other three, attending a distant university was also a means of leaving home and all four spoke of having felt relief and freedom to be themselves, and to pursue their dreams. Whatever the differences between Canada, Germany, Japan, and the United States, the availability of education to a tertiary level was a common factor in the participants' narratives. Children in those countries were required to attend school to be educated and to be prepared for work and other adult responsibilities. It was assumed that children were capable of learning and would develop some level of independence by the time they finished school. As they grew up, each participant developed a sense of self that included assumptions of autonomy – beliefs that they were able to achieve, to succeed, to support themselves, and that they were free, once they were old enough, to make their own choices.

In addition, to varying degrees, all four had relative safety; and they grew up in one version or other of post-war meta-narratives of technological progress, economic growth, and assumptions that opportunities were available for them as individuals, beyond those possible for earlier generations. They believed in their own capabilities, partly because – socially – that was expected of them, and partly because that was a conclusion they drew from meeting personal challenges. As Carola put it, she knew that she would always manage, always "find a way", and throughout her life, although many things were difficult for her, she said, "I never felt that I would not be able to do it". Despite sound educational foundations, all four also experienced times of economic difficulty, yet they took for granted that education, employment, housing, the freedom to travel, and other opportunities were available to them.

More personally, each one's sense of self was impeded by a lack of self-worth at different stages, and in various ways. For Connie, a sense of low self-worth began very early, and resided in longing to be "normal", and to have a happy home with "normal" parents, rather than grandparents. Jun, shy as a child, thought that he was "not very brave", because, when he was bullied in elementary school, he became a bully himself for a time so that "the tough guys" would accept him. He also says that for a long time he thought badly of himself for not standing up to his father. In Louisiana, Jun worked in a competitive job he hated, again allowing himself to be manipulated, until he collapsed with arrhythmia. Back in Oregon, he returned to university for qualifications that would improve his employability, and, feeling responsible by then for a wife and child, he pushed himself almost to the point of breakdown. Finding the university counselling service unhelpful, he turned to self-help books, and said that he began to realise for the first time, "my psychology is a product of whatever happened and whatever I was born with . . . and now that I am an adult, I can help myself, I can choose".

Carola says she often still experiences a "loss of self" " when with other people, and a need to withdraw to reconnect with herself in solitude:

> I had to learn, and literally have to keep reminding myself that I have to put myself first without feeling or thinking that this is selfish. That's taken me a long time, and it shows up everywhere – it can be at work where I find myself tired in the morning, because I've been on call, being demanded of all the time, and I get cranky and I have to shut the door, and say to myself, "Why am I here?" and get back, reduce it down to "this is what I'm about, it's about families, it's about patients, it's about what I want to do about healing", but I have to look after myself.

That regime of practice began early in her childhood, when Carola felt she had to look after her mother, and decided she must put other people's needs ahead of her own. It was a pattern she also connected to what she described as "a component of guilt just for being German". As a child, she did not understand it, but was aware of an undercurrent of angst in the adults around her from their various experiences including her parents' wartime imprisonment. Later, she learned the history of Germany's role in the Second World War. Carola was not born until almost thirteen years after the war, and yet her sense of self was deeply impressed by the social and familial narratives within which she grew up. Questioning the assumptions of those narratives, and seeing the meanings she attributed to herself in that process, in recent years, Carola has changed some key beliefs: "There is so much guilt, almost like you can't be proud being a German, because of all that history, but it is becoming less so . . . there's a lot about being German I can laugh about now, and a lot that's really good . . . and there's a lot of me that doesn't fit that picture anymore".

As a child, Carol knew the shame of poverty. In her words:

> Toxic shame is the biggest thing that undercuts everything. You know, *secretiveness* . . . to try to keep up the good front, you'd have one good suit, you'd take it down to the pawn shop, you'd drag it out again when there was a special event, then you'd take it back down to the pawn shop. We had a great distrust of – well it was difficult to own property; it was the *gentry* who owned property – *we* were people who rented. You distrusted rent collectors. People who had property and rented out *we* saw as the scum of the earth, and I suppose to a certain extent that still affects me today in terms of having things – I always feel strange about making that leap to buying something, *we're* not people who do that. It's a *mindset* about the efficacy of being able to imagine yourself being able to buy something. It's like tennis: '*We* don't play tennis, the *gentry* play tennis' – and it wouldn't matter how much money I would have, *I* don't play tennis. It's something that *other* people do.

Socially, Carol was further shamed by becoming pregnant at sixteen and having an *illegitimate* child – a label still common in the 1960s. But worse, in Carol's view, came later. In spite of excelling academically at a prestigious university, Carol was unable to cope with the vast gap she felt between herself and other girls, who came from rich backgrounds:

> I fell desperately in love with a young man at Trinity who took a shine to me. He was just *so* out of my league, a private school boy, and you know, that skin! Where do they get that skin? The white skin, the apple cheeks, the black crisp curls; he was going to be a doctor, he was going to go to South America and work with the poor people. He was *perfect*. And I wanted to marry him. But his mother, she smelled me coming a mile away, and she planked down on that really fast, and that *hurt*. In fact, if there was any part that I got really shamed by, it was that experience. That summer, when this boy dropped me – he hardly looked at me, and my girlfriend had told someone about the baby . . . I was kind of in a bad state.

Individually and together, these narratives are suggestive of what Brené Brown has described as *embodying shame*.[10] Based on social research involving some thousands of people in the United States, Brown finds shame to be fundamental to human experience, and writes:

> The constant struggle to feel accepted and worthy is unrelenting. We put so much of our time and energy into making sure that we meet everyone's expectations and into caring about what other people think of us, that we are often left feeling angry, resentful and fearful. Sometimes we turn these emotions inward and convince ourselves that we are bad and that maybe we deserve the rejection that we so desperately fear. Other times we lash out. . . . Either way, in the end, we are left feeling exhausted, overwhelmed and alone.[11]

Carol, Carola, Jun, and Connie each acknowledged that they had felt ashamed, and inadequate at various times. As children they did their best to develop and express what they learned was considered to be good behaviour, what was expected of them; and to control, or at least hide, what they thought was wrong with themselves. Deborah Du Nann Winter describes this process as one of building a *false self* in which the requirements of others are taken as one's central being, a way of living that has a high personal cost.[12]

Each of the participants also shared with me the sense that various challenges in their lives led them to question early beliefs, and to further develop their senses of self and regimes of practice. That process was stimulated by their moves from places of origin to live elsewhere, including by going to university, and in particular by their experiences of migration. For example, Jun found life in the United States and people there very different from his background in Japan. Coming close to breakdown he learned to question his assumptions and considers that was an important turning point from which his adulthood really started. Becoming more aware of himself, he also became more aware of others, and he feels that allows him to be a "better person".

Both Jun and Connie think of *self* as being half what they were born with, and half acquired, added to, changed, and developed throughout life, and especially by their moves to different countries. Jun reflects that he likes diversity, or unknown territory, "I actually want that half of me to keep exploring and keep moving into something better", and feels it is important to keep the two halves of himself in harmony, working together. On one hand, Connie told me, "My *self* is something that is unchanging, it's that thing, that inside thing – it's the same, no matter what". At the same time, her strongest feeling of self was being "the mom" – a role she takes very seriously. Emphatically, she added:

> Wait a second now; I was somebody *before* I had children. I had a *self* happening *before* I was married, thank you very much; and I was happy, and it

was a *good* self or person or life or whatever. When I learned I was pregnant I was happy, but at the same time I thought, "Oh crap! That's it, then, that's it". Because I thought then, and I still think now, when you become a mother, that's your life from now on.

Through Carola's experience of migrating to Australia, she says she came to an awareness of herself as neither German, nor Australian, but as a person in her own right. Carola describes her sense of self as a feeling of being strongly connected to her inner balance:

> It's like a sense that's right in the middle, that sense when you know a word is spelt correct or not, that centre – almost like a physical perception, quiet, peaceful – a very strong sense of "this is who I am", and out of that comes how I am in the world.

Carol sees herself as a survivor, and over time came to value that capacity, as well as her accomplishments. For instance, she is proud of having established Canada's first provincial day-care centre for unwed mothers – women on welfare, who could not afford day care, and wanted to go back to school. Carol's various migrations between Canada and Australia were very difficult for her, associated, as they were, with divorce and other personal problems. Nevertheless, she says her sense of self grew consistently. "*Passionate*, with a huge appetite for life" is how Carol describes herself, very caring, yet able to be ruthless to ensure survival of herself and her children. "If we were in a war, or a famine, I'd say, 'Stick with me, kid. *I'm* going to get the potato!'" Having gone through what she calls "some lumpy periods" in her life, Carol recognises that "there are several aspects – the person I reached is a sort of cohesiveness that pulls together all of these senses of myself – I'm nobody's *concept* of me, I'm just *me*".

To one degree or another, through varied experiences of migration, all four of these regular migrants have developed self-awareness: they have questioned at least some of the conditions of truth within which they grew up and challenged their own beliefs and assumptions, clarifying their senses of self in the process. In later chapters, I investigate how they have handled their relocations, but next, I introduce the participants whose journeys involve irregular migration.

NOTES

1. Serov, 28.
2. Knox, 1999.
3. Pocahontas, the daughter of an American Indian chief, married an Englishman and supported English settlement in America. Romanticised, she is the heroine in popular versions of the tale.

4. At the end of the Second World War, Germany was partitioned. The Soviet Union controlled the eastern sector, and called it the German Democratic Republic (GDR). The Berlin Wall was erected by the GDR in 1961, officially to protect against fascist elements, but in practice to prevent emigration and defection to the west.

5. In old age, people who had been living in the GDR, commonly called East Germany, were allowed to reunite with relatives in the west.

6. The Pestilence was another name for the bubonic plague, or Black Death, that swept through Europe in the fourteenth century, killing millions of people.

7. Australian slang: a fool, idiot, daggy, uncool.

8. Marano, 2008.

9. Ibid., 21.

10. Brown, 2008.

11. Ibid., xvi.

12. Winter, 126–27.

Chapter 5

Irregular Migrations

In the habitual terms in which human identities are narrated [refugees or asylum seekers] are ineffable. They are Jacques Derrida's "undecidables" made flesh. Among people like us, praised by others and priding ourselves on arts of reflection and self-reflection, they are not only untouchables, but unthinkables. In a world filled to the brim with imagined communities, they are the unimaginables.[1]

It can be difficult to grasp the enormity of challenges that we – as a global community – face in relation to refugees and asylum seekers. The language used to describe these people can strongly influence opinion about them, and responses to them. For example, charitable organisations typically publicise heart-rending pictures of individuals, usually children, against a background of chaos. News media tend to sensationalise numbers and to further catastrophise events with descriptions of waves, surges, and deluges of random hordes of *foreign*ers threatening to inundate places not their own. Frequently, governments use similar language and imagery to garner support for increased border controls, and reduction of aid. At the extreme right, fundamentalists exploit social insecurities, contestably claim that *illegals* take employment and other benefits from local people, and seriously threaten quality of life. Then there is *hate speech*, demonising people, primarily – but not only – Muslims. It was 2001 when Australia's then incumbent prime minister claimed refugees threw their children overboard. It is chilling to note that, in the relatively short period since that politically contentious affair, phrases that once would have been seen as defamatory, inflammatory, and racist have fallen into such common usage that they frequently pass without challenge or question. Whatever its origin, such language prompts reaction based on fear, insists that we need greater barriers to hold back the flood, and encourages people to dehumanise others knocking at the door, rather than to find ways to respond to them. The white supremacist hate killing of people at mosques in New Zealand in March 2019 and the murder a short time later of Christian worshippers in Sri Lanka shows the horrors to which such reaction can escalate.

At some point, we need to address the greater issues of which people seeking asylum are merely a symptom, such as the social, economic, and political situations from which people flee. Meantime, however, a first step towards any change is to recognise these *others* seeking asylum as people. Notably, opinion can shift rapidly when there is opportunity for refugees to tell their stories – to bear witness to their journeys, and to be heard. With all their differences, and sometimes strangeness, their stories make these others human again, and it becomes possible to treat with them, to respond to them, and to cooperate with them.

KIROS

Kiros was born in 1967 in Ethiopia, a country in East Central Africa that has seen decades of natural disasters, political unrest, war, drought, and famine.[2] These events forced millions of Ethiopians from their homes to seek refuge as internally displaced persons within their own country, or in other countries.[3] Nevertheless, Kiros' early childhood was spent in a relatively peaceful farming community in the province of Tigray. He grew up as an Orthodox Coptic Christian in a town with a population of about twelve thousand. He says, "Christians and Muslims lived in harmony", and he felt the whole community was his family:

> Growing up in that place, you are not only *of* that place, but you become part of that place, because it is a community where everyone knows everyone . . . us kids, we used to play outside, soccer, volleyball, and we run everywhere. If we end up in one house, if there are ten, the mother of that house is supposed to feed all of us . . . so growing up in that way makes you so part of that place there, you would never be able to let that go. For me, everyone that I knew from that time are like my brothers, my sisters . . . still if I find someone whom I grew up with together, the bond is instant.

From the age of six, with the end of the regime of Haile Selassie, violence entered Kiros' life with almost continuous fighting between rebel groups and the new socialist government: "Armoured groups would come during the night and attack . . . I grew up in a sort of continuous fighting, a war zone". To prevent young people, most of whom were from Tigray, from joining the rebels; on Sundays children such as Kiros were indoctrinated in socialist principles, and imprisoned if they failed to attend those political sessions:

> It was in a way very difficult, but at the same time you learned to be disciplined, and we were living beyond our age. We were contributing. At the age of fourteen I decided to join a club – we travelled maybe two or three hours on foot to teach in the dry areas – basically teaching people how to write, because the illiteracy rate in Ethiopia was high at that time. We were helping that.

At sixteen, Kiros left home to go to a distant university with several other students from the region. Students nominated the university they wished to attend, and the government – not the education department – allocated places. Kiros says he was fortunate to be sent to the agricultural university that was his first choice because that would qualify him to get "a meaningful job" in his home region. However, he did not return for many years because his homeplace had become a war zone. After graduating, he became a university lecturer, married, and had a daughter. In 1991, war brought about a further change in government, allowing Kiros to return home, briefly, for the first time in seven years. He was shocked by the devastation left by the years of war, "everything was dust . . . it doesn't even look that there is life there". Soon after, he went to the Netherlands for six months: "A shift in the way I think started happening. I felt that being in the university was a waste of my time. I felt uncomfortable with the way we were teaching. Everything was based on the western style of farming, teaching subsistence farmers to milk with machines. What is the use?"

Kiros left academia to work first with an organisation using a participatory learning approach with farmers, and then with an international non-government organisation leading an ambitious project, "recharging" the land in Tigray, and building infrastructure: "I had to do something personally to contribute, to change the situation . . . hills, wheat, lands, trees, water, even a high school". By that time, he had three daughters. In 1998, clashes at the border between Ethiopia and Tigray developed into full-scale war, leaving more than 80,000 dead and further destroying both countries' ailing economies.[4]

> My wife is from Eritrea and I am from Ethiopia, so my position as a person was immediately questioned. My wife was imprisoned, and to be deported to Eritrea. She doesn't even know Eritrea very well; she grew up in Ethiopia, and Eritrea was part of Ethiopia until 1991. Now there was war. Our girls were with her, but they were released. This changed our situation. We knew that we were in danger, so we decided to flee. We left our stuff and drove to Addis Ababa. I never knew that was the end of it, but that became the end of it. We would never go back.

Kiros worked in Addis Ababa for a couple of years but, in political trouble with the government, he was imprisoned a couple of times, and his wife and children were always afraid; so they moved on to Kenya and became refugees. There, he refused to go to the refugee camps, afraid that they might not be safe. As a refugee, he could not get a work permit, but survived for several years by teaching on a cash basis; then, with a contract that had to be renewed monthly, working for Canadian, U.S., and Australian refugee programs. Two years after applying to relocate to Australia, Kiros and his family arrived in Hobart, in 2006 – eight years after they fled their home (see figure 5.1).

At the University of Tasmania, Kiros completed a master's degree, and then a PhD focused on empowerment of people, particularly in new communities. For a time he was a policy officer with the Department of Economic Development, then moved to Melbourne's Swinburne University where he continues to research development and social change at local, regional, and international levels.

Figure 5.1. Kiros, now a university lecturer and researcher, living with his family in Melbourne.

NENE

The youngest participant, Nene, was born in 1991 in what is now South Sudan. It was at a time of conflict that has been part of civil war in Sudan for more than fifty years. Nene's father, a soldier, was killed when she was three months old. "My mum thought it wasn't safe for us, they could come after us, so she took me and three of our kids and she escaped with us; and two of her children were taken by my uncle, and I haven't seen them until now. I have only seen them in photos".

For four years, seeking safety, the family kept moving from village to village, along with many others, because "you don't really know who was fighting who". In 1995, they went to Kakuma Refugee Camp, in Kenya, and stayed there until they were resettled in Australia in 2005. The camp is administered by the UNHCR under the jurisdiction of the Kenyan government. When Nene was there, the population of the camp was close to capacity with approximately fifty thousand refugees.[5] A semi-arid, desert environment, it has dust storms; average daytime temperatures of 40°C; poisonous spiders, snakes, and scorpions; outbreaks of malaria, cholera, and other hardships.[6] Nene remembers that, to enter the camp, they had to have a ration card, which took two weeks to obtain. Once they had the card, they and other refugees were taken by truck to the camp:

> In the camp there is peoples from different countries – Ethiopians, Sudanese, Congolese, Eritreans, Somalians, Ugandans – about eight nationalities all came there, running from war to Kenya. So the UN has to give everyone basic food, and you wait for a fortnight to get your food, and usually many people in a family. If you get rations of food, if you finish it before the time, you have to wait another two weeks before you get more.

In addition to food shortages and disease, there was crime and violence, not least, tribal violence between refugee groups; and the local Turkana people did not want the refugee camp to be there:

> They say that this is their place, the refugees don't belong there, and they should go away. So, the Turkanas can come in the night and take away food. They ask you to give them food or give them money. If you don't give them, then they will kill you, and they rape womens [*sic*] and girls.

Taps put in by the United Nations provided drinking water for a couple of hours each day, but Nene says there was not enough: "You will have to queue and if two hours is finished, and the water stop coming from the tap, you have to go to the river . . . mostly people get water for like taking shower, or cooking, or washing clothes from the river". People also had to cross the river to get firewood, and sometimes timber for repairing buildings, but the Turkana lived in the forest. Children from the camp collected wood and water morning and afternoon. By evening, it was too dangerous. Houses were built from mud and grass, so when it rained, they leaked, and sometimes collapsed. Nene says there was a lot of sickness in the camp, including malnutrition, cholera, and malaria, and usually sick people would die:

> The UN built a hospital for refugees, but there is not enough medical supplies or nurses, and usually when somebody gets sick in the night – like here, when someone gets sick you call 000 and you get an ambulance to take you. But there, if you live very far away, if someone gets sick in your house or your family, you have to take them to the hospital. You have to walk all the way, in the night. Sometimes it is they die on the way, without you reaching there.

The UN set up schools with teachers drawn from among the refugees. If there were not enough classrooms, "we learn under a big tree, with a blackboard". Nene says it was not a full education but limited by what the refugee teachers knew. Children had time for school, to help their parents, to fetch water, and to play with their friends, but they were always aware of danger, and often hungry. Nene says, "I didn't have a good childhood – not like what is normal for children here, in Australia".

Nene, her mother, and two brothers were accepted for resettlement in Hobart, when she was fourteen years old. On arrival, Nene recalls:

> The first thing that goes in my mind – it is *safety* – like here you feel just the atmosphere of how Hobart looks, and it just feels safe. Back there, every time you feel afraid in the night time, you hear guns, you hear tomorrow morning someone was killed, and like that, so when I arrived in Australia, the first thing that came on my mind is safety.
>
> I could see that there were volunteers and people helping us around, and I could see like here there is help, you can get help, no matter what you are going through, you can get help, so it was kind of a different way. It kind of make me a bit forget, like finally I can feel that I am safe, finally I can feel that all is well. I feel like there is new beginning, it is a new chapter of starting a new life, and what I was thinking was, "Try to leave everything behind, whatever happened, forget", but it's hard to forget what happened.

Since arriving in Australia, Nene has completed her secondary and tertiary education. In the final years of high school, she helped to found the Students Against Racism movement and became a primary spokesperson at events in Australia and New Zealand. After working for a year, she did a Bachelor of Arts degree in Sociology at the University of Tasmania. Still involved in tackling racism, after graduation she began work at the Hobart Women's Shelter.

KHADGA

Born in the Dagana district of Bhutan, in 1982, Khadga describes his life as "mixes of happiness and sorrow". Khadga says that, following a census in 1988, the Bhutanese government categorised the population into seven groups, and split families by putting members into different categories. Men and boys were jailed and women and girls raped, and people were tortured. In 1991, when Khadga was nine years old, his extended family fled to Nepal, because "the Bhutan government decided to *cleanse* the Nepalese speaking, Nepali-ethnic people from Bhutan". For six months, the family lived in a camp on the bank of the Kanki River, in "horrible" conditions, very hot in the middle of summer, with "no good drinking water". In extreme hot weather conditions, and without medical services, three of the family's children died; so, the family moved again, to Beidangi II camp, higher in the mountains; the water was still rationed, but cleaner, and conditions were better. A health service was introduced a few months after they arrived. They stayed there for nineteen years.

School in the camp, run by a local organisation, Caritas Nepali, and funded by the UNHCR, taught up to tenth grade. With limited resources, the children sat on the floor on carpet, until in the older grades they had benches and seats. Numbers were high. Khadga says that in eighth grade, there were twenty-five sections, and each section had sixty students. Lessons were in English, and Khadga says the education was of high standard. Gaining a partial scholarship, because he was capable at maths and science, Khadga attended a private boarding school for years eleven and twelve. He worked as a tutor to earn money for rent and other expenses, and his brothers helped with the balance of school fees. Khadga says that refugees were supposed to stay in the camp, but the rule was not enforced.

Khadga applied to go to university to study food technology, but when he went to do the entrance exam, he was asked for citizenship papers; as a refugee, he was not allowed to sit the exam. The following year, he went to Kathmandu and was able to study at the oldest university in Nepal, because citizenship was not required, and the bachelor's degree in microbiology was open to all. He supported himself by teaching maths and science at a local school. While he was in Kathmandu, the UNHCR established an International Office for Migration, opening opportunity for resettlement of refugees in the United States, the United Kingdom, Australia, Canada, New Zealand, Norway, the Netherlands, and Denmark. Khadga was immediately interested, because he knew there was no hope of going back to Bhutan.

My father is now eighty-four years old, he is born in Bhutan, he has got citizenship, he has got all the documents; and my mum, born in Bhutan; but still the

Bhutan government said we are not the original from Bhutan, and said we don't
have enough documents to prove the citizenship of Bhutan.

There is no future living in camp. There is no chance to go back to Bhutan.
It was very clear to us. One of my brothers is still in Bhutan and when we talk
to him on the phone, all the time he explain the situation – what is going on
inside Bhutan. And we used to read newspapers, listen to news, thinking that we
may hear good news that we can go back to Bhutan, but each news all the time
adds us some depressions, and some kind of losing hope. We are very aware of
that, and it was clear that we cannot be assimilated in Nepal, because we are in
the camp. To go outside and live, it is a big money, health cost was really high
for refugee, and we don't have citizenship for Nepal as well. We are homeless,
citizenshipless people.

When the UNHCR opened the doors to resettlement, Khadga made up his
mind to migrate to one of the countries offering places, but achieving that
was complicated because his family is large: "We have twelve brothers and
seven sisters, and all brothers they have their own family, all sisters their own
family – if you count all the links together – around three hundred family".
Khadga explained that most family members are uneducated, and it was hard
for them to choose which country would best suit them. Khadga, one of his
brothers, and a nephew, who had been living together in Kathmandu, decided
they needed to help their families. After some research, they chose Australia:

> We picked Australia, especially Tasmania, because we compared Tasmania
> with Bhutan and Nepal, and we found that the geographical topography of Tas-
> mania is similar – climate, it is not the same, but it is similar – and demography,
> it is not densely populated, it is not big city where we are lost.

Advised by the Australian Ambassador that applications would need to be made
from within the camp, Khadga stopped studying and returned to the camp, about
six hundred kilometres away, to help the families make decisions and apply.

> I am the youngest, but I have education. It was a really, really tough time for
> us to make the decisions. My family member didn't believe [the process for
> resettlements] when I asked them first time. Each time I explained, when I make
> them clear, next day someone will give them different informations [*sic*], and
> then they change the decision. My mum and dad are very strict in their religion
> and the cultural thing, and they got very wrong informations from other people
> in the camp. They said that when you go to Australia, you need to be a shep-
> herd, in a big farm looking after sheep. There is no any communications. You
> will be alone. And another thing, and it was really a bit funny – they said that
> if you go to Australia, you find very dangerous snakes, and animals, and all the
> time you have to put injections – each morning you have to put injections. So,
> it was really, really hard for us to make them clear. Finally, we were successful
> to explain them, and where I was trying to take them.

Figure 5.2.   Khadga and his wife, Naina, on holiday in Nepal in 2017.

It took three years, "making decisions for whole families", and completing paper-work for applications. Some family members migrated to the United States.

> In 2010, 2nd of March, I got chance to come to Australia. From my family I am the first person to come to Australia to live in Tasmania – I came with my wife, she was pregnant, and my mum and dad – and slowly other family came, and now family is big. I am really happy now.

Khadga and his family – including children born in Tasmania – live in Hobart (see figure 5.2). Initially, Khadga earned money fruit picking and was a voluntary Red Cross bi-cultural worker. Studying for a nursing degree, he travelled a long distance to Launceston campus each week. "I am pretty much sure that I will finish my degree and *I will have a job*" – an outcome he has since achieved as a registered nurse.

SHOUKAT

A Hazara man born in Afghanistan, in 1985, Shoukat has happy memories of his childhood, until he was seventeen:

> When my father was alive, I was very happy. I don't remember many thing [*sic*] but at that time I was studying, and in school; and because my father was

working, so I was only studying, and nothing else, only school, from the school go home and play. Then Taliban did kill my father, and two younger brothers, then, I escaped from Afghanistan to Pakistan with my mother and other brothers . . . because the Taliban attack many time to our village, and they would like to kill our all family members . . . so after that my life is changed.

As background, the history of persecution of the Hazara people in Afghanistan goes back at least to 1880, following the second Anglo-Afghan war.[7] A new ruler of Afghanistan, supported by the British, embarked on an expansive, state-building project, which led to the so-called Hazara wars from 1891 to 1893. Until that time of invasion, the Hazarajat was totally independent. The wars were incredibly ferocious, killing almost 60 per cent of the Hazaras. Some of those left escaped to Pakistan and Iran, establishing the present-day communities in those countries. Some were sold as slaves, and the rest became a pariah group. In more recent times, the Taliban (Sunni Muslims) have persecuted and massacred the Hazaras (Shia Muslims). Since 2001, there has been no official discrimination against Hazaras, but the capacity of the state to offer realistic protection for them against predatory groups such as the Taliban is negligible.[8]

In Pakistan, Shoukat's mother was ill. To support the family, for a couple of years Shoukat worked hard with three older brothers, selling vegetables, and studied after work. Then he saw "Taliban killed our eighteen vegetable seller people" and his mother encouraged her sons to work elsewhere. Shoukat worked in many different places, continued to study, married, and fathered a child. Then, in November 2010, attacks on the Hazara people escalated:

Taliban did kill our eighty people, Hazara only, where we were living in Pakistan. During that time I saw and I cried for eighty people, so there is not any way to live there. Because I had not [*sic*] choice of anything else, so my mother said I should escape from Pakistan. So that's why I thought, "What should I do? What should I do? What should I do?"

I was really worried and at that time I had not enough money to escape from Pakistan to Australia, so I borrow some money from my relative, and all the friend. During that time Taliban again did killed our fifty people in bomb blast in our mosque. No any life in Pakistan for our Hazara people. So, I said, "There is nothing left, so what should we do? What should *I* do?" During this time my mother, because she was sick, she has died. So, after her death, I thought I should escape from there to a good and nice life for my family, for my brothers, sister, and my wife, my son.

So that is why I escaped from Pakistan, and I came to Malaysia, from Malaysia to Indonesia. So, my journey was illegal. Everything was illegal. My document was illegal, because in Pakistan I was illegal.

From Jakarta, Shoukat was a passenger on a people smuggler – a small fishing boat, carrying fifty-five people. In mid-sea, the boat broke down. For three days, they drifted closer to Christmas Island, working in shifts to boil water to drink. "Navy force, they caught us, so they brought us in detention centre". Shoukat spent about two months in the Christmas Island detention centre and then he was sent to Curtin detention centre, in Western Australia. He says that "the situation was very worse" in those detention centres. A contemporary Amnesty International account of conditions in detention centres on Christmas Island, in Curtin, and in Darwin, reported on escalating numbers of suicide attempts, and other incidents of self-harm, lack of appropriate services, and extreme psychological problems resulting from indefinite detention.[9]

After about six months in Curtin, Shoukat was sent to Pontville, in Tasmania, and says he was very surprised: "When I came to Pontville camp in Tasmania, so I heard my name, wow! Serco[10] already knew my name, immigration also, they were calling my name!" Shoukat said that in Christmas Island and Curtin detention centres, Serco and immigration personnel never used the detainees' names; "they called with our ID, for example LMN24, PUK36 – like a criminal!" Shoukat says the difference at Pontville was "a good pleasure" for all the detainees, as well as himself. "After one year, I heard my name, and I feel, oh, now I am human!"

While in Pontville, Shoukat was finally given an Australian permanent visa and came to Hobart, where he lived with friends. He was free, legally resident in Australia, and beginning to make a life for himself, but his situation continued to be very painful, because his family was still in Pakistan, and in danger:

> Everybody knows, Taliban again they are busy to killing only Hazara. Taliban think if they kill one Hazara they will go to heaven, because they think we are infidel. I don't know why they think like this. So that is true, and so they are busy to killing once a week, once a month. One month ago, two Taliban, they came in our town – in Hazara's town [in Pakistan] – and they did suicide bomb blast . . . and they did kill about ninety Hazara, so at that time we were in hunger strike, with our innocent dead bodies peoples. Our ninety dead bodies people on the road, so we were on hunger strike for three days.

The attack to which Shoukat refers was in Quetta, on 10 January 2013. As well as those killed, about two hundred more people were severely injured. News reports say that after this most recent attack, Hazara leaders in Australia and Pakistan called for the Australian government to ease restrictions on asylum seekers and those with pending family reunion visas.[11] One month later, there was another attack in Quetta, with similar numbers of casualties. Shoukat lived in fear for his family. Recounting the history of persecution for more than two hundred years, he explained that the dominant group in Afghanistan is Pashtun, ethnically Aryan, and the Hazaras are Mongolian, "Mongolian face, Mongolian", whereas the Pashtun, which includes the Taliban, have typically "Aryan" noses and eyes. "They can recognise us very well. So it is very easy to kill a Hazara in Pakistan, also in Afghanistan".

Shoukat's application to bring his family to Australia was refused for several years. He submitted a claim for a "spouse visa" and was told it would take more than five years, probably closer to ten years before his family would arrive. He was given an option to submit $AUD2,700 to the Department of Immigration, in which case "they will bring my family in between two years and one year", but it was hard for Shoukat to raise that amount of money.

> After prison, after I lived in Hobart for more than one year; so again I should wait. I don't know how long. So that is also painful for me. Taliban is busy to killing only Hazara, so any time anything maybe happen. Sometime, I feel it is very difficult to study, very difficult to live in Tasmania, in Hobart, or in Australia, without my family, because I think I live in between two part. My one part of brain at Pakistan, and the second part of brain in Tasmania. So how can I do a proper work, and how can I study like this? It is very difficult.

While waiting for family reunion to be approved, Shoukat studied for a certificate in aged care, and, like Khadga, he was a voluntary Red Cross bicultural worker; he was also the secretary of the Afghani Association and provided information about health to the small Hazara community in Hobart. One way he handled his emotions, particularly his longing for his family, was by writing poetry in Persian.

Subsequently, there were significant, very harsh changes to Australian government policy in regard to asylum seekers. In January 2014, the Australian Minister for Immigration and Border Protection issued a directive that family migration visas would not be processed for anyone who arrived in Australia by boat after September 2001 (people now officially classified as illegal maritime arrivals) and that if application had already been made, and visa application charges paid, there would be no refund.[12] Offshore detention was escalated on Nauru and Manus Island, and restrictions further tightened.

The state of limbo Shoukat experienced continued for several more years, but finally was resolved. More than seven years after he began his journey from Pakistan, Shoukat became an Australian citizen and, at last, he was allowed to bring his family to Australia. They settled in South Australia and, in 2019, Shoukat's wife and children also became citizens.

HONING SENSES OF SELF

I am humbled before these stories and deeply aware of what it took for these four people to share their journeys with me. Each of them said that they had had to tell their stories so often, to so many functionaries along the way, that they had become resigned to the process. Yet, there were poignant, tragic, touching moments in each telling, and I felt they spoke from their hearts. Each one hoped that voicing their stories once again might help others. Certainly, they contributed to this work: their narratives provide rich material here and in later chapters on sense of self and sense of place, and understanding of how these senses have influenced their migration and resettlement processes. Conversations with these people revealed significant differences as well as nuances in the experiences of asylum seekers and refugees that distinguish them from those of regular migrants.

Conversations with Shoukat, Khadga, and Nene were quite different from those of the other players, and shorter. Each spoke English well enough for our purpose (and they have since become fluent). Nene, who by then had been in Australia for seven years, far longer than the other two, was the most settled. They were quite willing to talk to me, but spoke of such painful memories it was inappropriate to press for detail. The trauma of certain experiences meant they had simply shut off clear memory of some events – a typical result of trauma – at times making it very difficult for people seeking to establish their claims to refugee status.[13] Shoukat was also deeply preoccupied with fears and longing for his wife and child, still in mortal danger in Pakistan. I also felt there was a limit to what the three *could* say because of a subtle difference in the way they thought of themselves – identifying their senses of self *through* family and community, rather than with a more individual sense of self common to the other participants.

The narratives shared by all four people indicate significant differences in how irregular and regular migrants experience and express their senses of self. To start with, none of the irregular migrants spoke much about childhood, which regular migrant participants emphasised. Shoukat, whose story is perhaps the harshest, spoke of a happy childhood; but in a single sentence, as if it had become unreal, wiped out by the murder of his father and brothers, and subsequent terrors. Khadga, at nine years of age, watched three children of his family die of disease and hardship in a refugee camp. Kiros spoke of a happy childhood truncated by violence that started when he was six years old. Nene's was not so much an account of her experience of *being a child*, but rather a description of conditions in the camp from a child's perspective; when one is constantly hungry and afraid, play is nothing like experience common for children who know themselves to be safe. Significantly, all four faced challenges to their survival and lived with fear from an early age, experiencing violence and atrocity at various times.

At first, I found some difficulty in discerning just how these four players experienced their senses of self and place. Kiros was by far the most articulate, at least in part because he has spoken English fluently since his youth; he has tertiary education, and, since migrating to Australia, has spent several further years at university. His explanation provided insight that helped me when interviewing the others. As Kiros expresses it, in African countries, generally, "the self is *defined* in light of the immediate family, the immediate community". He thinks that there is "a core philosophical difference . . . a difference in worldviews" that is common between Africans and people in the west, with its focus on ideas of individuality. Traditionally, in Africa, "the individual can be seen *only* in light of its own community", and although one's ethnic group is important, community is the source of what is most valued. In sharing this observation, Kiros used the term *relative* not just for blood relations but also for extended family members of the community where he grew up. If a relative, so understood, was experiencing financial difficulty, for instance, "you would just send everything you have, because that's where your value is – you see yourself *through* that".

Kiros' community-based sense of self deeply affected his experiences as a refugee. When first he fled from Ethiopia to Kenya, he was shocked to realise that he was "only Kiros". Disconnected from his community, he felt that he no longer had "the respect that I earned in my own community" and thus, he had no way to be known as himself. Disconnected from his country and without a passport, he says defined him as "I am not any more a person". He was shaken that he had to apply to even be recognised as a refugee. Resonant with Shoukat's experience of being known only by a number, this namelessness is dehumanising; and fits Arendt's argument that without any identification other than one's individuality, a person becomes "a human in general . . . and loses all significance". This idea is consonant with Foucault's understanding that, historically, the denial of names – to "slaves and other non-people", effectively denied that they had any "real" existence.[14] Thus, having a distinct name and identity is "an important precondition for being truly human".[15]

Faced with the likelihood of becoming a number in a refugee camp for an indefinite period, Kiros' response was to strongly assert himself in what he saw clearly as a fight for the survival of his family. He relates his self-worth to his capability to contribute towards his own existence, to his family, his community, and to his world. Given his experience of doing all those things up to that point in his life, he refused to be defined by his situation. Determined not to go to a refugee camp, he found unorthodox ways to make money, and opportunities for migration that would not have been possible in a camp. This experience stood him in good stead when he arrived in Australia.

Kiros says that making a new life in a new country requires accepting that this is a new start from "zero". First, on arrival, he was unknown, and the status and credentials he had in his country of origin were not recognised by the new community; and, thus, the place reflected back to him a self that was lacking in worth. Second, less obviously, but perhaps even more significant, was his realisation that in this new place he was ignorant of all the minutiae of culture and place that any person acquires in the process of growing up in any somewhere. Evident in Kiros' account is the importance of acknowledging that, although "zero" was a critical base from which he could begin to build freshly, what he had, what he brought with him, was *not nothing*, and was perhaps immeasurably significant in terms of his capacity to make a new life in a new country, for his family and for himself. What he had was a strong, honed, developed, and asserted sense of self: honed in a wartime environment, where early values of community were challenged; developed in his early efforts to educate others and to "recharge" the land; asserted in his refusal to go into refugee camps, and in his belief that he could find work, and that he could find a way to have his family be safe. Even the fact of Kiros' arrival in Hobart within a comparatively short time of leaving Ethiopia, with his family intact, testifies to the strength of his sense of self. Nevertheless, Kiros feels his relocation as a loss of self. After several years in Australia, he came up with an analogy for his experience of the loss of self that he feels is involved in the separation from his community of origin. He says it is something similar to the way people who have lost a limb speak of a phantom pain. To him "phantom pain" makes sense as a way to explain his ongoing feeling of displacement.

Similarly, Shoukat expressed a loss of self when he spoke of feeling as if he was "living in between", with one part of himself in Pakistan with his family, and one part in Tasmania. He did not have these words, but the sense I got from him was that he felt almost like a memory, or a ghost of himself. At that time, when I asked Shoukat how he would describe himself, or think of himself, he said,

> according to my history, so I am nothing really: I am nothing because I am Hazara, so when I think Hazara history, there is many painful story, so I think "wow, I am nothing really". I am nothing. I have lost my language, I have lost my culture, and I have lost many things in my history, so that's why I think I am nothing.

However, when I asked, "On a personal level, do you think you are nothing?" he replied:

> No. When I see on my personal level, I belong with the Hazara community, which is a true thing. My personal, I am Muslim, I love humanity, which is very necessity for me. I love only human. I don't love like Hazara, or Pashtun, or Dari, or Englishman, or other – for me I love humanity.

Shoukat's response here goes some way to explain his sense of self. The question of personal worth did not elicit an individual sense of identity or mission as it might for a Western self, but rather saw him broaden what he defines himself with exponentially, from Hazara to Muslim to humanity. It was as if his experience of being "nothing" erased his personal definition, and he defines what has survived of his sense of self in terms of the collectives of which he is part, and in relation to his care for their members. Separated from his family, it was impossible for him to do anything to protect them from violence at such distance. Such helplessness testifies to the desperation Shoukat and others like him feel in such circumstances, and it underscores the extraordinary courage they show in making the dangerous journey away from those they love in hope of saving them.

Although Khadga and his family lived in a refugee camp for nineteen years, in Nepal they were comparatively safe; what constrained them was their lack of citizenship and concomitant lack of hope that they would ever be able to move beyond the dreadful poverty of the camp. For Khadga, the opportunity to migrate to another country was never simply an option for himself alone; it was *for* the extended family, and even though he says, "*I* was the first to come to Australia", in reality he came *with* his wife and parents – for him, *I includes* those immediate family members. He was only really happy when more members of his extended family arrived here, and numbers were enough to re-form their community. For our conversations, Khadga invited me to his home. On arrival, I was introduced first to his parents, then his wife and son, then other relatives; and although we talked alone, it was clear that our conversation took place in context of the family.

Regardless of how my questions about Khadga's sense of himself were phrased, his answers were all in terms of his family. For example, I acknowledged his persistence in all he had done to bring his family to Australia, even though he was the youngest brother, and asked if he felt that showed that he was strong. He replied that "it was really hard, I did really struggle hard when I came first with my father and mum, because there were no other brothers here, no 'sisters'. Again, *I* must have included his wife, because he didn't name her. I asked Khadga what he thought helped him, what inside himself made him able to do that, and he replied: "I was pretty sure that one day my family would be happy here, because other of my family members, they are also doing their process to come to Australia. Sooner or later they will be here"; so, what sustained him was his belief that the family would regather. Khadga comes across as a person who is assertive, confident, clear about what he wants, and with an expectation that others will hear him, and support him in his endeavours. But very little of that is actually personal – a heightened sense of pride resides in speaking for his family. When I asked what is most important to him, he said: "The first thing in our culture is myself-and-my-family members", and it was clear that he was unable to articulate a sense of self other than as part of that greater whole. Khadga also said Australia is the first country in which he has ever had the opportunity to become a citizen, and his pride in the fact that he was eligible to be an Australian extended to knowing that his children would also be Australian citizens.

The orientation of sense of self in terms of family, extended family, community, and ethnicity is clearly very strong for Kiros, Khadga, and Shoukat and it is belonging to, and caring for family that sustains them. Because of my orientation in a Western culture, and embodiment of a concept of self as individual, while I recognise and appreciate that these people define themselves through family and community, sense of self in those terms remains outside my experience, but not outside bounds of empathy. Awareness of that predisposition led me to be particularly alert, when interviewing the participants, to individual nuances indicating their senses of self. Thus, with Kiros, Khadga, and Shoukat as comparators, a clear difference was apparent in Nene's sense of self. Those three all came to Australia as adults. Nene has grown from the age of fourteen to adulthood in Tasmania.

At the time of our conversations, Nene's sense of self was still emerging – at least in Western understanding – and "it is [likely] not until adolescence . . . that we are able and motivated to conceive of our lives as full-fledged, integrative narratives of the self".[16] Dan McAdams, Ruthellen Josselson, and Amia Lieblich draw a correspondence with Erik Erikson's description of adolescence as "the period of identity development".[17] They remind us that according to Erikson, "adolescents and young adults in modern societies are challenged to formulate meaningful answers to the twin identity questions: Who am I? How do I fit into the adult world?"[18] The challenge for Nene is to find answers to those questions from not one, but two cultures. Nene comes from a background within which defining self in terms of community could be considered the norm, and this applied even when living for ten years in a refugee camp. However, from early adolescence she has lived in a modern, Western country. In her words, she is "juggling two different things that I have to put together to make it work". Nene wants to retain, and says she feels comforted by, practices of her original culture; and yet, she also wants to adapt to the new one. She lives with her mother in Hobart, two brothers live in other Australian states, and the rest of her family is scattered, some still in the refugee camp. Extended family, for Nene, now includes members of the Students Against Racism group, to whom she has grown close. Juggling the mores of her native culture and Western constructs of self and individualism, increasingly, she makes decisions about her life independent of family. Asked to describe herself, Nene said:

> What I found in myself is, it is hard to forget the past. It is very difficult for me to forget the past, like I guess I just want to ask: "Why did it happen to me? Why it has to be my family?" And also, that I didn't see my Dad, so it is hard to forget the past, even though I want to go forward to the future.

"I am safe now" and "I am still afraid" are statements of identity, not just Nene's acknowledgement of the way she sometimes feels. The tension that shows here between past and future is common among refugees, and "the interaction between the individual and their own culture and both the group and individual interaction with the new culture becomes a complex one".[19] Nene exhibits a growing confidence in herself and her abilities. Her sense of self-worth is deeply grounded in her work, participation in Youth Against Racism, and the valuing of all human beings for which the group stands.

Contributing to the broader community and place that has received them as refugees is important to all four of these irregular migrants, and typical of many others with whom I have had contact. The high value they place on contribution might be understood as deriving from, and as an extension of their culturally strong family and community values. What each of these irregular migrants brought with them was an ontological experience of finding and knowing themselves through a collective history and identity that persists despite their persecution as individuals. They also made their journeys with hope, and belief that – given the chance – they have the ability to make good lives for themselves and their families as part of the broader community in their new country.

NOTES

1. Bauman, 45.

2. A brief summary of Kiros' narrative was first published as a conference paper, and subsequently in Walthrust Jones, *Diversity and Turbulences in Contemporary Global Migration* (online), and in Dugan and Edelstein, *Migration Matters*.

3. *Ethiopia Booklet*, edited by Australian Department of Immigration and Multicultural Affairs.

4. UNHCR, 'The State of the World's Refugees 2000: Fifty Years of Humanitarian Action.'

5. The population of Kakuma camp is more than 186,000, and there are rumours that the Kenyan government wants to close it, along with Dadaab. Tom Odula, UN Document Shows Kenya Seeking to Close Somali Refugee Camp,' Associated Press, March 30, 2019, accessed April 14, 2019, https://www.apnews.com/d4e1e25788034 d98a4258afe5e473e4e.

6. About Kakuma Refugee Camp. Kanere, A Refugee Free Press, 2010, Accessed April 26, 2013. http://kanere.org/about-kakuma-refugee-camp/. This account reports the camp population in 2010 as about 50,000 – less than a third of the number in March 2019.

7. Ahmed Rashid, Javed Saleem, William Maley, and Grant Farr, The Story of the Hazara People, interview by Anabelle Quince. Rear Vision ABC Radio National: Rear Vision, August 5, 2012, accessed September 8, 2014, http://www.abc.net.au/ radionational/programs/rearvision/hazara/4165942#transcript.

8. Ibid.

9. Louise Allen, Stories from Detention; Shrapnel, Stress and Self-Harm, Amnesty International, 1 November 2010, accessed April 15, 2014, http://www.amnesty.org.au/refugees/comments/24021.

10. Serco Group is a private – for-profit – international corporation, headquartered in the United Kingdom, and provides security and other staff for military bases, detention centres, and prisons worldwide.

11. Amanda Hodge, Aussies Die in Hazara Blast in Pakistan. *Australian*, January 16, 2013, accessed February 13 2013, http://www.theaustralian.com.au/national-affairs/immigration/aussies-die-in-hazara-blast-in-pakistan/story-fn9hm1gu-122655469 9633.

12. ASRC, Asylum Seekers Resource Centre. Family Re-Union Applications of Those Australian Permanent Residents Who Came by Boat Won't Be Processed by DIBP. http://www.asrc.org.au/.

13. Bhugra, Craig, and Bhui, Mental Health of Refugees; Goodall; Manzo; van der Kolk; van der Kolk, McFarlane, and Weisaeth.

14. Danaher et al., 2000.

15. Ibid.

16. Cobb; Erikson; McAdams, Josselson, and Lieblich, Identity.

17. McAdams, Josselson, and Lieblich, Introduction, 3.

18. Ibid., 3, 4.

19. Bhugra, Craig, and Bhui, Conclusions, 301.

Chapter 6

Mobile Lives

> The term "mobile lives" suggests an increasingly complex, detraditional-ized patterning to personal life. People with substantial network capital learn to live with the making of personal and social worlds "on the move", fashioned on shifting ground.[1]

While the term *mobile lives* has other meanings, here it relates to global travel, international migrations, and relocations within countries, which last accounts for an estimated 8 per cent of adults worldwide moving domestically each year, while 21 per cent move at least once every five years.[2] Motivations people have for migrating internationally apply also to relocations within countries. Wars or other significant conflicts, and catastrophic political, economic, or environmental events contribute to the numbers of displaced persons; and such events compel the relocation of people within territories in addition to emigration.

In countries that are relatively peaceful and stable, economic and political factors are the strongest drivers of internal migration.[3] Levels of internal migration are far higher in "advanced economies" than in developing ones – the United States, Australia, New Zealand, Finland, and Norway exemplify this trend.[4] In Australia, for instance, close to 41 per cent of the population relocated in each of the five-year census periods leading up to 2011 and 2016, and 15 per cent of the population changed their address in the year prior to the 2016 census.[5] Referring to such frequent changing of domicile as urban nomadism, Juhani Pallasmaa notes that "the average period of living in one location in the US is barely over four years" and can relate to lack of, or opportunities for employment, education and social services; availability and affordability of accommodation; and changing circumstances in personal wealth.[6] The World Bank makes explicit the neoliberal argument that economic efficiency requires a mobile workforce.[7]

Anthony Elliott and John Urry point out that "an individual's engagement with [an expansively] mobile world is not simply about the 'use' of particular forms of movement", but involves processes through which "an intensively mobile society reshapes the self' "[8] In this way, we are witnessing new expressions of what they call *portable personhood* – a "stretching of self" psychologically and socially.[9] Whether people physically relocate or not, they engage with a mobile world that affects their senses of self and of place through wider events, movements of other people, changes to places, direct and indirect impacts of globalism, the Internet and World Wide Web, and other media. As Doreen Massey writes, few people's lives can today be described as "simply local" or as "entirely untouched by events elsewhere".[10] In turn, Steve Pile and Nigel Thrift assert that mobile lives produce "possibilities of hybrid identities [with] new capacities for action".[11] Such possibilities arise through and in relationship with varied cultural and social influences, and in and through diverse places, giving new and varied "shape and form to human beings" and their governance.[12]

Yukari and Julian, whose stories follow, have relocated often. Julian could be classed as a regular migrant, Yukari has lived in the same building in Tokyo – albeit intermittently – for about thirty years; nevertheless, both their narratives emphasise many relocations and provide glimpses of distinctive and distinctly mobile lives.

JULIAN

Born in England, in 1947, by his own telling Julian is a seeker and an adventurer. His British parents both came from long history of military and civil involvement in colonial India, a background that influenced Julian's life "mostly by way of rejection of a lot of the values they stood for". Within months of Julian's birth, his father, a British army officer, was posted to Burma (where one of his forbears had been Lieutenant Governor General), then to India, briefly back to England when Julian was about three years old, then to Norway for a few years:

> Dad blotted his copybook and got court-martialled – I think he overdrew his pay, or something like that. I can't remember back that far, but we've always been a bit, sort of "out of the family" in that sense. The next posting was to Jordon, and I do remember Jordan. I was six. I used to play with the servants' children. My sister was sent off – as happened with so many children of British families – to boarding school in England, but when she visited us, she used to call me "the dirty little Bedouin boy".

That posting lasted for about three years, until the Suez Canal crisis.[13] The British contingent had five days to depart Jordan, and was shipped to Cyprus, and then transported back to England. Julian was nine years old. "I loved Jordan. The hardest part for me was leaving my donkey behind. It was called *Faddua,* which sounds very exotic until you learn that it's just *donkey* in Arabic. My Dad stayed behind; he was invited to work with the Arab Legion".[14] Julian was sent to a local primary school in England, "a horrific experience. I remember being caned in front of all the rest of the students. I can't remember what for".

Next the family went to Malaysia and was based in Kuala Lumpur for about three years. Julian was sent to a private school in Penang, then to the local army school, and next to boarding school in England. "I'd had a pretty ropey schooling, lots of different schools. I was terribly envious of kids who'd had friends for lots of years. I got bullied, yet I was physically okay, captain of rugby, and I did boxing. It wasn't a happy place". Julian escaped into Arthur Ransome books – stories of sailing adventures set in the Lake District, the East Coast of England, the Caribbean, China, and the Outer Hebrides that fired the imaginations of generations of schoolboys – and wanted to go to sea: "Even before that I used to look at atlases and plot journeys". That probably influenced his later choice to attend merchant and navy training school rather than one for the sons of army officers. Eyesight problems kept him out of the Royal Navy, so he studied mining engineering at London University.

In some ways I had a very troubled childhood, and I know that sounds a bit trite, but I grew up in other countries, and my parents separated, and one became an alcoholic and the other became a bankrupt, and yet it was a strong family in some ways. My sister wanted to convert us all to Buddhism. I was influenced by her, and by *thinking* that was happening in India. My mum had become a Theosophist.[15] One of the leading thinkers, Annie Besant,[16] was very supportive of Mahatma Gandhi.[17] She used to complain that keeping Gandhi in poverty was a very expensive business! Then there was this amazing character who we all thought was absolutely fantastic, J. Krishnamurti.[18] Brought up and educated in England to be the leader of the Theosophical Society, just months before he was to be declared the world leader, he upped and said he didn't want to be. He didn't want that role, he didn't believe people should follow him, and proposed that we really need to find our own path, and be, rather than just follow.

To us, young people in the sixties – well I wasn't a hippie type, but I was certainly part of that generation and that music, and looking for a better lifestyle – we thought what Krishnamurti had said was really good. However, I did a year at university, played a lot of rugby, failed most of my end of year exams, got invited to come back after a year if I'd like to go and grow up, so I went to South Africa and worked on a couple of gold mines.

Julian did return to England to complete university, then joined the predominantly Dutch company, Shell, as a petroleum engineer. After six months training in The Hague, he was posted to Qatar, in the Persian Gulf. He liked the work, but the "urge to learn more about life and life's purpose was very strong", so early in the 1970s, near the end of the Indo-Pakistan war, he resigned and travelled deck class to India.

> I had to choose: "Do you turn left and go up to Kathmandu, or turn right and go down to the beaches of Goa, where all the hippies hang out?" I decided on that [latter] path, partly because it was a lovely coastal trip on a lovely little boat; then, I hung out on Panjim Beach for a couple of weeks, but I didn't like it. I think the hippie movement had some very good ideas, they wanted a better world, there's no doubt about that, but they got a bit diverted by the weed, and other, just lostness. Lovely music, but just lost its way. Anyway, I had higher purposes. By that time I had a shoulder bag with a Bhagavad Gita in it, but I hadn't, like some, abandoned my passport.[19] I had a bit of money because I'd been working, and I had a dhoti and a jubbah [garments traditionally worn by Muslims in India], so I went travelling.

Julian settled for seven years in remote farmland in the south, where he was a volunteer worker at Seva Nilayam, a medical clinic for the poor run by an English woman, Dora Scarlett.[20] After a year, he worked in the laboratory:

> I was looking mostly at faecal samples for hookworm and pinworm, and I remember thinking: "Julian, you wanted to get to know the real India, and here you are peering down the microscope at samples of human – Indian – crap! How much closer to the real India do you want to get?" I did a whole range of tests, extending to tuberculosis and leprosy. Having used a microscope as a petroleum engineer, it wasn't a big leap, actually. At the clinic we worked bloody hard, six days a week, seeing two hundred and fifty to three hundred people a day. There were female, male, and children's wards, and a farm worked by the inpatients as, really, part of their cure.

It was a formative time for Julian. He was in contact with a group of Catholic monks, the Little Brothers of Jesus, working to treat leprosy. Each month he went to a Catholic Ashram run by "an amazing Benedictine monk", an English man called Dom Bede Griffiths, who was "on a quest for a dialogue between Catholic monks and Hindu saddhus". Julian says he nearly became a novice, "but I met Kay, an Australian volunteer, and that was a bit of a diversion". Through Dom Griffiths, he also connected with Vipassana [a sitting meditation that is a practice of self-transformation through self-observation and introspection] and its exponent, S.M. Goenka, whom he describes as "a very traditional sort of teacher, not whacko at all". Although this meditation practice came from a Buddhist tradition usually passed on by monks, it was "for anybody", and Julian liked it "for the same reasons as I liked the clinic – it was very spiritual, but it wasn't connected to religion".

Julian and Kay married and then worked for about six months with an organisation that was developing agricultural projects and schools in line with Gandhi's principles. They adopted a little boy, called Christopher, from one of Mother Teresa's homes.[21]

> We added the name Natarajan – a Hindu name relating to the god, Shiva – because we knew he was from a Hindu family. Living in India, and thinking about the future, especially for our adopted son, Christopher Natarajan, we decided that Australia would provide a future with greater opportunity than the UK. Our perception was that there was still a bit of the pioneering spirit and adventure in Australia, whereas the UK was well established, getting over-crowded, and did not have as exciting prospects. Nowadays, we feel that our perceptions were about right!

First, however, Julian and Kay went to England. Inspired by Maria Montessori's philosophy and method of education, and Jean Piaget's seminal work in childhood development, Julian trained as a teacher in a "very progressive education department" at the University of Sussex. Then they moved to Australia and lived in Melbourne. Julian worked in a fibreglass boat factory until his teaching qualifications were transferred, then taught at a Jesuit school, Xavier College. Then they saw a Community Aid Abroad advertisement for two people to work in Somalia.[22] Julian said, "It was just made for us", so they went to Somalia for a couple of years, only leaving when war broke out and "everything started disintegrating".

> I'd become a Quaker by that time, because I felt – although I was really interested in Hinduism and Buddhism, and considered myself to be a student of religion – the early, archetypal working of my brain was based on Christian religion, and I found Quakerism was a wonderful bridge between East and West. I wanted to work in a Quaker school, so we came to Tasmania.[23]

Julian and Kay have now lived in Hobart for more than thirty years. When I asked Julian how it felt to settle in one place after such a diverse and mobile life, he replied that he and Kay had often thought of going overseas again to work in other countries, "but it is true, we've bought a house, a boat, had a career – the full catastrophe!" However, he said they had also travelled during those years.

> We have taken two groups of students for one-month trips to South India, and introduced them to village life in a non-industrial part of the country. Once our son was independent, we decided to go adventuring – it turned out to be for five years! We sailed our little catamaran from Hobart up the east coast of

Australia to the Torres Strait, where we lived and worked for a couple of years. We had a dream to sail to the places we had lived and worked in before: Port Moresby (Kay), Penang in Malaysia (I schooled there), India, Somalia, Jordan, and through the Suez to Europe. But the boat was a bit small, and parts of the journey too dangerous – Somali pirates also take yachties!

The boat trip was my wish. Kay wanted to do the Trans-Siberian railway. So, we sold the boat, travelled to Europe, visiting friends and relatives, and to St Petersburg in Russia, where we took the rail to Moscow, and then the Trans-Siberian. We turned right after Irkutsk, and came down by rail and bus to Mongolia, China, Vietnam, Cambodia, Thailand, then flew to Burma, where I worked in a school for six months. We then returned to Australia and had to learn to settle down and behave ourselves!

At the time of our conversations, Julian still worked at the Friends School, as Quaker Coordinator – supporting the heads of school, leading gatherings, doing professional development, and implementing a program that brings Quakers to Tasmania from all over the world. Since then, he has retired but is still very active.

YUKARI

Yukari was born in Japan, in 1960, in Oiso, a town by the sea in the Kanagawa prefecture adjacent to Tokyo, with a population of about thirty thousand people. Her parents had met at university at a time when it was still unusual for a woman in Japan to have such education. Her father was not in Japan when Yukari, the youngest of three daughters, was born. He was in the United States, doing postgraduate study as one of the first exchange students from Japan, and on his return brought "a sense of living in a foreign country" into the family:

> When I went to his room, the radio has got Far East Network. It was the American Army radio so it was in English, and he bought a whole bunch of records of English lullabies for his baby. And the breakfast, I remember, was often tea and pancake, which was very different from the normal Japanese. So having a different culture in my own house was the beginning of my life.

Describing her father as "a very individualistic person – distinctive, and self-focused" – Yukari says he had no idea how to be a father, and "not knowing what he should do with these three children" he left when she was very small. "He didn't really support the family. He had the income from being a university professor, and that money he used for his car and his books", leaving Yukari's mother to provide for their three daughters. By the 1960s, Japan's economy was recovering from the devastation of the Second World War, and living standards had considerably improved.[24] Nevertheless, there was no social welfare support for single mothers.[25] Because of her education, Yukari's mother was able to earn money by doing home teaching, but that income was insufficient, so she also made clothes. Yukari says that when she was small, she wanted to understand rather than to be rebellious, but would complain to her mother:

> "Why don't I have what other people have? Why don't I have the father?" Because it was the mother that was taking care of, I didn't have the feeling of rebelling against her, because I could feel that she was doing her best, and I think that that was one of the survival mechanisms of a child, to accept and find meaning in the situation. Of course, to please Mother, I tried to be as good a girl as possible, and at the same time I had the sense that I am so different, and that played out as a sense of superiority. I felt like all the children were really childish, and with the sense of inferiority that I don't have the father, I don't have much things, so that was a mixture, going back and forth from feeling inferiority to superiority.

Even though she had little time with her father, Yukari feels she was strongly influenced by him: "He didn't hide himself being very different, very rebellious to what was going on politically, and he was a very interesting, eccentric person in the university". By the time Yukari was in junior high school, where she did not feel any sense of belonging, she had taken on his way of identifying himself, "that being different is my identity".

Fishing and farming were traditional ways of living in Oiso, but Tokyo people also had summerhouses there – artists, politicians, even the Prime Minister. Yukari says the presence of these people, whose outlook was broader than most locals, made the town interesting; as did an orphanage – "a secluded place" – that she passed on the way to school.[26] Yukari attended compulsory schooling in Oiso until she was fifteen, and then, allowed to choose, she attended a "free school" recommended by her father. Explaining that "free" is not about money, but about ideas, Yukari says the school was established before the Second World War by "a bunch of creators" such as writers, artists, and architects.

Yukari says her parents had very advanced ideas about education, and the school encouraged the students to express themselves, for example, as a writer, or an artist. Yukari started painting and began to develop a more individual sense of self than was common then, especially for a Japanese girl: "People do something else than the crowd does, so that makes me have the sense of freedom of not being one of the sheep. The basic idea that was given to me there was that you have a choice of deciding what you want to do. That was very, very useful".

While still a college student, at the age of twenty, Yukari went to India – also a highly unusual thing for a young Japanese woman to do at that time.

Her boyfriend was already travelling and wrote to invite her to join him. Yukari acknowledges that "for anybody, India is a big impression", but for her, learning to bargain in street markets shockingly challenged her notions of proper behaviour. "You are asked to pay twenty times as much as the normal regular fee, and you have to show you are being upset [to bargain the price down]. It is totally, totally different in Japan, but learning I could do this gave me a sense of strength". Yukari backpacked through India, Nepal, and Thailand, and recalls that she felt "if you get sick or something your life is over, so this is a survival experiment".

Yukari says that one of the reasons she "started to look out" – beyond Japan – was that she had always been interested in "people who are different to us" and her desire to communicate with foreigners visiting Oiso led her to learn English, and to travel.

> As I was travelling, I started to have an idea of being dissolved in the society, in the culture. It was very helpful. It is a very basic rule of survival, I think, that if you stick out you will be attacked. So it is a basic survival kit that I started to take in, in order for me not to get robbed, or have much of a problem. You have to know what the other people expect, what they do, how they function; to develop the eyes that you can observe the differences, so you can have the choice of whether you want to be together or not. And also, not the behaviour itself, but the emotional aspect of it: how they respond, how they get upset with it. You have the idea that what I grew up with is the same, but one way or another I was shown this doesn't work here.

Yukari explained that she wanted to learn what was customary in places foreign to her, and to understand the feelings of people there. Her *visible* difference in other cultures – as a Japanese woman – did not concern her because she had always felt herself to be different: "I was raised as somebody different, not at all in ordinary Japanese culture, because American culture was in my house. In Japan, I always have a sense of being a misfit". However, on her return to Japan from that early experience of travelling she says she thought her only choice was "to try to fit in, so it was quite a difficult time". At first Yukari sought to be an artist, and worked in an art gallery – a job that was of short duration "because I found the artists had to do business". Disillusioned, she quit the job and gave up painting. Proficiency with English led Yukari to work for the next ten years for a television production company, as a producer creating programmes about foreign countries:

> So, I started to go places, and I also started to have a lot of communication with Japanese co-ordinators living in different countries. It was very interesting; all of them were different, because how they developed the sense of themselves is influenced by where they are. For example, there was a Japanese co-ordinator living in France, and French people are a little bit always snobbish, and I have

never seen such a snobbish Japanese. So, I was experiencing what it seems the culture does to people and I am quite intrigued by that.

The television productions were for a popular series introducing other cultures to Japan. Yukari said it was a "bubble time", with plenty of money available to film exotic cultures in distant locations:

> Japanese people were very hungry for that in the nineties – twenty years ago. When I was small, in the sixties, the country was still quite poor. By the eighties, people started to consider spending money on travelling – going abroad was highly unusual until then. For the first time people started to have the room to see what's out there, so thirty years after the war, the second generation starts to see. It is a generational thing – the ones that worked their butt out became grandfathers, and the one after was getting quite affluent, so they started to take the abundance of things for granted.

As a reaction to the highly commercial television work, during her twenties, Yukari also sought "something completely alternative, nature friendly" and became an environmental activist "doing demonstration and hunger strike". She became involved in protests against old forest logging by Japanese and European companies in Sarawak, on the island of Borneo, and with its nomadic people of the rain forest, the Penan, said to be one of the last hunter-gatherer tribes in Asia.[27] Yukari says Japan was at least a decade behind the west in becoming aware of humanistic and other alternative ideas, but in the 1980s, "alternative" workshops began to be presented. Among other things, Yukari participated in a sweat lodge ceremony with Lakota Sioux people; a peace walk with Ainu people, indigenous to Japan; and another with native Hawaiians.

Yukari recalls that the television work became increasingly incongruent for her: "The times' need was there, I was playing a role to feed what was wanted, but it was manipulative of people". Also, with the constant travel from "cold country to hot country, from North Pole to South Pole, I started to get sick, so with these two things I decided to quit". Another factor in her decision was an offer of marriage:

> A man showed up and said "I'm going to feed you, I'm going to take care of you". That's what he said and I never had the idea of what it was like to be taken care of by somebody else. So I decided to get married when I was twenty-nine. It sounded good, why not try it. I gave myself a try, and that was that. The basic values of my husband and myself were too different.

Yukari says her husband wanted her to stop involving herself in activism and other alternative interests, "in order to have his baby". She experienced his demand to conform to the role of a traditional Japanese wife as a threat to her sense of self, and decided "not to continue".

In the 1990s, Yukari met Morten, a Danish man who became her life partner. Yukari feels the ideas to which she was introduced – by Morten, and through her relationship with him – expanded her consciousness. She says that "Northern European people have especially the idea of individualism more than anywhere else, I think, and being equal; and again, this idea is very different, because they take the idea of women being equal to men for granted, as a society". Northern European women might disagree with that assessment, but Yukari compares her experiences in Europe with contemporary Japanese views and "through the differences" has expanded her thinking. Also, beginning to appreciate concepts of self-development and self-actualisation, Yukari travelled to Hawaii to train as a healing therapist: "It was a totally new idea to me – that as a human – you have the capability to respond to what is going on, and the basic tendency is to restore the balance and go for better". For eight years, each winter in Maui, Yukari and Morten taught a healing method with students from Australia, Europe, and the United States.

Early in the new millennium, Morten visited a friend in Guatemala, who had started an eco-lodge in a small, still-primitive town. The couple bought a piece of land there and built a tiny house. Their lifestyle now is highly mobile: Yukari is an interpreter for international seminar presenters, mostly in Tokyo, translates books on topics ranging from physiology to philosophy, and is a bodyworker, healer, writer, and photographer. Morten travels the world teaching the Franklin Method – a process, which uses movement and neuro-plasticity to

Figure 6.1. Yukari celebrating her birthday in Europe, 2010.

improve body and mind – in Europe, Japan, and the United States. Yukari and Morten live for part of each year in Tokyo, a few months in Guatemala, and spend some time in Denmark and other countries (see figure 6.1).

GLOBAL SENSES OF SELF

In addition to having what Doreen Massey calls "a global sense of place", Julian and Yukari have developed and given expression to what might be called a *global sense of self*.[28] Although it could be argued that this simply reflects their continuing mobility, from the interviews it seems they each have awareness of having developed such a sense of self over time through on-going processes of relating to many people and places. Their experiences fit the oft-quoted description of

> people who belong to more than one world, speak more than one language (literally and metaphorically), inhabit more than one identity, have more than one home; who have learned to negotiate and translate *between* cultures and who, because they are irrevocably the product of several interlocking histories and cultures, have learned to live with, and indeed to speak from, *difference*. They speak from the "in-between" of different cultures, always unsettling the assumptions of one culture from the perspective of another, and thus finding ways of being *the same as* and at the same time *different from*, the others amongst whom they live.[29]

Julian, for example, is not simply a product of the hegemonic order of late-imperial Britain into which he was born. His sense of self has been modified by his lived experience of vastly different cultures and places and conditions of truth, as well as by engagement with different ideologies and spiritual and philosophical precepts. He describes himself as "a bit of a cultural sponge", able to absorb and be absorbed into the culture of wherever he is. He has an ability to adapt that he believes is based on a confidence that he can be open to difference, which comes from his sense of self-worth. Julian believes that this openness to other cultures probably came from his childhood experiences in so many countries. He feels it would not have happened if he had been isolated from the local children, and emphasises that his engagement with them in various countries led to a continuing openness to difference. A significant part of accommodating difference has been to accept and value people as they are, including himself.

Yukari says that because of the cultural influence her father brought to the family from the United States she was *raised* as somebody different, "not at all in ordinary Japanese culture". Although she grew up in one location, Yukari was deeply curious about foreigners she saw in the town, and about the rest of the world. At the "free" school she was encouraged to think broadly and creatively, and to develop a sense of herself as an individual. That encouragement was unusual in the contemporary – still very traditional – Japanese culture, which emphasises community and conformity, and within which the self is viewed as interdependent rather than independent.[30] As Yukari explains, having an individual sense of self was "not at all something people were looking at, maybe never happens".

Early experience in foreign countries was not always easy for her, and at first, Yukari thought that she had to change herself to be accepted in different places. Over time, she felt she strengthened what she called the "self-sufficiency" she had developed as a child. Her idea of self-sufficiency began by accepting that her mother was doing her best, and concluding that what worked best was to accept prevailing conditions, rather than resenting them. She recognised that rather than hankering for what was not available, when she decided something was enough, it became enough; and thus, she found she began to have more positive experiences. Applying that learning in varied locations, Yukari came to realise that, by accepting people and places as they were, she came to accept herself, and, concomitantly, she experienced others accepting her more readily. Rather than developing a sense of self conceptually, Yukari considers that she continues to strengthen her sense of self by having many kinds of experience in different countries. Variations in place provide opportunities for her to "have another look" at herself, by experiencing the distinctive conditions and practices woven into everyday life in those locales, and responding to the unique needs and demands of each place and its people:

> For example, Denmark is a country where I used to feel I was inferior, not because there is a prejudice, but because of the colours – because I was different, people start to look at me with my dark hair – I started to feel a bit of inferiority because they are gorgeous blonde, physically beautiful people, and that didn't apply to me. To be self-sufficient in a place like Denmark you have to have some sense of *okayness* in being *me*. That is the requirement there. Whereas, in Guatemala, the people's psyche functions in a totally different way from in a developed country, so appearance doesn't play a part in being self-sufficient in Guatemala. In Guatemala, to be self-sufficient is to know what food you can eat, where you can eat it, to start feeling if your physical condition is changing, so you can be pro-active – that kind of self-sufficiency is needed there.

Because Yukari still lives for part of the time in the country of her birth, she does not have a sense of having moved from one place to another. She explains that moving annually to different places and then returning to her place of origin feels like an expansion of her sense of self. Through personal connection with locations that are different to each other she has a growing sense that "this planet" is where she lives: "So I don't feel that I am becoming one person to another to another in order to fit there, to enjoy or anything; it is the sense that I am simply expanding my area of living".

Both these participants are aware of a high degree of openness to experience difference. As Yukari put it, "You have to develop the eyes"; Julian describes himself as "someone who is *looking*, and I mean *looking*, rather than *looking for*". Each exhibits a lack of self-consciousness, in the sense that they are more interested in getting to know people and places than in wondering what others might think of them. In common, their narratives reveal that their mobile lives have involved processes of letting go of attachments – for example, to any idea that there is just one right way to do things, or to be, or to think. That process has extended to letting go of limited definitions of themselves. Speaking of her experience of a pilgrimage on a fourteen hundred kilometre peace walk, Yukari describes seeing in herself and others "what is not real is falling off them", a letting go of attachments. Yukari concludes, "I get *detached* by moving places, but I don't get *dissociated* – that's one of the realisations of moving places".

The examples provided by these participants raise interesting questions. In chapter 3, I discussed contested ideas that dissociation, disembedding, placelessness, and alienation can result from high levels of mobility.[31] What factors have allowed Julian and Yukari to experience their highly mobile lifestyles without those results? Is the state of being they experience something they have brought about themselves? Or, has it happened to them? Certainly, there is similarity between these people with mobile lives and the regular migrants introduced earlier. Both groups take for granted that opportunities and choices are open to them – including in relation to mobilities; and even though they have experienced considerable challenges at different times, fundamentally they assume that they are, have rights, and are safe. On that basis, they have come to expect to thrive, develop capabilities, interact effectively with others and their worlds, give and receive, and to experience well-being.

The well-being of these participants could be attributed to their current status as educated, middle-class, economically independent professionals, but that was not the case throughout their lives. Many people might be held to have a similar narrative base without experiencing the well-being these participants describe. Elliott and Urry write of "increasingly mobile and uncertain lives" for people in some parts of the world, and point out that "people may hanker after the celebrity-inspired, jet-setting lifestyle, but many of those who in fact lead such lifestyles suffer high levels of anxiety, emotional disconnection and depression".[32]

Julian and Yukari – whom I have introduced as exemplars of mobile lives – are not placeless, dissociated, or alienated. In their own ways, they have developed Massey's "progressive sense of place . . . a global sense of the local, a global sense of place" and I suggest, *a local sense of the global*.[33] They relate to place openly and sensorially, and engage with people and place wherever they happen to be, but more than that, they tend to *immerse* themselves, rather than simply remaining as travellers. These two do not limit self-identification or belonging to one culture or place, and both express a global sense of self. A global sense of self can lead to a notion of global citizenship, which implies some sense of global responsibility as well as of rights, and they each exhibit that. They express their awareness of that responsibility as a concern with matters beyond the local and in their behaviour in various ways. For Yukari, that expression has included environmental activism, and being of continuing service; and contributing to increasing harmony in the world, professionally and personally, is important to them both. Julian thinks of himself as "just one very small dot in this whole mass of humanity . . . just one little blip who's around for a very short time", but it matters to him how he spends that time. Within the Quaker community he is recognised as "a sort of an elder in an informal way", an acknowledgement by which Julian feels privileged.

Significant themes characterising the narratives of these two people include accepting and valuing themselves and others and embracing the openness to difference that follows. Each of them feels that with such openness comes respect for the wonderful diversity of people, and cultures, and places; and a visceral recognition that we have our humanity in common, and our home is the Earth.

NOTES

1. Elliott and Urry, 11.
2. Australian Bureau of Statistics (ABS).
3. Esipova, Ray, and Pugliese, 4.
4. Ibid., 3.
5. ABS.
6. Pallasmas, 144.
7. World Bank report, 2009.
8. Elliott and Urry, 3.
9. Ibid., 97.
10. Massey, 'Conceptualisation of Place', 60.
11. Pile and Thrift; Bergmann and Sager, 10.
12. Nynäs, 172.
13. The Suez Canal in Egypt connects the Mediterranean and Red seas, providing a passage for shipping to travel between Europe and Asia without having to navigate around Africa. A neutral zone under protection of the British until 1954, the canal was

nationalised by Egyptian President Nasser in 1956, to finance building of the Aswan Dam. The crisis began when the United Kingdom, France, and Israel invaded Egypt to keep the canal open.

14. The Arab Legion was a military force instigated and commanded by the British in the British protectorate of Transjordan until it was nationalised in 1956 and merged with the Jordanian National Guard to form a unified Jordanian army.

15. Theosophy is a spiritual philosophy developed by Helen Blavatsky and contemporaries in the late nineteenth century. Through the Theosophical Society, it remains an active philosophical school with presence in more than seventy countries.

16. Annie Besant (1847–1933) was a prominent Theosophist, women's and human rights activist, writer, orator, and supporter of Irish and Indian self-rule.

17. Gandhi (1869–1948), known as Mahatma – great soul – was the leader of the Indian nationalist movement against the British rule, and is widely considered the father of his country. His doctrine of non-violent protest to achieve political and social progress has been hugely influential.

18. Jiddu Krishnamurti (1895–1986) was a writer and speaker on philosophical, psychological, and spiritual issues, who considered that schools of thought caused conflict, and advocated respect for all of humanity and social change through radical change in the individual.

19. The Bhagavad Gita is a 700-verse Hindu scripture.

20. Dora Scarlett (1906–2001), a writer, broadcaster, and communist activist, founded and worked for forty years in an organisation providing medical care to the poor in India, which grew to serve hundreds of thousands. Awarded an MBE in 1994, she died in India at the age of ninety-five.

21. Mother Teresa (1910–1997), a Catholic nun of Albanian ethnicity and Indian citizenship, founded Missionaries of Charity and ministered to the poor, sick, orphaned, and dying in Calcutta for over forty-five years. Awarded the Nobel Peace Prize in 1979, and beatified by Pope John Paul II in 2003, she is a controversial figure, praised by many, and criticised by others, particularly for her strong stance against contraception and abortion, and belief in the spiritual goodness of poverty.

22. Now part of Oxfam.

23. The Friends' School, which takes its name from the Religious Society of Friends, more commonly known as Quakers, was established in 1887, and is the only Quaker school in Australia.

24. Goodman et al.

25. Fujiwara Chisa, Single Mothers and Welfare Restructuring in Japan: Gender and Class Dimensions of Income and Employment. *Asia-Pacific Journal: Japan Focus*. January 2, 2008, accessed April 18, 2014. http://japanfocus.org/-Fujiwara-Chisa/2623.

26. A Christian orphanage, started and run in 1948 by Miki Sawada, a daughter of the Mitsubishi family, and named after the first person to donate money to support it, it was known as the Elizabeth Saunders Home, and was for abandoned babies of Japanese women and American soldiers. At the time, children of this mixed parentage and their mothers were ostracised, and single mothers often left their babies in the street.

27. Bruce Parry, Penan Tribe' BBC Bruce Parry Newsletter, updated March 2008, accessed August 11,2012, http://www.bbc.co.uk/tribe/tribes/penan/index.shtml.

According to Parry, the population of Penan people in Sarawak was reduced over a few decades from about 10,000 to less than 200 by 2008.

28. Massey, 'Global Sense'.

29. Stuart Hall, 'New Cultures', 206. Attributed by Hall to Homi Bhabha (1994), by Pile and Thrift (1995, 10) to Salman Rushdie (1991), and by Morley (2000, 207) to Hall. Not found verbatim in Bhabha or Rushdie.

30. Kan, Karasawa, and Kitayama.

31. Adey; Cresswell, On the Move; Sheller, 'Mobility'; Urry, 2007.

32. Elliott and Urry, 6, 9.

33. Massey, 'Global Sense'.

Part III

CHALLENGES OF RESETTLEMENT

So many factors challenge both immigrants and existing residents in a place when newcomers arrive and begin to settle that in this part of the book an *extrasectional* interweaving of accounts from theory and narratives of lived experience is particularly valuable. Complete books that focus on some of these factors already make up a substantial body of literature on place making and ethno-cultural community building. Here I bring this prior work together with participants' narratives to elicit insights into social-material processes of resettlement that may prove significant to understanding about how to increase well-being in circumstances of migration.

In chapter 7 ('Settling in New Places'), I consider the moral and political implications of sedentarist ideas, and geographers' and others' understandings of a range of senses of place. I also reflect upon how mobilities affect both the participants' senses of place, and how those senses develop. I apply the model of self-place relating most fully in that chapter to throw light on how varying strengths of senses of self and place correlate with the participants' lived experiences. Then, in chapter 8 ('Dilemmas of Difference'), I explore challenges of racism, how people's regimes of practice may need to adjust in new places, and other factors in the politics of recognition. First investigating meanings attributed to 'Identity and Belonging' (chapter 9), I reflect upon how these concepts relate to morality and power, inclusion and exclusion, citizenship and rights. Then I show how distinctions between identity and self significantly affect well-being, and dynamics of strengthening or weakening those senses.

Chapter 7

Settling in New Places

> If places are indeed a fundamental aspect of man's existence in the world, if they are sources of security and identity for individuals and for groups of people, then it is important that the means of experiencing, creating, and maintaining significant places are not lost.[1]

The sedentarist idea that well-being is best achieved when people commit to one place has strongly shaped environmentalism in Western societies, particularly among advocates of the political philosophy of bioregionalism. Defining it, an early proponent writes:

> a wonderful Spanish term – *querencia* – usually translated as "love of home" . . . is the deep sense of inner well-being that comes from knowing a particular place on the Earth; its daily and seasonal patterns, its fruits and scents, its soils and birdsongs. A place where, whenever you return to it, your soul releases an inner sigh of recognition and realisation. That's pretty much what bioregionalism is.[2]

Describing bioregionalism as broadly anti-urbanist, Jonathan Olsen considers it was a move, influential in the radical environmental community, to "reverse our modern alienation from nature through the creation of decentralized, small-scale, and ecologically sustainable communities".[3] Nevertheless, Olsen cautions that ambiguities in bioregionalism's formulations, "especially its notion of human 'rootedness' – can have unintended and disturbing political manifestations". For example, he writes that advocates of right-wing ecology in Germany "argue that each human community, distinctive as it is, must be protected from the foreign and non-native".[4] Such views underpin legislation that compels newcomers to change their conduct and beliefs in order to become assimilated, as noted, for example, in Denmark.[5]

If staying in one place is seen as a *good*, then *who* is to determine just who belongs where? And on the basis of what criteria? As noted on page 22, Tim Cresswell writes that when place is held as "an essentially moral concept", mobilities are seen as "antithetical to moral worlds"; and by implication as "the absence of commitment and attachment and involvement – a lack of significance".[6] Especially in places to which others migrate, people who stay in one place often apply such moral and political judgements to immigrants. As importantly, many people who migrate apply such judgements to themselves.

Deep attachment to a place is about the significance given to it through the experiences people have, the relationships and activities that occur there, and its social, cultural, ecological, and personal meanings. Such strong identification with place may – but does not always – mean a strong sense of place. If we consider the descriptions in the model of self-place relations (figure 2.1), a weak sense of place is associated with both the *marginalised and displaced* and the *independent from pace* nodes. A strong sense of place is more likely to align with the *dependent on place* and *interdependent with place* nodes.

Many people have a strong attachment to the place they feel is home – often their place of origin, where their ancestors lived, where they grew up, where they developed their sense of self, and of identity. Yi-Fu Tuan writes that "profound attachment to the homeland appears to be a worldwide phenomenon".[7] In like vein, Harvey Perkins and David Thorns consider that "place-based experience is a defining characteristic of everyday life for most people, notwithstanding the fact that they are influenced by, and contribute to, wider social, economic and cultural currents".[8] Among those currents the mobility of people's lives is one highly significant variable. First, the arrival of migrants to an area inevitably introduces changes to the contexts of existing residents, it may lead to environmental changes, and has diverse and often unintended consequences for all concerned. As John Urry explains, "Large-scale system change normally results from 'small' changes". Second, immigrants generally arrive in a place entirely new to them, so for them all is changed.[9]

The term *solastalgia* has been coined to name the distress caused by environmental change, and people's mental well-being can be so threatened by the "severing of 'healthy' links between themselves and their home territory" that they suffer *psychoterratic* – that is, earth-related – mental illness.[10] Solastalgia was first applied to people's experiences of changes to the environments in which they live, but the term is also used to describe the distress many people experience when they migrate and relocate in places unfamiliar to them. If migrants have deep attachment to places elsewhere, challenges of resettlement can be exacerbated. However, developing multiple senses of place in a new location might mitigate the difficulties. John Eyles and Alison Williams consider that "experiencing multiple senses of place may instil a particularly strong sense of place-identity with one particular place, given that any one individual has experience of places which they can compare".[11]

The participants' stories reveal multiple and overlapping senses of place. By the time we spoke some had found that one place to call *home*. Others still felt themselves to be *in between* – neither fully departed from one place, nor yet fully settled in another. Some participants thought of sense of place mainly in terms of an appreciation of landscape, rather than as inclusive of people and society, and the environs and aesthetics of places are important to them. There is a distinct difference between the senses of place felt by irregular migrants, and those felt by other participants, although Kiros' version is different again.

A common theme in participants' narratives is reference to those features of landscape in new places that remind them of their places of origin and that help them to feel at home. Kiros thinks that happens because the features of one place remind people of other, childhood senses of place, memories of community, and other attachments. His remembered sense of place contributed to Kiros' choice to migrate to Hobart, because he felt it was geographically familiar, "The mountains, and the temperature, and the way things are set up, it looks like home. You find comfort in a place if it looks like the place you are from; and sometimes you recreate the place for it to look like home".

He pointed out that Tasmania's first settlers from England had done that, naming their newly constructed streets after English names and events, building houses and planting gardens in the English style – a practice evident in colonial settlements worldwide. In childhood, Kiros probably was *dependent on place* but his university years and time spent in the Netherlands expanded his perspectives. In early adulthood, marrying and starting a family, his focus was predominantly on making himself *independent from place*. Fairly soon, his work for an NGO, revitalising land laid waste by war, brought in elements of *interdependence with place*, because he was involved in projects to make rural areas of land, and the communities in those places, sustainable. The outbreak of war between Ethiopia and Eritrea pushed Kiros and his family into *marginalised and displaced* situations. Although they survived in Addis Ababa for a couple of years, his wife had no legal identification, Kiros was in trouble with the government, and their lives "became a nightmare", so they fled the country. As irregular migrants in Kenya, support was only available for them if they went to a refugee camp, where their lives would fully be *marginalised and displaced*. Kiros' response to that situation was to assert a strong sense of self, and he was able to achieve a level of control sufficient to provide for his family. He kept them out of the refugee camp for several years, until they were able to migrate to Australia. On arrival, they were *dependent on place* for a time, in that they were identified primarily according to ethnicity and country of origin, but fairly quickly Kiros again gained relative independence. When we spoke, he felt that he had increased his certainty of self and place and had come to enjoy some level of *interdependence with place.*

Tasmania's mountains hardly measure up against those of Shoukat's birthplace in central Afghanistan, but he could "find a mountain here", and felt that "Tasmania is looking something like Afghanistan – I can find trees here, and green, water view, and rain" – all of significance to someone of rural and agricultural origin. Until he was seventeen, when his father and brothers were killed, Shoukat lived in a rural village in Afghanistan, in conditions strongly oriented to *dependence on place.* For more than fifteen years from that time, his life was *marginalised and displaced.* In those circumstances, his journey to seek asylum in Australia certainly demonstrates the *heroic* quality – indicated in the model – that can arise from the need to survive and to take action to ensure the survival of others. In spite of the fact that, in Australia, he was physically safe and living in materially better conditions, for so long as Shoukat was powerless to protect his family, and in the limbo experience of being *in-between*, he was *placeless* without them. His sense of self was strong enough for him to survive the journey, but, in those circumstances, it was steadily eroded. In his bid to express agency, and to become self-supporting, his orientation fluctuated between the *marginalised and displaced* node and the *independence from place* he is building, now that he is reunited with his family and working towards material security.

In altogether different circumstances, when Carol was a small child in Scotland, her family's poverty and lack of adequate housing located their experience as *marginalised and displaced.* This narrative was modified by her parents' recognition that they could migrate to Canada, where they began to move towards greater independence. For Carol, emphasis remained on *dependence on place* throughout her childhood, and into her early adult years. Lacking a sense of self-worth, and often feeling deeply ashamed, she missed Scotland, and found solace by creating fantasy worlds in the nearby ravine. It was not so much that she romanticised Scotland, but valued it as familiar, and as home.

Gradually, Carol transferred her attachment to Canada, and her next migrations showed that familiarity continued to play a significant role in her feeling of safety. Carol's sense of place in Australia has changed greatly since she first migrated in the 1970s. Arriving then, with her Australian husband, she felt herself to be an outsider, and hated the place:

> The sun was so bright I couldn't see. The light in Scotland is soft, misty – the light in Canada could be harsh – but the light in Australia was obscene! I had never worn sunglasses in my life; only a person in Canada pretending to be a San Francisco cop would have a pair of sunglasses. And the food! It's changed now, dramatically, but then . . . it was its obviousness! In Canada everything came in packages, so it doesn't look like what it was. When I first came to

Australia and I saw food come out looking like a lamb, I felt like Alice in Wonderland where suddenly the plum pudding gets up and starts talking to her, or a fish with its eye looking at me, or prawns, with their little beady eyes looking at me, and I thought "I'm not eating that!" I still don't think I'm quite over it.

The couple returned to Canada and then moved to Australia again some years later with two small children, but they separated soon after. Carol's husband took out a restraining order to prevent Carol taking the children back to Canada, and for a time, Carol lived alone in Sydney:

If you ask me, how did I cope in that place, in that situation, I remember I would be on the bus and I would just shut my eyes, and I would hope that if I could just shut them for long enough, I would open them again and I would be in a streetcar in Toronto. That, somehow, I could just literally transport myself out of this place by just thinking of Toronto . . . I didn't cope, I didn't. There was no place in the landscape that I could make any sense of, I hated the flat. Some places I loved, I used to walk down to the wharf to take the ferry across . . . and I loved that standing on the wharf, getting on the boat, being on the water, that was lovely, but I couldn't attach myself to this place at all.

Carol flew back to Canada to retain her citizenship there, and then returned to Australia to fight for custody of her children. That time, her second husband, Richard, was with her, and it made a difference that they were "Canadians making sense of it together". Carol says her first husband was "forever telling me that I should just love the things he loved", especially when she did not. In contrast, Carol and Richard often had similar reactions to their new environment and felt free to comment to each other in ways that might have offended someone local. Nevertheless, at first it was difficult:

Our first Christmas, it was so hot! We could not believe it. We were devastated. Richard couldn't get a job – he had qualifications for things they didn't even have in Australia yet. We went to Coogee Beach, and we were lamenting the family, the snow, and suddenly, I got it: The ocean was crystal clear, just beautiful. I looked at Richard and I said, "What *is* the problem here?" And he said, "There isn't a problem, this is just gorgeous". And in that moment, it was so clear, not comparing, but taking this country on its own terms.

After many moves within Australia, the couple settled in Katoomba, in Sydney's Blue Mountains area. Its similarity to their places of origin was a significant factor in their choice of that location. For Carol, the mountainous area of Katoomba combines Scotland, Canada, and Australia all in the same landscape:

I've got the cliffs; the mauve, the indigo, the maroon; the sky changing the way that it does, the light being more filtered than it is down there [on the coastal plain]; I've got the coldness, the smell of cold on clothes. Spring here, it's glorious, and you really get the Canadian feel where you get tulips, crocuses, everything; but there's also snowdrops from Scotland, and it's like Scotland. When I look out over the cliffs, it's like looking out over an ocean almost, and it's bush; I can smell the eucalypt and I can hear the bellbirds and the whipbirds – and it's a place where I can claim just me, so I'm not defined by somebody else.

And what of Carola? It is likely that her early years fit the *dependent on place* description. Experiencing safety and stability with a nurturing extended family, and "everything social – sport, music, youth groups, school, church – in one, small, traditional German town", she grew up with a strong sense of place and confidence in herself. To some extent, her self-worth was challenged by the difficulties she experienced in her relationship with her mother, but her sense of self grew in the supportive environment of her community and her undoubted place in it. Carola easily stepped into an *independent from place* mode when she left home to attend university to study medicine, and was involved with other students in extra-curricular training in humanistic and other modalities – "it was experimental and experiential, and amazing!" In the stability and learning of that environment for about ten years, Carola thrived, and her sense of self strengthened. The university was in the heart of the mining, industrial Ruhr area, which Carola experienced as very culturally different: "the people there are a lot of working class and very straight down the line", whereas, in her hometown "you have to find the right words . . . middle class, nice talk, but you don't know where you are at with someone". Carola says it was a relief to be with people "that talk straight and what they say is what they mean". She found it relatively easy to travel for study and to work in different countries but was attracted to a significant difference she felt in Australia. Shortly after her arrival, an Aboriginal elder asked if she was born in Australia, because he felt she was very connected to the land. Carola says:

> There is a lot of truth in that. I can't explain that. It is to do with the land. It's almost the colours of the land – it is not the political Australia – it's the actual land, the actual place. And that's got to do with space, just space to breathe, space to be yourself. From my very first experience being here, I could just *be* myself, and I am at home.

The pattern of moving from *dependence on place* to *independence from place* and then to *interdependence with place* also fits Yukari's narrative. As a child, she says she felt a mixture of inferiority and superiority when comparing herself with other children. Travelling outside Japan in her early adult years, Yukari felt that she needed to change herself to fit local conditions, and to learn how to be in control of her well-being in foreign places. This chameleon-like behaviour applied most strongly whenever she felt inferior in others' eyes, especially for being Asian – a new identification – rather than simply being Japanese. She came to understand that, while it was appropriate to adapt her behaviour in different cultures, making such adjustments had nothing to do with her value as a person. On the contrary, she discovered that through being open to understand and appreciate difference, and to learn from it, she expanded and strengthened her sense of self. Concomitantly, her sense of place deepened through immersion of herself in many different environments. Yukari's sense of self and of place is expressed in her recognition that being alive *is* interacting and exchanging with place, and inextricable from it in every moment, wherever she may be. Acknowledging that it is a very abstract description, Yukari explains that the more she feels connected with a place, the more aware she is of connection with the planet as a whole.

Moving "from pillar to post" as a child, Connie's experience cannot quite be fitted into either the *marginalised* or *dependent on place* descriptions. Growing up in the United States, and strongly pushed by circumstances to stand on her own feet, she developed individualistically, and wanted to travel as "a free spirit", independent of people or particular places. However, she told me that since meeting Jun, her relationships with others are most important to her. Her immediate family comes first, and she likes to be recognised as a mother and as a contributing member of community. Bred in Washington State, Connie said she felt like a foreigner when the couple lived for a year in Louisiana, even though it was another part of her own country.

> I didn't really understand that within the United States, there really are different cultures. Someone could have told me that and I would have said, "oh, yeah, well", but I didn't really get it. It really was a different culture – people are different – you feel it in the grocery store, you feel it walking with a baby stroller down the road, houses look different, things people eat are different, accent is different. I did not like it. I used to think that *homesick* meant I miss being with my family – the family things that I am so familiar with – but I don't think that any more. I recognise now homesickness has not been the people, it has been just the familiarity of sort of expectations. When you know the name of the game, you know how to play the game, you know at the grocery store when you have an interaction with another person, you know where you stand, and you know what to expect.

Connie's description reflects Kiros' earlier observation that starting from zero when ignorant of the customs of a place can lead to self-doubt and alienation; and Peter Nynäs' view that relationship with place is contingent on knowing 'the rules'.[12] As Connie put it, "In a place you're not familiar with, even if you think you know how to play the game, if something falls off in an interaction with someone, you tend to think it is you, and then you blame the place".

Although Jun is from a culture that is strongly oriented to community, he was left largely to his own devices from the beginning of high school, and became very self-focused. His identity was culturally based and located, and *dependent on place*, although his sense of place seems to have been limited to familiarity with his environs rather than with any particular attachment to a place. His narrative suggests he has remained connected to the aesthetics of the Japanese environment – that he says he sees in cities and countryside, and people's expressiveness and sense of fashion – but he is not attached to, nor really engaged with place in any particular location and mostly fits an *independent from place* orientation. Connie's desire to travel encouraged the couple's early sojourn in Japan, but very different factors motivated their subsequent moves – primarily their desires for security and financial independence, once they had children. When their application to settle in Australia – their first place of choice – was rejected, they decided to return to Japan rather than to the United States. For Connie, this was a very conscious decision to reject her country of origin.

All Jun's moves were motivated by a combination of desires to move *away* from some places and *towards* others. For instance, he left Japan to get away from his parents; and moved towards the United States, excited by the adventure of living in that country and improving his English. He left the United States to get away from difficult economic and social conditions, and a political environment he did not like, and moved towards Australia after careful consideration of what it offered in terms of living standards and social conditions. He preferred returning to Japan rather than to the United States, but still chose to relocate in Hokkaido to keep distance from his parents. He moved to Sapporo attracted by the richness of Japanese culture, the familiarity of Japanese food, a quality of service he prefers to Western ways, and recognition that "in Japan you can access almost anything" – meaning technology, goods, and services – far more than in Australia. However, he says the main reason for choosing to move to Hokkaido is the feeling he has there of open space, because it is not as crowded as the rest of Japan:

> There is great nature, this northern climate, rugged mountains, and dark blue, navy blue ocean, great seafood, wild animals, different from the rest of Japan; it has more of a nature, wild, feeling, and agricultural rather than industrial. I like that kind of place. Also, Hokkaido is the newest place in Japan. In Edo time, Hokkaido was almost neglected. Ainu people [indigenous] were living there, no Yamato people – the Samurai people – were interested in that piece of land, so it is only after Meiji time that Japanese people moved to Hokkaido; so what that means is that Hokkaido is not as traditional as the rest of Japan.
>
> The rest of Japan, because each region has long history, especially during Edo time, each region was closed off from each other. You had to have a pass to go to another region. It is a small area, but because of the history and dividedness, each region developed its own culture, accent, and dialect, just like in the UK.

The rest of Japan has long history, very strong tradition – you are supposed to live like everyone else. But Hokkaido is where people from different regions in Japan had to live together – there was no common sense. So in a way Hokkaido is like the US or Australia, where people from different parts of the world came together and they have to learn how to live together. There were no set rules, no accents. People speak Tokyo standard Japanese, and they tend to be more open, to say what they think, and I like that style, I want people to express their true thoughts, so that would be the second reason.

Jun said he would like to visit many places, and is open to experiencing variety, but his sense of place seems to be more instrumental than affective. The most challenging relocation for him was his initial move to the United States from Japan, when he found language and cultural differences most confronting. As his English improved and he adjusted to the culture, he was excited to move to other places in the United States. However, of Louisiana – which his American wife, Connie, had found so culturally and environmentally challenging – he said, "It was just another State in the US". Relocating to Australia was more comfortable because he said the difference from the United States was so small compared to the difference between Japan and the United States. Nevertheless, he attributed a strengthening of his sense of self to living in other countries, and said he is now more able to recognise that 'Japan is not my parents, and my parents do not speak for Japan – they are separate entities'.

Until she was fourteen, Nene's life experience was *marginalised and displaced*. Her infancy was spent in Sudan with her mother and siblings, fleeing from village to village to avoid violence and war until she was four years old, and then they lived in the refugee camp in Kenya for the following ten years. I can only guess what Nene's sense of self would have been like as a child in that camp. She says she felt comfort in being with family, and in religious practice, but was often hungry and thirsty, lacked adequate shelter and basic amenities, and was constantly afraid because rape, violence, and disease were common. By her account, she lacked self-confidence for the first few years in Australia and felt diminished by her experience of racism; but given the opportunity and support of a teacher, and participation in the group of Students Against Racism, she blossomed. If *dependent on place* is interpreted to include strong attachment to culture, then Nene's experience would fit there to a large extent, but she is also increasingly confident in herself and has become an independent young woman – graduated from university, working in a job she feels is meaningful, planning future travel and a career that she hopes will contribute to making her world a better place.

Living as a child and young adult in a refugee camp in Nepal, Khadga's situation was *marginalised and displaced* yet, even with the severe deprivations of the camp, it provided a minimally safe and stable environment – compared with Nene's experience of the camp in Kenya, for example. Khadga's sense of self is likely to have been more linked to the nexus of *dependence on place*, in that his identity is so strongly based in being part of his extended family culture and ethnicity. There seems to be a direct relationship between the strength of his sense of self and his pride and certainty in belonging to, and representing that community. Support for this in the camp came from the many refugees of similar origin, who also maintained that cultural and ethnic integrity.

Khadga's self-confidence was such that he managed to go out from the camp to work and to gain senior secondary and tertiary education. He learnt how to take advantage of whatever was available within the limits of conditions for refugees in Nepal. By the time there was opportunity to emigrate, he had taken charge of his own life to a considerable degree. He had achieved some level of independence, and his broader experience away from the camp played a strong role in his ability to organise for the whole of his large family to migrate. Relocated in Tasmania, settling well, and working towards owning his own home, his self-confidence is reinforced. He is building a life for himself and his family that is *independent from place*. In Australia, his sense of place is finding expression as he puts down new roots, for the first time in his life knowing that he and his family actually have and can depend on a place of their own, yet they are not dependent on it; having rights of citizenship and belonging, Khadga is becoming *interdependent with place*.

Julian's family background was primarily *independent from place*, though there are elements of *dependence on place*, particularly relating to the family's civil and military history in colonial India. As a young adult, Julian's return to India was an act both of rebellion – against his family's expectations – and of independence, suggesting that he was confident of his abilities, and that he assumed that he had rights: to go adventuring, to seek knowledge, and to live in India. His experience in India gave him back the pleasure he had felt as a child relating to the people and places of exotic cultures. During the years in India, his deep engagement with people and place expressed mutuality – contributing to and receiving sustenance from both – and his sense of self and sense of place deepened in the process. From his narrative it is obvious that place, including the richness of people and culture within it, has been of great significance to him. There were elements of claiming *independence from place* in his moves to England and Australia, but his current way of life predominantly reflects *interdependence with place*.

DEVELOPING SENSE OF A NEW PLACE

Proponents of methods for developing a sense of place recommend paying attention to place and all that is in it, engaging with it sensorially, and learning from, as well as about it.[13] All the participants spoke of a need to interact with place to build relationship with it, but their methods and focus varied (see figure 7.1). Kiros was perhaps most conscious that it was something he had to do intentionally, to accept being in a new place, to "reground" himself, to become involved in community, and to establish professional and social connection: "It's good to connect with nature, but connection with nature cannot replace connection with people". Kiros spoke of taking his wife and daughters for bushwalks to get to know the country, "intentionally!" For him, "the landscape remains foreign, so it doesn't come naturally. For our girls, it is natural, that's the difference".

Yukari feels that she interacts well with new places and people, but recalls being reluctant, at first, to establish a new home in Guatemala because of the language.

> It took so much time for me to learn the English and now I go to a place where that English doesn't work, and the first sense that I had there was so foreign. But as the tree grows and as the tree flowers that we planted in our own garden, and then see some kind of relationship to the nature like that, and also to the people, then you have the sense of home.

Carola feels her roots have shifted from Germany to Australia:

> I'm clearly at home here, and that's got to do with the ground, it's got to do with me planting things in our garden – very much to do with the soil, with the actual

Figure 7.1. Locals helping a newcomer with fishing tackle. Courtesy of Creolumen Photography.

land. Feeling at home somewhere means that I'm taken care of, it's being welcomed, belonging, but it's not people, it's the land.

Now, Carola's experience could well be described as *interdependent with place*. Given the intensity of involvement with people in her work, at times Carola needs solitude to regather and centre her sense of self, and for her, also, gardening and place-making are important balances.

In maturity, Carol also enjoys a greater sense of *interdependence with place*. Her early sense of self came across as a fierce determination to survive, and to make a place for herself and her children. Gradually, she took charge of her life, developing a sense of self-worth and becoming increasingly *independent from place*. She found ways to make place, not only in different countries, but also in the various places within a country to which she has moved. Carol very consciously draws on her creative, imaginative use of sense of place. She describes what she does as "smelling, touching, physically sensing a place" to give herself back to herself. In any environment, she says, "You pull out the elements of it and then assemble it into a story that works for you at that time" beginning by physically connecting with, and touching something concrete. In her words, "I'm certainly not dependent on place, because I'd be dead by now, wouldn't I?" Having strengthened both her senses of self and place, Carol says she is open to and engaging with place – she likes "to smell dirt"; she has a sense of the earth caring for her, and a sense of the sacred in special places. To balance her busy life, she restores herself by gardening.

Considering ways they deepen their senses of place, both Carola and Carol speak of the importance of looking for beauty – or finding ways to create it – wherever they are, and of connecting with place through regular gardening and walking. They experience and consciously develop sense of place as a physical connection, through the senses. Carola experiences it as "a mutual taking care of". Carol describes it as "getting your ear in, and your tongue in"; that what is required is for her "sensibilities to learn" to stop comparing, and to hear, taste, smell, feel, and see freshly: "Look at the colour of the sky, embrace it on its own terms and don't try to interpret it – you can feel scared and lonely and strange, or you can say that's a place of spirituality, make a narrative of it, *this* is what this is'". Through such sensory awareness of place, Carol developed insight into how differently she came to terms with a new landscape as a child and as an adult:

In Scotland there are things I *know*: I know a snowdrop coming through the snow, I know gooseberry. These are things that I know intimately. I have taken a gooseberry off the bush, I have been prickled by its prickles; I know what it is like to fall into nettles. Scotland is a prickly country, and I know the smell of that, the way to work with that, the leaves, all of those things.

When I first came to Canada, when I was still a little girl, one of the things I had to get used to was maple trees and oak trees; and oak trees have those wonderful little things that look like little people in hats – acorns – and because I was going to school there I got to do things with the leaves – I've waxed an oak leaf, I've waxed a maple leaf. I've climbed those trees, I've seen them shed their leaves, I know why the chlorophyll shuts off during the winter; this is something I'm very intimate with. When I came to Australia as an adult, one of the hardest things I found is I have no intimate relationship with a palm tree, or a gum tree. I haven't climbed a gum tree. I've been told about it, so I'll break a leaf and I'll smell it and I'll think, "that's lovely", but I haven't had a childhood relationship with it.

This understanding highlights the value of providing opportunity and encouragement for children to engage with their environments as part of developing their senses of place.[14] It underlines the importance of supporting migrants – both children and adults – to intentionally interact with the living as well as built aspects of places that are new to them. While features of landscape reminiscent of places of origin can help people to feel at home, sometimes the places to which they migrate have no such features. As the participants' stories show, part of what opens the possibility for people to begin to feel at home in any place is for them to become familiar with it.

Understandably, a new place may look and feel foreign, and require new or newly tapped forms of knowledge and behaviours from newcomers. There is a need for *haptic* learning – experiencing place sensorially and building bodily awareness of place.[15] For example, for people who come from rural areas, cities can be overwhelming; and for those from inland places, coastal environments can be daunting. Growing up in a place involves countless interactions that become so familiar they are taken for granted. In cities, there is a need to discover the location of services and shops, schools and churches, parks and playgrounds, and to learn how to use those facilities. In country areas, it may be important to be aware of and to learn respect for things such as snakes and insects, birds and animals, plants that are edible and those that are poisonous. For someone who has learned to swim in a lake or lagoon, a surf beach can be treacherous. Carol, for instance, discovered she needed to "learn mechanically" to deal with unfamiliar shores:

> The first time I walked into the ocean, I walked straight in and kept going, because I thought I was in a lake. I'm not used to walking into water that is moving. Water is supposed to stay still. I got scared to death by it, I got pulverised. I kept standing up and the water would kick me back down again. And somebody came out and said, "you dive under the wave", I'd just never thought to do that . . . oh, and that is an *exhilarating* moment of control.

Carol's story also draws attention to the value of immigrants learning from and collaborating with locals in becoming familiar with place, as exemplified by a gardening initiative created by Hobart's Phoenix Centre's migrant resource service. About twice each month, refugee immigrants spend a day working together to create gardens at different homes tenanted by immigrants. Depending upon the site, there may already be a few old fruit trees and some areas of flowers. Often the group clears overgrown bushes and grass, tills the soil, and builds up beds, then plants out a variety of vegetables. The vegetables are a welcome source of food for these people, who usually have low incomes. The project affords opportunities for immigrants to discover what will grow in their new land in different seasons; and fosters cultural exchange that sometimes amuses all involved. For example, immigrants were excited to recognise rhubarb, a plant familiar to them, and said they ate it raw, with salt. When the project supervisor told them Australians commonly eat rhubarb cooked, with sugar, there was amazement and laughter.

There is a considerable body of literature discussing the role and importance of gardening in migrant place making (see figure 7.2). Authors describe gardens as places where people and plants both carry on traditions and work out relationships with new social and biophysical environments.[16] Sonia Graham and John Connell consider that the "actual garden produce and type of environment created by the garden helped to emphasise and maintain cultural relationships, provide a space of nostalgia, and give a sense of ownership and control".[17]

Figure 7.2.   Gardening helps migrants to settle in new places. This community garden is in Japan.

Participants emphasise that, in addition to interacting with place, an attitude of openness is important for developing a sense of a place. They found that an attitude of openness helped them to settle, begin to feel at home in new places, and maintain a sense of place wherever they might be. Julian and Yukari both hold as essential the precept and practice of being open to "*really see* what's actually there". With their experiences of Jordan, India, Japan, Guatemala, Ethiopia, Kenya, and other locations, these two and Kiros stress that it is critical to learn and know what works in a place, rather than – or at least before – superimposing other notions on it. Describing village life in India, Julian said, "Bullocks are just wonderful because they don't need wide roadways, and they produce more bullocks – tractors can't do that!" and Yukari told a cautionary tale from Guatemala:

> The local people have a totally different idea about time, efficiency, pride – everything is different – so if you try to apply your ideas to them, they rebel against them. So that is giving us an opportunity to have another look at what kind of ideas we have. There was an Italian guy who was building a house there. It started a year ago. It is a whole manual building – they are building the blocks using the earth from the land. They have been building for a whole year. One day he came and saw no progress. He got upset and said something like, "if you are not going to change your behaviour you don't need to come". Next day nobody showed up. So, who has to change to get the house built?

Julian believes that it is necessary to drop stereotypes, be tolerant, and "celebrate difference"; and also to learn about other people's cultures and places, for such an approach has the advantage of increasing awareness of self. Yukari has long known that immersion in new places brings out new knowledge of herself. Connie began to discover the opportunity of such new knowing of herself during her time in Tasmania:

> One of the first things I noticed were the trees – from a distance you don't think anything, but when you get closer to them – they're like Doctor Seuss trees, and that just made me happy. I just wanted to laugh at them because they are just so new and different to me. And then, since we've lived here, I've just taken pictures of so many trees – dead trees, live trees, flowering trees, green trees – I love the trees! I take leaves out of branches and boil them up and dye fabric with the leaves and bark. I love trees, but I've never been so inspired by trees; so living here has changed me, and brought out things that are different, from me. Going to Japan this time – whatever neighbourhood, whatever house – will bring out parts of me, inspire parts of me. That would happen anywhere I go.

Connie likes to take control and adjust any new place to suit her preferences. She says that she needs to know what to expect and was pleased to anticipate that – as she had previously experienced – service in Japan, for example from tradespeople or shopkeepers, would be reliable and predictable. Although somewhat nervous about having to become fluent in Japanese, she was deter-mined to do that quickly. Contributing is important to her, but a component of it is to have others rely on her, to ensure their acceptance of her, and to give her access to reciprocal community support. These factors align her, too, with *independence from place*. However, by opening to a new relationship with place while she was in Australia, she has begun to appreciate places differ-ently and is keen to learn from place – a shift indicating that she has begun to experience a greater sense of mutuality with place, and opening towards experiencing greater *interdependence with place*.

Sense of self and sense of place are always related, but as these accounts show, openness to place has been concurrent with a deepening of partici-pants' senses of self. They felt able to *be* themselves, experiencing a clearer, fuller sense of self. Through experiences such as those described, these people have become more open to allowing and developing their senses of place wherever they might be.

SEEKING SAFETY, TERRITORY, SOVEREIGNTY, AND CITIZENSHIP

With the exception of Shoukat's feeling of being at home with mountains, he and Nene expressed their relationships to place in ways that contrasted with those of other participants. In part, that may have had to do with limits of language, although Nene, at least, was already fluent in English. It seemed to me that this difference had far more to do with the degrees of trauma they had experienced and was associated with their priorities at the time. It may be that I could have pressed harder to elicit more from them about sense of place. However, being with each of these people through their interviews, I felt it would have been insensitive – and not in the spirit of ethical research – to per-sist in asking for more detail about what was either a source of pain and fear, or clearly of small relevance to them, at least at that stage of their resettlement.

Nene spent most of her teenage years in Tasmania, growing up to be a young adult and quietly excited about her future. Nene is articulate and con-fident in sharing her story, especially because of doing that many times with Students Against Racism. Yet, she exhibits a reserve and serene demeanour that is, in part, very culturally and religiously based. Notwithstanding, Nene's reserve also comes from fear, because she cannot forget either her experience of trauma or her fears for family still in Sudan and still threatened. Those fears affect her sense of place. Aspects of the environment that she associates with traumatic experience are anchored in her neurology, and when she sees simi-larities in other contexts, memories of trauma are triggered. For instance, Nene is afraid of the bush. She has travelled to Melbourne on mainland Australia, and to Auckland in New Zealand, and looks forward to widening her travels overseas in years to come. Cities do not frighten her, countryside does:

> Because there is not much houses, and forest, kind of . . . just reminded me of how – that's where the Turkanas used to live, the forest side – they come in the night and invade the camp and stuff like that. If you went to the river to get water, to get firewood in the forest . . . it's kind of on the side of the forest and where the Turkana stays, so you have to make sure you are home by six o'clock because it may be dangerous at night. When Turkanas get you, you be in trouble, they kill you, and stuff like that.

Travelling through country Tasmania, Nene explains, "just gives me the feeling of back then in the camp" and she confirms that any place that reminds her of the Turkana area – "it's a bit forest, no houses" – brings back the same feeling of fear.

Although Shoukat was glad that Tasmania was a quiet place, "no rush – a very good country for me", in the years he lived there he found it very difficult to think about anything much else than the safety of his wife and son, and "our Hazara people" still in Pakistan:

> For example, when I study in Polytechnic, or anywhere, if I try to forget for a while, "oh I am in class", after thirty minutes, again, I think "oh, where is my family? They are in Pakistan, but just leave it, okay". I study again, I just look to teacher, but again after thirty minutes or so, "Where is my family? Is something wrong?"

A summary of what underlies Shoukat's emotional sense of place might be: Afghanistan – death, pain, loss, and fear; Pakistan – death, pain, loss, and fear; his journey to seek asylum – acute danger, pain, loss, and fear; in detention – imprisonment, pain, loss, and fear for his family; Tasmania – personally safe, but deeply missing his wife and son, and his people, afraid for them, grieving over Hazara people regularly being killed in Pakistan, and helpless to protect them. His sense of place then might perhaps be described as *in-between* or *liminal*, and until his family arrived, he was never fully present. In our first conversation, Shoukat said, "Now Australia is my mother home", and he lived with hope that sometimes ran thin, as expressed in a poem he wrote in Persian and translated as:

> I become sad for my joyful son
> I become desperate and sad
> I become sad for my dear ones.

Khadga's nineteen years in a refugee camp in Nepal is almost unimaginable to anyone who has not had such experience. Children of his extended family died on the way to that place, undernourished and in flight from terror, yet he has no direct memory of war, or torture, or the death by violence of anyone close to him. He grew up in an environment of poverty, lack of rights, and humiliation, yet he managed to get education, and migrated as soon as that option became available. When selecting Australia, a cool climate and features of landscape such as mountains were important, but Khadga's sense of place is strongly socially oriented, centring on rights, services, and opportunities. Recall that earlier I wrote that Australia is the first country within which Khadga has ever had the possibility of citizenship, and so, he says, "I love this country! I am very proud to be Australian now":

> I think we made the right decision to come to Tasmania. I visited the mainland, because my in-laws are in Adelaide; it is quite hard, it's too big, and it is quite difficult, especially for migrant people to explore the services that are available to them in the big place. In Tasmania you don't have to struggle as much to explore all the services that are mainly for people like us.
>
> I was very small in Bhutan; I didn't have much experience my area, what is Bhutan looks like. When I read interviews and when I listen news, now I certainly feel that Tasmania is the best place, and Tasmania is my home, because the people who are living in Bhutan, they are not enjoying all their rights. Even one of my brothers is in Bhutan. Before we left Bhutan, his citizenship is ceased by Bhutan government – he still has not got that citizenship – it is more than twenty years. He is stateless, and because of that, his sons and daughters, they are not getting opportunities to studies and to their own business; they are also restricted by the rules and regulations of the country, not having citizenship. If I were there, I would also have to face the same situation. Here, I am exercising all my rights, freedoms, liberty; I am feeling free. I can walk with my head is straight. In Bhutan, when someone from the offices is coming, you are not allowed to look them straight, you have to bend your head. And in Nepal, the life in the camps is pretty horrible.

When we spoke, Khadga planned to stay in Hobart, where he says he is already "habituated" to the place and the facilities. He is close to his extended family, his children can get an education, and, like his brothers, he is buying a house. In the backyard of his new home, Khadga and his elderly father established an extensive and productive vegetable garden. The garden and the family are thriving, and place for them is about community and social belonging.

All four irregular migrant participants are conscious that their relationships with safe territory, sovereignty, and citizenship are essential foundations for building well-being.[18] For others that relationship is no less important; but they take their citizenship so much for granted that it is almost unthinkable for them to consider that the freedoms and rights they presuppose might ever be questioned. Like Jun and Connie, they accept that they might experience restrictions in some other countries, but expect and assume continuity of freedoms and rights in their countries of citizenship. And some can claim such rights in more than one nation-state.

With all the variations, nevertheless, it is clear that correlations can be drawn between the state of the participants' senses of self and the quality of their senses of place. Exploring the relationship of these senses, thus far, reveals three significant understandings: first, when people are afraid, at risk, and have learned to be *helpless, hopeless,* and *worthless,* their sense of self is reduced, their focus narrows, and they are defensively closed, rather than open to place.[19] Second, when people are safe, free, and have learned to value themselves and others, their sense of self expands, their focus broadens, and they are more open to discover, experience, and learn from place. Third, when the sense people have of a place is that it nurtures them, and that there they are safe and free to be themselves, without needing to defend or put on a false front, then being in that place supports them to develop and expand their sense of self.

On the other hand, especially when existing residents are suspicious of migrants, or hostile towards them, dilemmas of difference arise, and it is much harder to settle.

NOTES

1. Relph, Placelessness, 6.
2. Sale, 41.
3. Olsen, 73.
4. Ibid.
5. Ellen Barry and Martin Selsoe Sorensen, In Denmark, Harsh New Laws for Immigrant 'Ghettos', *New York Times*, July 1, 2018, accessed October 1, 2018, https://www.nytimes.com/2018/07/01/world/europe/denmark-immigrant-ghettos.html.
6. Cresswell, On the Move, 31.
7. Tuan, 154.
8. Perkins and Thorn.
9. Urry, Mobilities, 279.
10. Albrecht et al., 95.
11. Eyles and Williams, 203.
12. Nynäs: 169.
13. Abram; Cameron; Cronon, 'Wilderness'; Macy; Mathews, Reinhabiting Reality; Naess; Roszak, Voice of the Earth; Seed; Thomashow.
14. Horton and Kraftl, 'Rats'; Kraftl et al.; Stratford, Geographies, Mobilities, and Rhythms.
15. Paterson.
16. Head, Muir, and Hampel, 326.
17. Graham and Connell, 375.
18. Elden, 'Conversation', 'Legal Terrain'; Fine, 'Immigration', 'Keeping Them Out'.
19. Seligman.

Chapter 8

Dilemmas of Difference

> The ways that migrants of colour are approached in the present . . . can be traced to the legacy of colonialism. Within the constructed binaries of difference, the ethnic other is not only considered as absolutely different but as inferior to the norm of the ethnic Western self.[1]

The assumption that human being is flawed clearly underlies racism and can be seen as central to many stressful problems people experience in processes of migration, whether they are new arrivals to a place, or already resident. These primary social challenges of migration are "dilemmas of difference"[2] – problems that arise, first, because people are different from each other, and second, because many people fear what the differences may portend. Both immigrants and existing residents in receiving countries have to cope with difference usually involving culture, ethnicity, religion, economic fears, fears of loss, fears of erosion of ways of life, fears of change – fears that compound into fear of the Other. These fears are used to influence various reactions and responses in the service of particular agenda. For instance, advocates of political policies slant public opinion to favour or reject migrants of particular origins, and decisions about issues such as increased border controls depend upon fear of difference.[3]

In recent years, the shift in public discourse is more than disquieting: manipulation based on fear has become extreme, public debate has become openly aggressive; *hate* speech is rife; and racist incidents proliferate.[4] Reaction escalates rapidly in the face of acts of terrorism, whether perpetrated by those we usually think of as terrorists, or by white supremacists. The horror is the same. The danger, however, is that if we do not stop to consider what is actually going on every day on a far less extreme scale, we will continue to enable a contemporary "banality of evil". It is critical that we notice how indifferent our societies are to everyday racism, the extent to which we accept and normalise and tolerate racism and don't question it. Of course there are individuals who do question, but societies as a whole reflect racism in their inequalities.

There are many problems associated with migration, and many practical issues need to be resolved to reduce causes of distress and fear – for example, those to do with employment, housing, health, equal opportunity, and discrepancies between policies and their implementation. Without minimising or disregarding these matters, however, one key to increasing well-being is to *respond to people's fear of difference itself.* To that end, it is important to consider again the assumption that human being is flawed. So long as that assumption is held to be true, then difference is seen to be threatening. Inequities and discriminatory practices are supported by the related assumption that some people are inherently better than others. People's beliefs predispose them to expect that their experiences will validate their assumptions; and beliefs based on ideas that there is something fundamentally wrong with people, and especially with different others, are self-validating reductions. These dynamics, of course, apply both to presuppositions about immigrants, and preconceptions immigrants have about the places and people where they hope to settle, and are central to the politics of difference.[5]

EVERYDAY RACISM

Gabrielle Berman and Yin Paradies write that is common to consider racism as "a combination of prejudice and power": people with authority attribute inferiority to other racial or ethnic groups and use that definition to propagate and justify unequal treatment of them; they base social systems on ethnoracial categories, and other reductionist and pejorative "premises about human kind".[6] In an attempt to overcome limitations they perceive in others' definitions, these writers define racism as "that which maintains or exacerbates inequality of opportunity among ethnoracial groups", and which can be expressed through beliefs, emotions, and practices.[7] They see racism as a form of oppression intrinsically linked to privilege, and point out that, in addition to disadvantaging minority groups, "racism also results in certain ethnoracial groups (for example, Whites) being privileged and accruing unfair opportunities".[8] In the Australian context, for example, Berman and Paradies provide evidence that there *is* racism, that it may be on the rise, and that "racism in the form of opposition to diversity in recent years has consistently been expressed by a significant proportion of those surveyed".[9] Others see social cohesion as the norm in contemporary Australia, but also write that racist attitudes and racial discrimination persist, with Indigenous Australians and immigrant minorities being the main victims.[10]

Participants all have experiences of racism, in different forms. Carol recollects a barbecue in a rural area that she attended on the day of her first arrival in Australia, in the 1970s. The graphic examples of racism Carol heard were not directed at her, but she felt very uncomfortable at this first exposure, and remembers them vividly:

> All the guys went to the garage and began drinking, and the women were standing in the kitchen, talking about making pavlovas. I had never been in – I mean the split between the female role and the male role – Canada is not like that! I ended up wandering into the garage because the men were talking politics, which was much more interesting to me. A cattleman was telling me that you could breed an Aborigine out in two generations because their genes are so weak, you know, and so they'd come out white! And then he starts to go on about how the Aborigine's brain is not as big, they can't help it, it's just not as big. . . . They were the antithesis of everything my family is. These guys were pro the war in Vietnam. One man was talking about building a tank in his garage, I kid you not, for when the Indonesians – the yellow peril – were going to come over.

Attitudes such as these epitomise the manner in which certain views can become commonplace assumptions in social and personal narratives, and become part of the constitutive *conditions of truth* in human experience – that is, as part of the environment within which people live, and conduct their lives. Carol's experience at the barbecue occurred over forty years ago, yet such opinions can still be heard in modern Australia, especially in rural areas. Hannah Arendt explains that whatever "touches or enters into a sustained relationship with human life immediately assumes the character of a condition of human existence".[11] The assumptions contained in narratives generate those conditions through practices that reinforce or substantiate those ideas, thus influencing behaviour and governing the quality of experience. In situations of migration, people's negative prejudices – pejorative and reductionist views of different others – become conditions of experience both for immigrants and existing residents. Reaction to those experiences can reinforce those ideas, but not immutably – such ideas are stable, often durable, but not immutable – and understanding how beliefs constitute conditions of human experience can open the way for assumptions to be questioned and changed.

As described in chapter 1, we are born into prevailing narratives, and the assumptions upon which they are based are continually reinforced, partly because they are self-validating, and partly because of memory. Bruce Fell writes of *internal* and *external* memory, both of which are "directly linked to how we neurologically process the world; how our priorities and attitudes surrounding self, [others,] sexuality, religion, design, politics and ecology are formed, reinforced and passed on to the next generation".[12] Internal memory is individually embodied. External memory, in Fell's terms, is a condition of experience that "constantly reminds us of the dominant discourse of the day".[13] Fell suggests that external memory reminds us how to think in certain ways, and he argues that "the memory system that underscores our day-to-day lives hasn't had a major upgrade since 1944".[14] He points to the involvement of history, politics, and media in forming and changing assumptions and narratives, and in constituting truths then reinforced by external memory.

By way of example, I take the phrase "the yellow peril" from Carol's account to follow one small thread in the history of racist attitude in Australia. This perceived threat of Asian hordes overtaking Australia can be traced at least from the days of Australia's gold rush, if not before. After all, the Chinese and others traded with Aboriginal people in Australia's north long before the advent of the British in these waters.[15] Fear of the peril is also instrumental in legislation of the White Australia Policy at Federation, and in the subsequent exclusion from Australia of Chinese and other Asian immigrants. Whether or not that attitude lessened or just simmered during the years between wars, in the Second World War, Japan was the enemy, fought on the Pacific front. Historically, the threat of invasion became real with Japanese bombing of Darwin, and submarines in Sydney Harbour. The regenerated narrative of "the yellow peril" was intensified by post-war revelations of atrocities in Japanese prisoner-of-war camps. I wonder if the nuclear bombing of Hiroshima and Nagasaki produced a pause – a moment, at least, of reflection that humanity had just done something that irrevocably shifted reality for *all* of life on this planet – or if it was just a fillip to mark another war's end.

Not so very long after the end of the Second World War, as Australia began to experience a flood of cheap merchandise from Asia, and the White Australia Policy began to soften in the 1960s, Australia joined in the Vietnam War. Public television, which went on air in Australia in 1956, for the first time brought live broadcasts from and about that war into people's living rooms. Asylum seekers from many places in Asia, particularly Vietnam, began to arrive on Australian shores during the 1970s. What impact did all of that have on prevailing attitudes? It was at that time – nearing the end of the Vietnam War – that policies of multiculturalism were introduced in Australia. Undoubtedly, there would have been many different and shifting attitudes. But, as Carol's experience testifies, for some people, in some places, the attitudes and prejudices of old narratives prevail in external memory long after the events.

HIERARCHIES OF BELONGING

Of course, both social and personal narratives can and do change over time, influenced by education, events, politics, media, and more. The length of time an ethno-racial group has lived in the country can affect acceptance and inclusion of immigrants, but negative and pejorative response also shifts from previous to most recent arrivals.[16] In a study of an inner-city suburb of Sydney that has become intensively settled by Chinese immigrants, Amanda Wise writes of "a deep-seated sense of displacement and disorientation" experienced by long-term elderly residents, particularly Anglo-Celtic, but also among several other, predominantly European, ethnic groups.[17] Wise focuses on the sensuous and affective dimensions of the experience of these elderly residents in coping with rapid changes to shops and businesses in the main shopping street. What is available in the shops is different, but also there is change to how they look – including mostly Chinese signage – and smell, and feel, and the mannerisms and behaviour of the Chinese are alien to the older residents. Wise writes that, in one focus group discussion she facilitated, the overwhelming discomfort felt by the elderly residents poured out emotionally in a dystopian description of what they felt the suburb had become.

> And then something extraordinary happened: one of the much older ladies – a widow dressed in black who, until now, had been quiet – began to yell back at the group. First she was recounting in tears, with all her body engaged in the telling, her misery at how her Chinese neighbours let their children wee [urinate] in her front garden. She described having fishy water hosed on her feet at the bus stop in front of the fish shop. The room was charged with emotion. But then she turned, almost on herself, and began to berate herself and the group . . .
>
> "My God, what are we saying? We can't say about the new people what the Australians used to say about us. How can we do this to them, how can we make the same pain for them? This is not right to say such things. These Chinese just want to feel a little bit at home, make this place a little bit more home. We don't like them but how can we take their home away from them?"[18]

Placing this event in context, Wise writes that the community to which the women belong was itself subject to a great deal of racism in the post-war years, until the 1980s and, sometimes, even today. Until the 1970s,

> Europeans were seen as "wogs" who ate "smelly" food and spoke with funny accents. Children were regularly teased and bullied at school. Much of the teasing was around issues of bodily hexis which, to Anglo-Australians of the time, was rather too "expressive" for their liking, and differing food cultures – which ironically have been embraced as "mainstream" in today's Australia.[19]

Growing up in working-class areas of Sydney and Melbourne in the 1950s, it was common for me to hear migrants from Mediterranean countries derogatively called *wogs*[20] – a slang term referring to any non-white person, but especially to dark-skinned natives of the Mediterranean, the Middle East, or Southeast Asia. In Australia's *Macquarie Dictionary*, the definition of *wog,* still classed as derogatory, is extended to mean "any foreigner". It was common to call immigrants from the United Kingdom *poms,* or *pommies,*[21] and sometimes *whinging* [complaining] *poms*, especially those whose passages were supported, but *pom* was also used in a friendlier manner.

In the 1970s, suspicion shifted to more recently arrived migrants from Southeast Asia, particularly from Vietnam; and then, to Arabs, Lebanese, Afghani, and Iraqi asylum seekers – often conflated as *Muslim* whether or not that was accurate – and who soon "replaced Vietnamese as the most suspect and despised 'others' in the landscape of multicultural Australia".[22] Pardy and Lee write that some immigrants "seek insider status, by fabricating others as more outside and thus less worthy of inclusion". For example, to distance themselves from more recent arrivals, some Vietnamese-Australians asserted that they came through "proper channels". When reminded of their similar arrival as asylum seekers, they protested that their situation was different, arguing that they were "genuine refugees".[23] Pardy and Lee also find that "hierarchies of belonging are in constant flux", and quote a Vietnamese-Australian woman, who has lived in Australia since 2001, as saying:

> I tell you there is a hierarchy here of how you are respected. Aussies and Viets are treated differently. In Myer or Centrelink or other businesses this is the hierarchy – Aussies first, then European-looking migrants. After that comes Asians and then at the bottom it's the Muslims.[24]

More recently, there has been focus on migrants from African nations, who are often categorised and stereotyped on the basis of their *visibility*. Kiros – from Ethiopia – says that identity is problematised because of visibility:

> If you are with a dark skin, it doesn't matter whether you come from the Caribbean . . . "African" is easy for people. When there is something good, which is done by an African-Australian, then the *Australian*-ness is what comes out. When something bad happens, everyone forgets that this person is an Australian. I have to remind people in a recent meeting, that this boy is an Australian, not a Sudanese. When there is any issue, then you pick what you want to demonise.

Sudanese people were more than half of all African migrants resettled as part of the Australian Humanitarian Program in the ten years from 1997 to 2007, and constitute the single largest black African group.[25] David Nolan and his colleagues write that "at least some media coverage of Sudanese people in Australia continues long-standing media practices involving the construction and problematization of visible difference".[26] Significant in their study is frequent reference to media assumptions of the *implicit whiteness* of Australia as a host country to migrants of *colour,* and they discuss views that, by constructing Australia as a white nation, media both overlook the needs of refugees, and deny Australia's Indigenous heritage.[27] Nolan and his colleagues' analysis of media coverage of Sudanese migrants shows that, in a period of a few months either side of an Australian federal election,

> media coverage created a particular set of discursive representations of Sudanese people that portrayed them as visibly different and as the outsider "Other" in contrast to the normalised "white" majority who are represented as belonging in Australian national space. In this way, and without being overtly racist, the media . . . contribute to an emergent integrationist policy agenda. Further, and resonating with previous media research . . . such representations also appear to situate Sudanese people as an undifferentiated group that is unlikely to integrate and thereby represents a problematic "Other".[28]

Given such attitudes, it is perhaps predictable that the irregular migrants participant here – all of whom are people of colour – describe personal experiences of racism. None was overtly violent, but all were unpleasant experiences, and sources of discomfort. And at subtle levels all such events affect people's experiences of enablement and constraint: as David Bissell writes, "Barely perceived transitions in power . . . occur in and through situated encounters", in a *micropolitics* of "bodies always transforming, however subtly, in relation to what is happening around them".[29] Nene speaks of her experience of racism in high school:

> I didn't know English very much, and people around me they said all these kind of words. I can hear them, but I didn't really know what they meant until when I started college and I started hearing, and also in the community when I hear people saying those words, then I realised what they meant it was actually racist words – like "negro".

Apparently innocuous questions such as "where did you come from?" or "why are you here?" to Nene are racist because of the tone and manner in which they are spoken:

> The way of their face expression can tell you that they are saying it to you like they are saying that you don't belong here – if someone says, "where did you come from?" I know they are asking me where I came from, but if they say it like with a very angry face. . . .

Since 2008, Nene has been part of Students Against Racism, formed when a teacher observed that several students who had come to Tasmania as humanitarian entrants were quite isolated and realised that most people had no idea of their backgrounds. With her help, these students began to share their stories through a dramatised presentation, *Living in Between*, which has successfully brought about greater understanding, and now has funding to extend its reach into the broader community. The importance of sharing stories as a step in recovery from displacement and trauma is becoming more widely recognised.[30] At college and in the community, Nene and others in the group had often been "called *nigger* – that's why we started the group". Nene says that racist remarks no longer happen much at the college, but still occur in the community and on buses. As a project officer for the group, Nene says,

> Some of them, when they came here, they can't really speak English, they can only say "hello", or "my name is such and such", and that's it. For them just to see how, through the group, through that problem, they have developed so much, they have self-confidence, and now they can speak and just be part of the group and connect – it makes them proud.

Shoukat says he is clear that not all Tasmanians are racist, but nevertheless he reports "a lot of abuse" of Hazara women, who are Shia Muslim, and wear headscarves. "Racist people, they think . . . she is Muslim, so she is going with Taliban . . . sometime they say, "Fuck off!" It is a painful situation". Understanding that the Hazara people are in Tasmania precisely because they have been extremely persecuted by the Taliban does make a difference, but, evidently, that background needs to be more widely publicised and acknowledged.

Khadga describes an incident on a bus when an African man was speaking on the phone in his own language, and a woman stood up and instructed, "If you want to speak, you speak in English, and do not use a language that we do not understand". On another occasion, Khadga said that he and his brother were talking in Nepali, and a woman said, "If you want to talk here, you talk in English". Khadga said he explained, "we find better understanding in our language than English", and assured the woman that to communicate with her, he would use English, "but we can use our language within our community". The two men had not thought that she might be uncomfortable because she could not understand them. "Oh, but we were not talking about her", he assured me. Equally, it might not occur to people speaking English in front of immigrants that this might make them uncomfortable, too. In this instance, however, hearing the two men talk, the woman might have been be frightened because it was at a time when there was deep fear of terrorism and a perceived need to pre-empt suspected attacks.[31] As they had no concept of themselves as possibly being seen as terrorists, such an explanation had not occurred to either Khadga or his brother.

POLITICS OF RECOGNITION

The examples cited above are far from extreme and exemplify every day or banal racism that sees people through the lenses of stereotypes. As Charles Taylor writes, racism denies recognition of who people actually are, and "can be a form of oppression".[32] David Morley calls this the "problematic gaze" that might be welcoming, hostile, or curious, and writes that a predominant lack of recognition undermines peoples' dignity and self-confidence and is deeply wearing.[33] Greg Noble describes racism as a form of social incivility that may include "name-calling . . . jokes in bad taste, bad manners, provocative and offensive gestures or even just a sense of social distance or unfriendliness or an excessive focus on someone's ethnicity".[34] Respondents to his study with immigrant Australians and their children reported this type of experience as pervasive.[35] Noble stresses that, although less dramatic than stories of violence or threats, this everyday feeling of social discomfort "reveals a more fundamental ontological relation underlying all acts of racism".[36] Everyday racism lessens the confidence or trust people have in the world around them, and thus threatens their ontological security:

> Crucially, our ontological security is founded on *our ability* to be recognised. Our "fit" in an environment requires the "acknowledgement" of other actors – human and non-human – that we fit. *Our ability* to be comfortable in public settings also rests on *our ability* to be acknowledged as rightfully existing there: to be recognised as belonging.[37]

I emphasise *our ability* in Noble's text because discourse on this topic usually focuses on the role of the perpetrator of racism and does not attend to the possible agency of the recipient. A person's sense of self is critical in this relationship – an understanding implied in Noble's wording – the *ability* to be recognised, to be comfortable, and to be acknowledged is *not passive*. It is significantly affected by the ability to acknowledge, recognise, and respect oneself. Noble supports his claims of the importance of recognition with Axel Honneth's argument that "the possibility of realising oneself as autonomous and individuated depends on the development of self-confidence, self-respect and self-esteem, and these can only be acquired intersubjectively through being granted recognition by others whom we recognise".[38]

   In short, we are social beings, embedded in a social world, and recognition and respect for each other – intersubjectively – is clearly necessary for people's well-being; it is a relationship actively involving both parties.[39] Within that relationship recognition and respect from a receiving community, including respect for difference, can provide significant support for new arrivals; helping them to maintain and grow self-respect, and engendering their respect for the people and place new to them. A fundamental sense of and respect for self is equally essential for the full benefit of such support to be realised (see figure 8.1).

François Levrau builds on Honneth's three dimensions of recognition – love, formal respect for equality, and social esteem – and, in his view when "recognition is denied, we are not capable of living autonomous and worthwhile lives".[40] It is generally understood that the degree and quality of loving care, nurturing, respect, and acknowledgement received by infants and children deeply affects how they develop self-confidence, self-respect, self-esteem, and autonomy.[41] However, once a person has developed a sense of self based on those attributes, lack of recognition does not result in the loss of autonomy; as exemplified *in extremis* by Viktor Frankl, referred to earlier. Even when a person is without freedom physically or behaviourally their freedom to think and to choose their own attitudes typically remains.

Figure 8.1.   Women immigrants now at home in Adelaide, South Australia, 2019. Courtesy of Creolumen Photography.

There is evidence of autonomy – indicative of sense of self – in participants' narratives. Seeking asylum, as Shoukat did, demonstrates belief in himself and his family as worthwhile human beings, and shows a refusal to accept others' pejorative judgements of Otherness. Kiros' strong sense of self was fundamental to his refusal to go to a refugee camp; it was critical to his ability to make his own way in Kenya, and to succeed in arranging for himself and his family to migrate to Australia. Although he was shocked by the experience of becoming *nothing* in others' eyes, and found it difficult to handle, he did not become nothing in his own eyes. Kiros believes that it is important for his daughters to develop a strong basis of self-confidence to withstand racist "pushes", such as rude remarks from boys in the bus in Hobart: "I usually tell them as long as you know who you are, it shouldn't concern you, and the more I reiterate that, the stronger they get".

Levrau proposes that there is also a need for another dimension of recognition, one of respect for individual and group difference, especially of ethnicity, culture, and religion.[42] Countless other authors draw attention to the need for recognition, acknowledgement, and respect as fundamental to ontological security. Certainly, all of that applies both to people arriving in a new place *and* to the people already resident there. Berman and Paradies distinguish between two forms of internalised racism, internalised *dominance*, and internalised *oppression*:[43]

> Internalized dominance (i.e. privilege) . . . is the incorporation of attitudes, beliefs or ideologies about the inferiority of other social groups and/or the superiority of one's own social group. Conversely, internalized oppression is the incorporation of attitudes, beliefs or ideologies about the superiority of other social groups and/or the inferiority of one's own social group.

This distinction reinforces the importance of sense of self in handling the challenges of migration on both sides of the relationship. Without a sense of self based on self-respect, people do not readily attract – nor do they truly accept or trust – any respect or esteem from others.

Racism in particular, and people's fears and disrespect of others and themselves, more generally, both provide evidence of beliefs that in one way or another, something is wrong with who people are, and that some people are better, or worse, more or less deserving than others. This observation is not the same as one asserting that some people have more wealth than others, or that they are better educated, or more skilled, or have some other advantage. Racism is based on beliefs about the *nature* of being human and such beliefs are versions of the generic assumption that human being is flawed. Those beliefs, in all their variations, are passed on in narratives from generation to generation. They are part of the conditions of truth in prevailing narratives, and govern peoples' conduct of their own conduct. They are reinforced socially, pervade external memory, and are involved in politics, media, and everyday interactions between people and places at all levels.[44] Racism is also a process of self-validating reduction in which attitudes and prejudices that lessen people result in their actual reduction. Because the prophecies of prejudice are self-fulfilling, people's behaviour begins to fit the descriptions, and the beliefs are proven in the end result. Racist reductivism affects those seen through the lenses of prejudice and results in alienation and loss to community as a whole.

COMMUNITY AND FREEDOM OF WORSHIP

In his own research on resettlement in Hobart of African immigrants, primarily refugees, Kiros writes of a "honeymoon phase".[45] He says that on arrival people are relieved at the end of their ordeals, and happy to have an opportunity for a fresh start. Then, days, weeks, or months later, what appears is "the culture shock phase",[46] when worry, confusion, and frustration sets in and they want to go home. Commonly, a subsequent phase involves recovery, making sense of new environments, proactively forging new connections, seeking to belong (see figure 8.2). Thereafter, there is an "adjustment phase"[47] in which immigrants sometimes defensively protect and maintain their cultural identities and reject host cultures; sometimes they identify with the local culture, and reject families and ethnic communities.

Sufficient numbers in any ethnic community generally make it possible to establish places of worship, maintain cultural practices, languages of origin, and traditions. These practices are common in Australia, and have both positive and negative expression. Suvendrini Perera describes many suburbs in Sydney where different migrant groups are concentrated as "ghetto precincts that operate to encircle, separate, control, and police racially othered populations".[48] At the same time, she sees demands for assimilation as a "drive to eliminate spaces of difference perceived as threats to "law and order . . . social cohesion [and, increasingly] national security".[49] Notably, discrimination pushes people to emphasise their devalued identities.[50] In like vein, Dinesh Bhugra and her colleagues write that attempts by migrant groups to stay together "may create ghettos and increase racial views and stigmas".[51] In later work, Bhugra and Susham Gupta point out that "mutual mistrust/misunderstanding can lead to social marginalisation of individuals and ethnic minority groups, contributing to behavioural problems, under-achievement, and over-representation of these people in mental health and criminal justice systems".[52]

Shoukat, Khadga, and Nene feel it is particularly important to have community with others from the same ethnic backgrounds, and the freedom and opportunity to practice their own religions. Shoukat told me that he felt relief and gladness when he was released from detention and welcomed in Hobart by the Hazara community, with whom he found cultural familiarity and shared concern for Hazara family and friends still in Pakistan and Afghanistan. Hobart's Hazara community is relatively small – with only about sixty people – and for Shoukat it was a special day when he first met with them: "They did help me to understand very good in Hobart, what is the life, what is the law", and he is glad to know those differences. "In Australia there is a good law . . . you cannot find any law in Pakistan or Afghanistan". Aware that there are far larger Hazara communities in Melbourne and Adelaide – where he later chose to live – Shoukat said that some Hazara people "are escaping from Tasmania to mainland". Asked from what they were "escaping", he replied that it was the absence of a mosque: "There is a mosque for Sunni Muslims, but not for Shia – and there is not any graveyard – so our elder people think, if they die, so what will happen with their dead bodies?"

Khadga and his extended family, actively involved in the Bhutanese community, hope that at some time in the future there will be a Hindu temple in Hobart. Meantime, Khadga says they are happy because they are free to

Figure 8.2. Salamanca Market in Hobart, Tasmania – a multicultural venue featuring locally made artisan goods, international cuisines – enjoyed by local residents from many cultures, interstate tourists, and more than 300,000 international visitors annually.

celebrate their religion, and "my mum, she went to mainland last month and visited two or three temples in Melbourne".

Nene finds comfort, support, and moral sustenance in the cultural familiarity of the Sudanese community. Going to church is a priority. At first Nene attended local churches, but did not experience the level of comfort in the Australian style of Christianity that she feels in culturally familiar services. Nene says her mother taught her "to know God", and that "the feeling of praising God in that kind of way" kept hope alive in the refugee camp.

> Back home, whatever worries you have, whatever problems you have, you pray, and God will help you, help you to take away the depression, to take away the pain and the sorrow, and the sadness that you have. So going to church and praying to God, knowing God, it helps me.

Recently, a pastor came to Hobart from the Congo and holds services in a library while the community seeks its own permanent church. Nene explains that "God says whatever has happened to you, you should let it go and try to focus on the future and who you are, so I love going to church, I love praying, I like singing, I'm in the church choir, and I play the keyboard at church".

Freedom to worship is one thing; ready access to places of worship is another. Inappropriate and inaccessible location of places of worship can contribute to marginalising and separating cultural groups, and to social unrest. In regard to civic planning, Leonie Sandercock writes that such is "our fear of the Other . . . that we try to make them [and their religious and other structures] invisible, by removing them – legally, of course (the law is always on our side) – from our neighbourhoods, our communities, our parts of the city".[53] Perera also comments that it is not uncommon for places of worship important to immigrants to be located in places that are considered inappropriate, such as "industrial areas, next to waste dumps or in the middle of highways".[54]

Immigrant cultures can enrich existing cultures, as well as attracting conflict.[55] Opportunity for enrichment can be lost through indifference as well as rejection of difference, and tensions are created when newcomers are ignored. For instance, as an African woman immigrant in the United States, Sobonfu Some, writes:

> Longing to belong to an environment that didn't want closeness and to people who were constantly struggling to remember or know who they were was much more difficult to digest than the distance I felt from the place I called home. In many ways, I found comfort in knowing there was such a place as home, where I could be seen and understood without having to explain myself. It certainly helped to diminish the bitterness that came with the realisation that people couldn't care less what country I was from, much less who I was or what story I had to tell.[56]

In Nene's account, she and other teenage refugees felt depressed and anxious when Australian students ignored them at school. It was not until they were encouraged to share their stories that the general indifference to them began to change. Nene says that she has made friends, but not many are Australian.

> I still try to figure out why this is so. I have a lot of friends from different countries. I have a few Australian friends but not very close. And that's one of the things that we try to discuss, when we do our Students Against Racism – because all these members say it is hard – the most difficult thing they are facing now, and we don't know why.

The group members think the problem has to do with cultural difference, and that motivates them to present their program in the hope that it will help them to connect with Australians. Most of them consider lack of common language is a major barrier, and they recognise that "we don't know how to connect with them, and it is also hard for them to reach out to us". Adolescence has its challenges regardless of culture, but in this instance, perhaps the cultural narratives are too divergent to allow for easy bridging. Amia Lieblich refers to this as a "loss of clarity of norms", for instance, confusion in areas of gender expectations: "How should a young, single woman behave, especially in the context of a possible development of heterosexual relationships?"[57] Australian teenagers generally take for granted a far more permissive social environment than is likely even to be comprehensible from the perspective of someone with Nene's background. I asked Nene (who was twenty-one at the time) if she had a boyfriend:

> No, I don't have a boyfriend, because in my Christian belief . . . boyfriend is kind of not something that you do. When you want to have a boyfriend, it is like you are sure that this is the person – you are going to start a relationship with them and it leads to marriage. It is not like have a boyfriend and after some time then you break up. I will decide it when I want to get married, then I know that I will start a relationship and I will know that this person I might end up getting married to.

Nene's underlying moral assumptions and cultural beliefs are likely at least to be at odds with those of many Australian young people, and to bridge them effectively is surely a challenge, not only to Nene, but also to the values and regimes of practice common to her original Sudanese culture.

LIVING IN LANGUAGE

Differences in language are perhaps among the most significant challenges for immigrants. Being able adequately to speak the language of a host country is sometimes prerequisite to acceptance as an immigrant, and setting such conditions into law is a way of excluding people judged to be undesirable. Dominant groups may also discriminate against others speaking in languages they consider inferior and refuse to include them.[58]

From a socio-cultural perspective, Joan Hall locates the essence of social life in communication, and she writes that "language is considered to be first and foremost a sociocultural resource".[59] For a person to learn the vocabulary and grammar of a language new to them is not enough, by itself, to give them full access to that resource because

> Languages influence the way group members view, categorise, and in other ways think about their world. Since different culture groups speak different languages, individual worldviews are tied to the language groups to which individuals belong. To state it another way, if individual thought is shaped by language, individuals with different languages are likely to have different under-standings of the world.[60]

It follows that when people learn new languages, they expand their world-views, or at least their understanding of what things mean to native speakers of those languages. This learning contributes to the blending of cultures, and new perspectives can lead to variations in people's experiences.

Fluency in a language affects a person's identity and sense of self. It affects how people feel and think, and colours how they experience themselves dif-ferently depending upon which language they are using. It is important, also, to recognise that a culture is soon lost when its language stops being spoken. This risk is highly significant for immigrants, especially when their children learn the language of a new country, and forget – or never learn – the lan-guage of their parents' origins.

Participants' narratives provide some examples of these issues of language. Shoukat speaks English and studies to improve his fluency, clear that English is the language of his new life. He is troubled, however, about preserving his mother tongue, *Hazaragi*, which, to a great extent, was lost when Dari was imposed as the official language of Afghanistan. He explains that, as a result, some Hazari think their mother tongue is Farsi, or Persian, which comes from Iran, and some think it is Dari, but that comes from Tajik, another ethnic group.

> Most of our educated people, they think "oh just leave Hazaragi, because it is the language of poor people or third class people". They think Dari is very powerful language and they can read and they can write. So that's why most of our Hazari think our mother tongue is Dari, which is wrong.
> My genetic is from Mongolia, my language family is from *Uralultai;* Hazara is part of *Uralutai*. Dari and Farsi is drawn from the family of Aryan people,

which is Indo-European, so this is two kind of family of languages; so how can I say that Dari or Farsi is my mother-tongue? I can't.

Acutely aware that with loss of language, culture is being lost, Shoukat says this is a very big disaster in a Hazara's life, because "without any language, everybody is anyone. Animal has no any language. Basically, we were and we are the Aboriginals of Afghanistan".

Shoukat appreciates that Hazaragi is a registered language in Australia, particularly because he believes refusal to register it in Pakistan and Afghanistan is based on racism. His passion to preserve his language fits Tuan's view that such desire arises from a need to support a sense of identity.[61]

Jun and Connie's desire to have their sons become fluent in both Japanese and English was an important consideration in their decision to settle in Japan, rather than return to the United States after their years in Australia. The boys and Connie spoke little Japanese, and they expected this would make resettling difficult to begin with, but they also believe that bilingual skills will give them great advantage in the future. Jun learned to read and write English at school in Japan, but was quite unfamiliar with it as a spoken language, so he says it was a "shocking experience" when he first went to the United States. He found the directness of the English language very uncomfortable:

In English it is hard to avoid what you mean. I can't give you any specific example, because every sentence I say in English is more straightforward and in your face than a Japanese sentence. Japanese language is very organic, very flexible. The English language is this subject, verb and object – this structure. It is so mathematical and direct. It was uncomfortable for a long time, communicating using that language, and wondering "so that doesn't offend them? So, okay, I guess that's how they talk, so I will learn to do it".

Part of Jun's discomfort, he says, was because "everyone is so different [from] each other . . . so lack of common sense is huge compared to Japan". By "common sense" Jun means a common attitude and behaviour among people. A primary example for him is that in a store or dealing with a business in Japan he can expect, and will receive, "nice service, politeness", and help to get what he needs. "In the US, you never know, depending on who you are dealing with, the outcome is going to be different. With Americans, some people can be very nice, others can be very rude, but you never know – you just have to learn not to take it personally". In Japan, customarily, people's communication – in language and manner – is deferential, unassuming, and often self-abnegating. By comparison, in Jun's view:

Americans *brag*. For example, they brag about the diversity and accepting differences, but, if you live there, you know that's not true. Americans have almost regulation dress – jeans, t-shirt and baseball cap. They all have to have perfect smile, they have to have bright white teeth that are aligned perfectly.

Jun says he was surprised at the intolerance he observed in the United States of any deformity, "some people are missing their arms or legs . . . most of them try to hide those things". Jun feels that he was more remarkable there when he wore different clothing than for being Japanese. He found it para-doxical that, in his experience, people in the United States were individu-alistic and different from each other in behaviour, and often ethnically, but conformed in their appearance; whereas, in the far more homogeneous Japan, people have "common sense", but embrace widely diverse and colourful ways of dressing. Jun thinks this might be "because Japanese people falsely believe that they are all the same, single race . . . so there's no outsider" and he concludes that certainty of sameness on the inside allows acceptance of expression of difference on the surface.

Having lived in Australia for most of her adulthood, Carola says she *thinks* in English and now feels more relaxed in Australia than in Germany. "I *live* in English, and that's where I've been in the last twenty odd years". She feels it has become harder to maintain a strong connection with herself in Germany, or when she is speaking German. "It's a bit rigid . . . a bit of stiffness in it for me" and she observes that use of each language changes not only how she feels, but also how she perceives herself, and whether or not she feels *at home*.

It might be said that multiculturalism in Australia is a work in progress. Whatever may be considered as being necessary for its fruition, both *old* and *new* Australians will be involved. Early in 2013, a group of recently arrived Rohingyan asylum seekers, in detention in Tasmania, were *welcomed to coun-try* by Tasmanian Aboriginal elder, Rodney Dillon.[62] Dillon spoke to them of Aboriginal history before and after white colonisation, and prophesied that fifty or more years in the future, life in Australia will be different again. He said that the future will be made by everyone in the country, old and new; and that it is up to "us" to do that together. Dillon said that it was important to tell the stories of where different people had come from, and what they had expe-rienced; that building a new future had to start on the basis of that acknowledg-ment. Acknowledging the original migrations of Aboriginal peoples fifty to sixty thousand years ago, he concluded that "we are all boat people".

Whomever we are, and from wherever we might have come, the many dilemmas of difference are just part of questions of identity and belonging to be explored next.

NOTES

1. Ghorashi, Davis, and Smets, 380.
2. Sandercock, 'Towards Cosmopolis', 3.

3. Rajaram, Nolan et al.
4. Anthias; Ghorashi, Davis, and Smets.
5. Modood, 35–36.
6. Berman and Paradies, 216.
7. Ibid., 217.
8. Ibid.
9. Ibid., 226.
10. Collins.
11. Arendt, Human Condition, 9.
12. Fell, 126.
13. Ibid., 127.
14. Ibid.
15. Blainey.
16. Pardy and Lee; Wise.
17. Wise, 919.
18. Ibid., 920–21.
19. Ibid., 922.
20. wog (n.) c.1920, 'a lower-class babu shipping clerk', Partridge; popularized in Second World War British armed forces slang for 'Arab', also 'native of India' especially as a servant or labourer, roughly equivalent to American gook; possibly shortened from golliwog: 'grotesque blackface doll', 1895, coined by English children's book author and illustrator Florence K. Upton (1873–1922), perhaps from golly + polliwog, Harper.
21. pommy (n) colloq. also pom, an Englishman, English; abbrev. of pomegranate, rhyming slang for immigrant, Delbridge et al.
22. Pardy and Lee, 307.
23. Ibid., 306.
24. Ibid., 306–7.
25. Australian Bureau of Statistics, 2011.
26. Nolan, 660.
27. Ibid.
28. Ibid., 668–69.
29. Bissell, Transit Life, 37.
30. Bhugra and Gupta, Migration, 3; Read.
31. Massumi; Stratford, 'Encountering the Circle Line' in Geographies, Mobilities, and Rhythms.
32. Taylor, Ethics of Authenticity, 50.
33. Morley.
34. Noble, 110–11.
35. Ibid., 112.
36. Ibid., 111–12.
37. Ibid., 114, emphasis added.
38. Ibid.
39. Dugan and Edelstein.
40. Levrau, 168.
41. Brown, Fisher, Piaget, Winter.
42. Levrau.

43. Berman and Paradies, 217.

44. Fell.

45. Hiruy, 79.

46. Ibid., 80.

47. Ibid., 83.

48. Perera, 142.

49. Ibid.

50. Gómez et al., 1040; Morley, 168.

51. Bhugra, Craig, and Bhui, 'Conclusions', 300.

52. Bhugra and Gupta, 'Globalisation', 64.

53. Sandercock, Cosmopolis, 21.

54. Perera, Insular Imagination, 142.

55. Bhugra and Gupta, 'Globalisation', 62.

56. Some, 172–73.

57. Lieblich, 'Looking at Change', 107.

58. Isseri et al., 45, 46.

59. Hall, Joan, 7.

60. Ibid., 17–18.

61. Tuan, 1977.

62. Rodney Dillon was the Indigenous Campaigner for Amnesty International. The account of this welcome to country is included here with Mr Dillon's permission.

Chapter 9

Identity and Belonging

> It is not a question of discovering what people are, but of diagnosing what they take themselves to be, the criteria and standards by which they judge themselves, the ways in which they interpret their problems and problematise their existence, the authorities under whose aegis such problematizations are conducted – and their consequences.[1]

Like self and place, identity and belonging are imbricated, an overlap evident in literature and in the participants' narratives. In everyday living, problems of identity and belonging exemplify primary challenges of migration: What do identity and belonging mean to different people? How does experience of identity change with relocation? What makes belonging problematic? How do people resolve these dilemmas? At stake in seeking responses to these questions is the possibility of finding ways to increase people's well-being when migrating and relocating.

Belonging is primarily about a quality and recognition of relationships of a person with other people and with places (see figure 9.1), and in the context of migration the *ability to belong* is a resource.[2] It is not easy to define belonging. Linguistically, *belonging* is a nominalisation of a *process* rather than a *thing*. It is inherently relational; it only makes sense in terms of the relationship of what belongs to what. From the perspective of philosophy, Linn Miller writes that belonging and identity are conceptually linked – "the *belonging* self and that to which it *belong[s]* has to be in relation – mutually constitutive".[3] This relationality implies that a change to one affects the other.

Definitions of belonging are obviously not universal; those taken from an English dictionary represent assumptions of meaning in a dominant Western meta-narrative and framed by capitalist economic and political relations.

Meanings of belonging from this source fall into categories of *relationship* and *right placement*, on one hand, and, on the other, of *ownership* and *possession*. These definitions manifest in divergent views that belonging is a state achieved through relationship, and that ownership of property endows belonging.[4] Further, the words *right* and *proper*, which also appear in definitions, can imply either the fitness or appropriateness of someone or something for some circumstances, or limits to belonging, associated with having *proper* social qualifications, conforming to established standards, and being entitled through having *rights*.

Etymologically, *belonging* comes from *longen* – "to go, to go along with, properly relate to, pertain to" and old English *gelang* – "dependent, belonging". In the first instance, human being is dependent on the Earth, on this *place* – Jeff Malpas' existential ground of being. Thinking along such lines, we might begin to comprehend or remember an Indigenous knowing of people belonging to places, rather than a usual Western view that places belong to people. Through appropriation and ownership, place has been fragmented, parcelled, and partitioned into territories.[5] Groups, tribes, princes, priests, dictators, and nations have endowed some people with rights to belong and excluded others from belonging. In the context of contemporary migration, some people are classed as *placeless* – and, therefore, as belonging nowhere. Some assumptions in the dominant Western meta-narrative generate beliefs and experience that belonging can only happen in particular places, or with certain people, or with *proper* rights and qualifications. Evidently, a person's experience of belonging is qualified by her or his identity – and being able to prove it.[6]

Identity is a contranym – a word with opposite sets of meanings. Used to *differentiate* one person or thing from another, it relies upon a persistent *sameness*.[7] Sameness is used in processes of identification. Differentiation is close to the common usage of *self* – to infer a particular person or thing as distinct from any other person or thing; confusingly, this often leads to *identity* and *self* being used interchangeably. Yet, as Gregory Bateson explains, no class can be "a member of itself" – that is, a self may have a number of identities, but an identity cannot have a number of selves – so identity and self actually are not interchangeable.[8] It is important to distinguish between them because they represent different logical levels, ontologically and experientially. Self is the realm of being and identity is the realm of doing – something a self performs. I discuss this distinction and its significance at the end of this chapter, but here draw attention to what happens when no distinction is made – to the consequences of conflating being with doing. When self is conflated with identity any direct challenge of identity is perceived to be a challenge to the self, that is, a person perceives that their *existence* is challenged.

Describing identity as "always incomplete . . . more readily understood as [in] process than an outcome", Michael Keith and Steve Pile see identity

Figure 9.1.   Locals and recent immigrants at a community picnic in Tasmania, 2018.

as contingent on context, and thus assert that it is open to change and to reconstruction.[9] Discussing what they describe as a "spatialized politics of identity", they draw attention to a reactionary vocabulary that, politically, is a "rhetoric of origins, of exclusion, of boundary-marking, of invasion and succession, of purity and contamination; the glossary of ethnic cleansing".[10] Although such rhetoric is used to attribute particular meaning to people's identities, "meaning is never immanent [but] *constituted* by the spaces of representation in which it is articulated".[11] Meaning itself is constructed so that terms mean different things at different times and in different places. As Steve Pile and Nigel Thrift put it, identity is a "fiction which must be continually established as a truth. Indeed, the practice of authority is revealed in the moment where identity is considered as a truth and forgets that it has been authored at all".[12]

The issue of authority is critical to understanding identity. Who is it that has the authority to determine any person's identity? In this regard, Paul Rodaway holds that "the subject is perhaps the location where human meaning emerges and is contested, and therefore [it is] a locus of power".[13] We give that power away when we determine identity in line with "Charles Horton Cooley's 'looking-glass self' theory, which clearly states that the individual

is not what he thinks about himself, nor is he what others think about him –
rather, the individual is what he thinks that the others think he is".[14] In social
theory, attempts to understand the power relationships between the individual
and the social world have usually been resolved in terms of concepts of *structure* or *agency*:

> On the side of structure, it is argued that circumstances by and large determine
> what people choose to do – from this position, it is a short step to believe that
> circumstances determine what people do and that people are unwitting dupes
> to the dominant logic of the social structure (whether this is named as capital-
> ism or patriarchy or . . .); on the side of agency, it is argued that people make
> history, though bound by certain constraints – from here, it is a short step to
> believe that people are completely free to choose what to do, without constraint
> on their actions.[15]

Pile and Thrift point out that we "should not be under any illusions that just
thinking new possibilities for practices of the body and subject will somehow
undo the regulatory and oppressive maps of meaning and power".[16] Nevertheless, as Michel Foucault observes, freedom from prevailing structures and
transformative change are possible; but first we need to question the status
quo – to develop questions that constitute "the point of problematisation
and the specific work of thought".[17] As long as we do not even think about
how or by whom our identities are determined, we externalise authority, and
remain relatively powerless to effect change. If we do not critically question,
but simply accept prevailing meta-narratives – the social determinations of
meaning – then we govern ourselves and others with those narratives even as
we may rail against them.

Kiros and Shoukat provide strong examples of agency in extreme situations.
Kiros challenged the view that the social identification of himself and his
family in Kenya *meant* that they would have to go to a refugee camp. Instead,
he saw himself as capable of providing for his family perhaps even outside of
hegemonic structures, and he found ways to do that. Kiros describes identity
as "an *interaction* between what you think you are and what others think you
are"; significantly, he assumed agency in his interactions in Kenya. Shoukat
is one of many who flee from persecution and oppression because they refuse
to accept being identified by others as deserving of such treatment. The fact
that they seek asylum demonstrates that they identify themselves as entitled
to fundamental human rights. Naming of them as *boat people* or *illegals* is
designed to identify these as people who have no rights.

Among others, Jon Austin writes that *identity* is frequently used to denote
identification, ranging from "what we produce and wear, key-in or display"
to legal documents attesting to who we are; a "surface-level labelling of each
of us as individuals".[18] Thus, identification distinguishes difference from one
individual to another, yet that is achieved by labelling what is consistent or

the same in an individual. For example, in order to confirm identity, a person needs to look like the photo in their passport, use the same signature, and have the same fingerprints. Perhaps the form of identification most fundamental to human experience is *naming*:

> Human beings across cultures and across history have named themselves, both as communities and as individuals, and have denied names – and hence "real" subjectivity – to slaves and other non-people. So an important precondition for being truly human is having a name which denotes an identity that is distinct from everyone else.[19]

It is not enough to have a name – it needs to be recognised by others. Populations are governed and controlled by mechanisms of identification that come within "Foucault's notion of the politics of calculation".[20] Without acceptable identification people seeking asylum, like Shoukat, can find themselves stripped of rights and protections. They can be locked up because they cannot prove their names or other aspects of their identities. Governments set policies to determine whether or not asylum seekers will be identified as genuine refugees or as *illegals*, and which forms of identification and qualification allow people to be accepted as migrants, or confirm them as citizens. Governments also change policies – for example to tighten borders – thus moving the goal posts in varying circumstances.

People are frequently subjected to persecution on the basis of certain identifications, such as skin colour, gender, cultural, religious, or political affiliations, even for something as simple as wearing or *not* wearing a headscarf, depending upon what customs prevail. For the homeless, lack of a fixed address – another form of identification – can deprive them of citizenship rights in some countries, such as the right to vote in elections.[21]

IDENTITY, PLACE, AND ETHNICITY

In addition to the sense of place people have through relating *to* places, often people also come to develop a sense of self and to identify themselves *with* places because of their attachment to them. Importantly, places include people's relationships with attributes and features of landscape, and of natural and built environments; *and* with a society encompassing friends, family, and other people, language, culture, customs; *and* with history, events, and personal memories. Noting that identity "evades simple definition", Edward Relph holds it as inseparable from identity with other things, particularly with place.[22] Yi-fuTuan says people feel that their roots are in one place, because they "have come to identify themselves with a particular locality, to feel that it is their home and the home of their ancestors".[23]

Malpas adds that ideas tying human identity to location have persisted through time and across cultures, and he holds that "our identities are . . . intricately and essentially place-bound".[24] Explaining that self and others can only be conceptualised in relation to place and our engagement with it, he writes that self-identity is not tied to any single location and makes clear that the idea of being place-bound does not mean bound to any particular place. Rather, sense of self might be tightly connected to a sense of place, especially through memory and narrative. In turn, Morley points out that there still is a "pervasive assumption of a natural – or originary – world in which people are (or in happier days, were) rooted in their own proper soils or territories".[25] Morley challenges the idea of homogeneity based on equating a culture with a people, and that people with a particular place, from which flow oppositional notions such as *us* and *them*. Although he considers that such assumptions strongly influence popular consciousness, Morley writes that they are contrary to the "actual [movement of peoples] in many parts of the contemporary world".[26]

Nevertheless, people often identify themselves according to their places of origin.[27] For example, Carol, who first migrated to Canada at the age of five, still identifies as Scottish first, then Canadian, and Australian. Carola identifies herself as neither German nor Australian, but both, and "maybe I will never be either. I don't think I will". However, she says her son, who was born in Australia (and has a Turkish father) "clearly is an Aussie".

Kiros realises that how he identifies himself has changed since he migrated to Australia. "In the old days, if someone said 'Who are you? Where are you from?' I would immediately say 'Ethiopian', without even thinking". More recently, he says he has a new, added identity as an African, an identity he said "you only take once you are outside your country. If I were in Ethiopia, no one would tell you I am an African". He also thinks,

> it will take a very long time for Australians, collectively, to accept that a person with a dark skin is Australian. Psychologically, it is a big mountain to climb. To change that in one decade, it doesn't happen; but recognising, knowing that, accepting that, helps. Because then you don't have to be upset when someone asks you, for the next thirty years, who you are and where you come from. You have only to answer positively, and remind them to change one attitude one per cent of the time. But if you consider that "no, I am an Australian, I have my passport, and . . ." then that is where the problem starts to come, so you can either contribute to the problem or to the solution.

Kiros says that there are times when it is important to reiterate the axiom that he is a human being, given that some people do not consider others to be so. He also feels strongly that it is problematic for refugees to be identified according to their country of origin because they may have been displaced and lived elsewhere for many years, "People want to know the origin, and then they put every assumption in that basket".

Identifying with a nationality is an issue of belonging that is not exclusively about place. The word *nation* refers to a large group of people usually associated with a particular territory, to the territory itself, and to an aggregation of people of the same ethnic family. It is important for Shoukat to be identified as Hazara, not as Afghani. He explains that this distinction matters because his country, originally called Ghargistan, was renamed by its Pashtun conquerors – *Afghan* means *Pashtun*, and *stan* means *place* – so *Afghanistan* literally means *Pashtun place*. Shoukat says "Afghani means the son of Pashtun. So it is a clear thing. My mother, my father is Hazari, my wife is Hazari. I am Hazara, so say me Hazara, because when you say Afghan you discriminate me". Although he values highly his Australian citizenship, it is important to him to identify himself as Hazara as an assertion of the continuity of existence of that ethnic group, despite the loss of homeland and sovereignty concomitant with repression and ethnic cleansing of Hazara in Afghanistan. It is also a way of maintaining his sense of connection with family still in Pakistan.

Khadga is another whose ethnicity is being erased from his country of origin by ethnic cleansing. A major difference between Shoukat and he is that Khadga came to Australia as part of a formal refugee intake, and was quickly and securely resettled in Australia with his family. With citizenship available to him for the first time in his life, he proudly emphasises that he is Australian. At the same time, he maintains his Nepali-Bhutanese culture at home and is active in strongly building the Nepali-Bhutanese community in Hobart.

The wider salience of deep attachment of identity with place, and loss of identity with loss of place is poignantly illustrated by the plight of Tuvaluans whose home is on islands in the Pacific that are fast being submerged by rising sea levels:

> It can be argued that culture is the only "possession" Tuvaluans have, for it is their language, traditional knowledge and rituals that keep Tuvaluans bonded together and recognised by other nations . . . we cannot create another Tuvalu in Australia . . . when we say that the impact of sea level rise in Tuvalu is diminishing of this race it does not mean that Tuvaluans won't exist. No, it's the identity, the unique identity as a people among peoples in the world.[28]

In coming decades, with projected "floods" of migrants pushed by climate change and other forms of environmental challenge, further study of the Tuvaluans and others who may be forced to migrate will raise questions about upon what identity is, or can be based, beyond identification with place and national sovereignty. Hopefully, those studies may further explore what might assist such migrants to settle in new places.

Limiting one's identity to strong attachment to any particular place can be problematic when, for whatever reason, people move from those places to live elsewhere. Sometimes migrants identify themselves with places of origin they keep alive in memory, only to find, when later returning to visit, that those places have changed.[29] For many people, and for various reasons, there is no place to which they can return.

DIVERSE PRACTICES AND PERCEPTIONS
OF PERSONHOOD

An influx of migrants from distinctively different cultures and places can be an immense challenge for people already resident in a place, inevitably affecting the identities of both groups, and changing society and place. From the perspective of an immigrant, one of the first things needed in the process of resettlement is to discover and find out how to adjust to whatever is different in practice from that which prevailed in their place of origin. This adjustment relates to everyday practices of living – from accessing food and other resources to knowing how the transport system works or how to post a letter – all the minutiae of moving from the known to the unfamiliar. Finding their feet in a new land, immigrants' attention is likely to focus first on those practical, obvious differences.

At a more subliminal level, the new arrival encounters environments arising from the host society's particular ways of conceiving and enacting personhood. Roger Rouse writes that he is troubled by "the widespread tendency to assume that identity and identity formation are universal aspects of human experience".[30] In modern Western cultures individualism is intentionally encouraged. If immigrants are from a similar cultural milieu then, to that extent at least, they are on relatively familiar ground. If, however, an immigrant is from a communal culture – for instance based on extended family, clan, and hierarchical structures – exposure to social mores and practices based on individualism can be profoundly disturbing. In a study of Mexican migrants in the United States, Rouse emphasises their moral reservations about American individualism, and their critique of the economic and social structure:

> Men and women frequently [spoke about] difficulties they encountered in their attempts to act as good parents, given both the greater freedom and autonomy available to children and the tendency of state agencies to intervene in family problems without proper reference to the mediating authority of family heads; men often expressed anxieties about their ability to act as good husbands under conditions in which their low-paying jobs made it difficult to support the other members of the family and to keep their wives and daughters in the home; and

women often underlined the problems that they faced as mothers given the frequent need to take on work outside the home.[31]

In this vein, Peter Nynäs writes that people feel deprived of their sense of responsibility, and experience "a deteriorating sense of being a moral subject" when the rules they are used to no longer apply.[32] In turn, Arnon Edelstein refers to the transition from extended to nuclear families, and the dispersal of families to numerous locations away from traditional forms of support from relatives and elders, shifts that affect everyone concerned.[33] In a study of Ethiopian migrants in Israel, he notes that Ethiopian women generally appear to acculturate more easily than their male counterparts, and often secure employment while men remain unemployed. Edelstein names this gender inequity as a cause of severe stress for people from a patriarchal society. He recognises that such change in function and status of husband and wife threatens the man's self-perception and public image: "an Ethiopian man fears the loss of status not only within his own nuclear family, but also among other Ethiopian men, who may treat him with disrespect, although they suffer from the same problem".[34] Edelstein attributes the disproportionate murder of Ethiopian women by their husbands, in Israel, in large part to such acculturation distress.

When considering communal ways of conceiving personhood, distinction also needs to be made between *communal* and *collective* orientations. As Rouse explains, "Collectivities are aggregates of atomized and autonomous elements, either individuals or subgroups, that are fundamentally equivalent by virtue of the common possession of a given social property" and they are "categorical and abstract".[35] Thus, for example, Ethiopians possess the "social property" of their common ethnicity, which makes them – in these terms – a collective. Therefore, they are treated collectively, and categorised – not least by being stereotyped – yet expected to function from individualistic notions of self, rather than communal responses. This discussion perhaps goes some way to explain why migrants often want to form and belong to communities of people who share their cultural origins; it is not just the comfort of familiarity that is at stake, but access to particular moral conditions or milieux. In this regard, Amia Lieblich considers that "one cannot shift one's sense of belonging without [also changing] values, norms, behaviours and choices" – a significant change to regimes of practice, which may generate a form of *hybrid* identity.[36]

EMERGING AND *HYBRID* CULTURES

A term originally applied to the offspring of two animals or plants of different breeds, varieties, species, or genera, *hybrid* refers also to *crossbreeding* in other domains, for instance, of unlike cultures or traditions, and has come into popular usage through scientific innovations, such as hybrid seeds and animals, and cultural innovations, such as fusion music.[37] It is used to encourage cross-disciplinary research, embracing, for example, the perspectives of both physical and human geographies. Hybridity challenges boundaries, seeks to create connections and to integrate "elements thought to be incompatible or conflicting", and brings about "something ontologically new".[38]

In the complex process of resettlement, individuals internalise more than one culture. Pile and Thrift write that this process is evident among people who will not be able to return to their places of origin, and will need to "refashion themselves [by] drawing on more than one cultural repertoire".[39] Individuals who blend cultures in such ways "can have more than one cultural meaning system [and] can move between their two cultural orientations quite fluidly".[40] Peter Adey writes of multiple identities, others describe such individuals as hybrid, sometimes maintaining old identities and developing hybridity rather than fitting assimilationist assumptions.[41]

Participants in this study demonstrate their capacity to move between cultures, but each narrative shows the nuance inside the generalisations. Nene says she is comfortable because she still has her own culture and another she has adopted, but feels that she is "juggling two different things I have to put together to make it work". Although she feels at home in Australia, she says that a Sudanese saying is that "home is always home, no matter what happens" and she has been told that "where you come from, you cannot forget it". Nene says she would like to visit Sudan and feel that sense of home, "but at the moment I can't because I haven't known anything about it. I was only three months old moving away".

Connie's strongest identification of herself is as a mother, and she feels that, because her children have both Japanese and American ancestry, she has a more international sense of herself. There is an interesting tension, however, in the way Connie identifies herself. Born in the United States and holding both American citizenship and passport, she says:

> I am American . . . I have to be something, everyone is something, and I am American, but *I* am not defined – I do not define myself by that. I can't say I'm pro-America – it just doesn't sort of fit. I feel like I had a long relationship with America and they did me wrong, so I broke up with them. I feel grateful that I can live there if I have to, but I'm thankful that I don't have to, that I have another option, so we are lucky that way.

Julian from England, his wife Kay from Australia, and their son Chris from India see themselves as an international family. Julian sees himself as a global citizen, and his spiritual search as a theme. He identifies himself as a seeker, based on a feeling he says he has had for years "that this time in history is a real time of interaction between east and west, and there is so much we are learning from each other". Yukari recognises that in terms of visibility people see her as Japanese, but she identifies herself in terms of a process of "exploring the context of self" rather than nationality or culture:

> I identify myself as somebody who loves to keep exploring, mainly by going past the boundaries and coming back to the original place, and find the bridge; and entertained by the differences, and being creative . . . the freedom of expansion is coming only from the idea that you are expanding from your original place.

Although Kiros and his family are active in the Ethiopian community, they live in an area representative of the more general population, and have a lifestyle in their home that is not culturally traditional. Kiros says that how he identifies is complex – that in practical ways, his identity changes because in different places he operates in different ways. At the same time, he says his central values do not change. He feels his values shape his identity, and give him a strength and certainty of self that stays fairly constant no matter where he is: "It's like a lighthouse; you don't change a lighthouse, the ship or the boat will have to change its direction looking into the lighthouse". He identifies as a human being with Christian values, and sees "spirit as broader than religion". Like Yukari, he concludes that "as human beings we have a lot more in common than the differences".

For these participants, hybridity is of culture and identity, but not of person. Applied in terms of personhood, hybrid means of mixed race and can attract racism. Racially a mix of Indonesian and Swiss, author Jessica Zibung grew up in New Zealand and experienced what she calls the "hypocrisy of hybridity":

> If we accept that race is a social construct, one that reveals more about history, economics and politics than biology, then we get closer to understanding the discomfort that racial hybridity produces. People like me are caught in between the guarded boundaries of static racial identities; our presence threatens not just essentialised identity categories, but also foundational narratives on which whole social, cultural and political histories are based.[42]

Zibung writes that *hybrid* assumes a distortion of purity – a mongrel offspring of the domesticated and the savage – neither purely one race nor another. She considers that as an outcome of colonialism, "Being mixed-race is only problematic when the combination involves a white/Western race and an 'inferior' not-white/not-Western race", but she knows, too, that the hybrid may be excluded by both racial groups.[43] Jun and Connie's two sons are hybrid – half Japanese and half American – and thus "permission-seeking rather than entitled" in both countries.[44] Japan was long closed to foreigners and, traditionally, white Western people were classed as inferior. During the Second World War, the United States imprisoned Japanese Americans, and after the war, during military occupation of Japan, the United States imposed significant changes at all levels of Japanese society. Clearly, many factors influence the way outsiders and people of mixed race are treated.

Growing up in White Australia in the 1950s and 1960s, I remember comments that Eurasians – children of European and Asian descent – were unusually beautiful, but exotic – the inference being that they were foreign, mysterious, and *too* strange. Although developing a suntan at the beginning of summer was considered to be a fashionable imperative, if anyone looked as if they were *naturally* dark rather than fair-skinned, someone might remark: "a bit of the tar-brush, there" or "a touch of the boong". Such appallingly racist attitude is an example of *truths* constructed in colonialist regimes, and it illustrates the strength and pervasiveness of such memes in external memory.

CREATING BELONGING IN A NEW PLACE

Learning languages, adjusting to cultures, and putting down new roots are among the ways immigrants settle effectively and with well-being in a new place. Relph describes rootedness as "a secure point from which to look out on the world, a firm grasp of one's own position in the order of things"[45] – a desired state for newcomers. From academic literature to personal accounts of experiences of migration and settlement in participants' narratives, there is evidence that when people relocate they want to be accepted and valued, and to contribute – to belong. If people are not accepted, if they feel their communities are "targeted because of their marginal identity and status", Michael Buzzelli writes that this sets up social justice challenges that result in a particular kind of sense of place, "one that is defined by territorial defence aimed at power and control over the quality of local environments".[46]

Relph sees having roots in a place as involving "responsibility and respect for that place both for itself and for what it is to yourself and to others".[47] Implicit is recognition of belonging as dependence on place, and of *mutuality* – taking care of place as well as benefitting from it. Ideally, that mutuality applies to all that place includes, and opens up interdependence. It is not a goal to be reached, but a process of active and on-going engagement. Thus, for people settling in new places a key to belonging can be – actively and intentionally – to establish mutuality with the place, and with the people in it. Khadga, for instance, works hard to ensure belonging for his family and community. His new roots are growing as he builds a network of relationships, does paid and voluntary work, and engages socially. His two children were born in Australia and by four years of age, the older boy was already rapidly learning to speak English, and coaching his parents in that language. Khadga's roots are also deepening literally: the garden he and his father have established in the backyard of the house he is buying has a few small trees, and vegetables are thriving.

Kiros feels that social connection is most important when it comes to settling in a new place. Rather than meeting people in a context of ethnicity, or nationality, he sees "a need to draw from a wider frame of reference" and to seek out people with common values, such as spiritual connections (including, but not necessarily religious), or concern for and care of the environment. He knows that many immigrants feel most comfortable settling and building community with others from their place of origin, but he thinks that "if people resort only to their culture, then they will be left isolated". Kiros considers that "actions of place making are expressions of both willingness and determination to belong to the host community". To that end, within a few days of arriving with his family in Tasmania, Kiros asked people to take him and his family to a church. There they met people who befriended them, and helped them to settle:

> If you draw your identity from a broader frame of reference, you are more likely to have more connections and it is easier – you are more likely to settle better, to communicate better, and also to feel better for yourself. When I went to the Netherlands it was exactly like that. And it is the same here. The more resilient ones will be those who draw from the broader identity, not from the narrow one.

Commonly, participants recognise the importance of interaction, communication, and sharing themselves in the process of entering new relationships. Each of them speaks of *making place* – in countless ways creating something new out of what they find, and what they bring with them, making home for themselves in new places. Connie, aware that relationships with people make a place easy or difficult for her to be in, has a clear strategy:

> I meet people and I *position* myself for someone to *rely* on me for something, and I come through, and that person can trust me now, I'm in! And when that happens with several people – neighbours or other parents at school – that's a bridge to me, I'm part of the community now, and that's important to me.

Shoukat relates belonging most strongly to direct and extended family. Until he achieved citizenship, there was no possibility for him to bring his family to Australia. Granted permanent resident status – which allowed him to visit his family, and return – he made one trip, but such journeys are expensive, and he was earning little. So, effectively, Shoukat was in limbo – "split between two places" – holding onto hope for a future policy change. Nevertheless, he continued to do paid and voluntary work, to study, and to involve himself in community as best he could, but was unable to settle. When citizenship finally allowed him family reunion, he moved away from the place where he had felt so alone and now is building home with his family in an Australian city where an Hazara community was already settled.

Jon Austin considers that home and place have both "a physical and a conceptual or imaginary dimension . . . an intersection of where we have come from and where we are", and bringing together a person's history and present in a place "embodies, figuratively and actually, our sense of belonging and identity".[48] That concept fits Connie's experience of making her own "nest", and using familiar, meaningful things to remind herself of who she is in a new country:

> No one would know who I was when I was ten years old! Nobody knows me, and I feel I want to be known, so my stuff, stuff that's not worth anything to anyone else, I bring it with me . . . a wooden spoon . . . I've seen it always, it was in my grandma's kitchen. It was always there, now it's here, and it will be there in Japan.

The "imaginary dimension" of place is especially significant to Carol, who intentionally uses her creativity to feel at home, to add colour and beauty to transform a place she finds ugly, and to enrich wherever she is through imaginatively bringing in characteristics and aesthetics of other places and times. Carol says she learned this tactic as a child:

> We never were just in the place we were in physically. When I was a little girl, everything was imagined. The ability to imagine something else is lifesaving. So when Dad would take us for a walk, he'd say, "okay, let's pretend we're going on a big adventure, and we're this or that". And off we'd go. So anywhere I go, I do that.

Carol is clear that it is not about using imagination or fantasy to separate herself from where she is, but to transform her relationship with places:

> I always decorate – I've done that in all the places we've lived in. You know people say, "oh we're living in it, but we're just renting this place, so we're not going to change it". I have to change the entire thing; I paint it, I make new curtains, I rearrange the furniture. I've got to do things like that, I've got to plant things in the ground, make it feel like my place, arrange my things around – that's very, very important to me.

Carol says she uses "individual objects and moments of connection with them as *touchstones*", fusing the values those touchstones represent into her present time and place. In that way the Scottish Highlands become part of where Carol now lives in the Blue Mountains, imitated by weather and seasons, mists and colours. She has a sense of belonging, walking home from the station:

> I feel like I've walked into a heartbeat . . . I can see the cliffs in the distance and it's wonderful, and I walk along and hear only my footsteps. And I feel like *Carol,* like gooseberries, because the colour of the trees can be like gooseberry green, the sky slightly mauvish, and it's the quietness . . . I walk down, turn the corner, and it's not the zim, zim, zim of the city. I just go around that corner and up, and there's my house across the road, and there's a smallness to it, a containedness to it, a quietness to it, a slowing down of time.

In this vein, Malpas writes that the fusion of past and present in place reflects the "connection between the formation of self-identity and the grasp of place", and that "as we grow older . . . past places and things associated with the past, become more important: Our grasp of the identity of ourselves and others, is always situated within and articulated with respect to particular places and with reference to specific objects and surroundings . . . memory, and identity, are tied to spatiality, to embodiment and worldly location".[49]

THE PRODUCTION OF IDENTITY

People tend to identify themselves on the basis of what endures, persists, remains more or less the same – and often they treat that identification, that description of themselves, *as if* that is who or what they really are. People tend to use the words *identity* and *self,* about themselves and others, interchangeably. As challenges of resettlement emphasise, failure to distinguish between them in practice creates problems. These conflations weaken sense of self and lessen openness to others and to place.

Imagine what it would be like to wake up in the morning and look at yourself in the mirror, and see an unfamiliar face. Most likely, it would be disorienting; probably, it would not be easy to reconcile that strange external image with the knowing of self on the inside. It might seem obvious that continuity and stability of identity is critical for maintaining a healthy sense of self, and for effective interaction and relationship with others and the world. In a study of commitment to identity, Koen Luyckx et al. state that "a well-developed and integrated identity provides a subjective sense of inner unity and continuity over time, providing adolescents and emerging adults with a sense of well-being and self-esteem".[50] However, *reification* of identity can lead to many problems. If people feel their identity is threatened by change they tend to try to keep it as consistently the same as possible, which can result in parochial, reactionary, bigoted, and racist behaviours and, at an extreme, in violence or other forms of breakdown.[51]

Identity forms throughout childhood, adolescence, and adulthood; it is a mutable *map* – a summary, and representation, made over many years of *this is me* – *this is who (or what) I am*. Many things influence that summary, particularly the relationships we have with parents and significant others, cultural, ethnic, economic, and social factors, and the environment. The maps we make – of ourselves, of others, and of our worlds – are not the territory; rather, they are *representations* of experience.[52]

Holding to notions of identity as being consistent over time, our maps of self, others and the world are likely to move further and further away from the territory. Consider what it would be like to negotiate your way around a large, modern city, today, with a map of that place from the 1950s. When we are relatively unconscious of the maps we have made from early childhood of ourselves, others, and our worlds, and we continue to hold them without questioning or updating them, it can be difficult to negotiate present-day living – an experience recognisable in some elderly people. This disjunction or disconnection between the map and the territory might not be much of a problem for anyone spending a whole lifetime in a single place where there is very little change, an increasingly rare scenario. When people function from identification of themselves as if the map *is* the territory, they associate with that identification, and over time and with change there is likely to be significant dissociation from self, and thus a weakened sense of self, resulting in at least some degree of dissatisfaction and lessened well-being.[53] Such weakening of sense of self can result from the changes people experience when they migrate and relocate in new places, especially if their self-understanding has been based on living in one place and one culture. It can also apply to people living in an existing community when newcomers move into that place, or when there is significant change to their environment.

People are identified and identify themselves according to various criteria at different times: for example, as individuals, married, single; belonging to a particular family, group, culture, ethnicity, gender, religion; having particular purpose, direction or affiliation; holding certain beliefs, being an optimist or a pessimist, courageous or fearful, self-determining or a victim, capable or inadequate; wealthy or poor; and according to behaviour, roles, and possessions. Identity in such terms obviously serves a useful function in our interactions with others, but it could perhaps best be recognised as what we are doing, rather than being taken as defining who we are. If identifications in different contexts are understood as *expressions* of self, the person's sense of self is central and likely to be strong. A far weaker sense of self is the result when a person conflates who they are with those expressions.

These dynamics of strengthening or weakening sense of self apply when people label others. For instance, participants' narratives exemplify what can happen when people are identified as irregular migrants, asylum seekers, or "illegals". Kiros and Shoukat both spoke of "becoming nothing". Shoukat's report of being known and treated as a number in detention centres is a small indication of the dehumanising process – the denial of a person's existence – implicit in the way people are often identified through immigration policies and practices. Racist epithets and other negative judgements of people can reify identity of the *Other* according to stereotypes, and as less than human. When people function from such identification – as if their ideas or maps of other people represent them accurately – there is likely to be significant dissociation from those others, and there is minimal possibility of rapport, empathy, or actually getting to know another person.

By adulthood it is common for people to conclude that they are as they have experienced themselves to be, and that their ideas about other people are probably right, until and unless they question upon what presuppositions, and what practices they have based identification of themselves and others. Such questioning might occur through an intentional reflexive process, whether informally – for example as described by some of the participants – or more formally, in a structured transformative learning situation such as counselling, coaching, seminars, and workshops. Perhaps most commonly, such questioning is likely to be stimulated by experience of major change, especially when the conditions of people's everyday lives are problematised. The ability to integrate new information and to adjust self-identification has been linked to having an integrated sense of self.[54] That is, if people have an integrated sense of self, they are able to incorporate and respond to new information and new situations and to adjust their identification of themselves. But who, or what *has* that *sense* of self, and those abilities, and those adjusted identities? Presumably, it is the *self*, whatever that might be.

It is not easy to articulate the distinction between identity and self that I am seeking to make here, especially because the idea of self eludes definition. Identity is derived from the Latin *idem* – same, precisely *that*; it combines the Latin *id* – it, and entity from the Latin *esse* – to be, essence, and *entitat* – yields, so it could be said to mean "to be, or yield *it*". If the self is considered to be a process of *being,* then identity might be understood as the expression, or product of that process at any moment, the *it* that is yielded in any circumstance. This is to assert that the self is always a work in progress, not a fixed thing or final achievement.[55] My concern here is to consider: what difference does distinguishing between self and identity make to a person's sense of self? If a person conflates identity with self, they do not actually have a sense of *self,* but only a sense of the limited idea of self that is what they have identified themselves to be. Necessarily, identity is less than the whole, which is inclusive of both identity – the product – and self, the *process* by which it is produced. Earlier, I showed that the conflation of being and doing was an example of Weston's *self-validating reduction*. Thus, conflation of self and identity is a self-validating reduction. Both conflation of being and doing and conflation of self and identity problematise understanding of what the self *is*, and reduce sense of self to sense of identity – in other words, to the map rather than the territory. If a person distinguishes between identity and self, then their sense of self is centred in their ability to learn and change and grow, and to express and identify themselves variously.

The participants' narratives support the idea that when sense of self includes distinction between identity and self, there are several important outcomes: First, people experience greater resilience, agency, and well-being than they do if their sense of self is limited to identity. Second, their sense of place is also affected because they are more open and responsive with a more active sense of self than with a fixed idea of themselves. Third, an integrated sense of self makes a significant difference to the quality of their experiences of migration and settlement in new places, and to their handling of these transitions – because they are more able to take in new information, to adapt, and to adjust. So what might best support people in developing these sensibilities?

NOTES

1. Rose, 96.
2. See also Stratford, 'Belonging as a Resource'.
3. Miller, 250.
4. Rouse, 357.
5. Elden, 'Government, Calculation, Territory', 578.
6. Stratford, 'Belonging'.
7. Relph, Placelessness, 45.
8. Bateson, *Ecology of Mind*, 189.
9. Keith and Pile, 28–30.
10. Ibid., 20.
11. Ibid., 23.
12. Pile and Thrift, 'Mapping the Subject', 49.
13. Rodaway, 241.
14. Edelstein, 146.
15. Pile and Thrift, 'Introduction', 2–3.
16. Ibid., 50.
17. Rabinow and Foucault, 24.
18. Austin, 7.
19. Danaher et al., 127.
20. Elden, 'Government', 578.

21. Morley, 26, 28, 33.
22. Relph, Placelessness, 45.
23. Tuan, 194.
24. Malpas, Place, 177.
25. Morley, 39.
26. Ibid.
27. Morley, Read, Slavkova, Tuan, Wendorf, 2009.
28. Farbotko, 'Representing Climate Change', 89, 241–2. See also Farbotko, Stratford, and Lazrus.
29. Read, 1996.
30. Rouse, 352.
31. Ibid., 371–72.
32. Nynäs, 169.
33. Edelstein.
34. Ibid., 141.
35. Rouse, 358.
36. Lieblich, 121.
37. *Dictionary of Human Geography*, 5th edition.
38. Rose, in Sui and DeLyser, 113.
39. Pile and Thrift, 10.
40. Miramontez, Benet-Martinez, and Nguyen, 431.
41. Adey, 25; Carruthers, Kymlicka, Morley, Pile and Thrift, Urry.
42. Zibung, 42.
43. Ibid., 41–43.
44. Ibid., 42.
45. Relph, Placelessness, 38.
46. Buzzelli, 172.
47. Relph, Placelessness, 38.
48. Austin, 111.
49. Malpas, Place, 183, 84.
50. Luyckx et al., 52.
51. Massey, 'Global Sense'.
52. Korzybski, 58.
53. Dugan.
54. Luyckx et al., 53.
55. Taylor, Sources.

Part IV

MOVING FORWARD

Having shown throughout the book that sense of self and sense of place deeply implicate the quality of people's experiences, and their assumption of agency, in this final part I consider what might usefully be passed on from such insights to mitigate suffering and increase well-being in future. In "Vital Sensibilities" I delve deeper to delineate how we weaken or strengthen senses of self and place and suggest how we might develop those sensibilities. Using fresh examples from the participants' lived experiences of developing their senses of self and place, I draw again on Foucault and others in the search for freedom from the constraints of unquestioned conditions of truth. Asking *What Legacy Will We Leave* for future generations, I return to the deep moral questions and issues of human rights raised in the introduction. Reflecting upon the growing intensity of extreme climate events compounding with social disruptions, I see escalating numbers of people migrating as a major symptom of world disorder, global economic inequalities, political polarisations, and social fragmentation. In such circumstances, I ask again: what might be possible if we were to conceive differently of the nature of human being?

And I propose that it is time for us to question, to think, and to make space for bringing substance to future imaginaries that might provide opportunity for people and place to flourish.

Chapter 10

Vital Sensibilities

> Our disregard for the earth is inseparable from our disdain for each other
> and ourselves. We treat the earth with deprecation in a parallel reflection
> of the exploitation and violence we do unto each other. The two are inter-
> twined and it is impossible to undo the knots of one without undoing the
> tangles of the other.[1]

Sense of self and sense of place deeply implicate the quality of people's
experience, and their assumption of agency. The participants' narratives demonstrate that when their senses of self or of place were weak they experienced
greater difficulty, and exhibited less agency, irrespective of the conditions
they were in. Conversely, as their senses of self and of place strengthened,
they experienced increased agency and well-being. If people know how to
strengthen these senses, they can be more in charge of their own well-being.
The question, then, is *how can people intentionally strengthen their senses of
self and place?* In order to respond to that question, a first step is to consider
what might hold people back even from recognising the value or possibility
of doing that.

What people most limit themselves with is *unquestioning acceptance*
of whatever meta-narrative they have embodied and demonstrate in their
regimes of practices. Sometimes people question the status quo, but may
not recognise, or may be reluctant to acknowledge that their acceptance of
a meta-narrative underlies their experience. When a meta-narrative's underlying assumptions, beliefs, conditions of truth, and practices are taken for
granted, it becomes a self-fulfilling and reductive prophecy.

If people believe that being human is intrinsically wholesome, then they
are likely to value themselves and their capability, and thus to develop strong

senses of self. If people have an entrenched self-understanding of human nature as flawed, then they are likely to disengage from and try to control whatever they assume is wrong with themselves, and thus to weaken their senses of self. Dissociation from what is assumed to be flawed focuses attention on developing only what is valued, and sense of self comes to be limited to and conflated with identity. If safety, even survival, comes to be associated with identity being recognised, accepted, defended, and justified, a person's identity can become reified and sense of self weakens.

Deliberate cultivation of individualism and competition promotes extreme disengagement and alienation of people from themselves, others, and place. This modern, neoliberal project is a version of control fitting Joseph Campbell's description of the characteristics of a priesthood – that is, it begins by declaring that something is wrong with people and then stipulates rules for acceptable behaviour; people are held responsible for their behaviour, and acceptable behaviour supports agenda of those who set the rules.[2] Campbell's distinctions in comparative mythology infer that the assumption of a flawed human nature is not limited to the Western meta-narrative, but underlies meta-narratives more widely, particularly those based on religious and other fundamentalisms. It is important to broaden this discussion beyond solely Western views, because migration confronts people with others from many and disparate origins, and because problems arising from migration affect the whole of humanity, not just part. If people meet different others in contexts that assume that something is fundamentally wrong with being human, then whatever is different about those others or in their behaviour is likely to be seen as evidence of their wrongness, and is to be feared. This self-validating reduction then determines the way people are seen, recognised, judged, acknowledged, and treated by others, which further affects – and can reduce – their senses of self and place. On either side of such confrontation, the integrity of the self and one's very existence is challenged. In such circumstances, some people defend, attack, try to control, explain, or justify – and some simply suffer.

What people do and think affects their beliefs, and what people believe affects what they think and do; and both thinking and acting are required for change to be sustainable. People involved in migration are faced with varied conditions that demand changes in their thinking and behaviour. If people adjust to meet those demands at a relatively surface level – that is, without questioning the fundamental assumptions of the meta-narratives that constitute their conditions of truth, and still holding their senses of self and place as identified, defined, and relatively fixed – then they are likely to find the transitions stressful. Questioning and change in both belief and practice are needed at a deeper level to engender well-being.

STRENGTHENING SENSE OF SELF

If people take the perspective that who or what they each are *is* the self, they can begin to explore their selections of and commitments to identity. Koen Luyckx and his colleagues describe the process of developing identity as an exploration of alternatives, and then a commitment to the identifications selected.[3] Their argument implies that the self is the developer, the explorer, and the one making such commitment – in other words, supporting the concept that the self is the *process* of human capability, and identity and behaviour are products and expressions of that process.

Works by Michel Foucault, Nikolas Rose, and Mitchell Dean provide ways to think about and understand distinctions between self and identity, and to appreciate how the two have been conflated. Foucault initiates and Dean and Rose further develop work encompassing relationships and conditions of truth and power; and how individuals, cultures, and authorities are connected and organised in modern society. These authors hold that the self is able to transform the regimes of practices by which the self governs itself. As Dean writes, we "govern others and ourselves according to various truths about our existence and nature as human beings".[4] Transformation is possible by analysing the practices we have used to govern ourselves, becoming aware of what is implicit – the underlying beliefs and assumptions – in those practices, and then responsibly *conducting our own conduct* differently. The point at which people realise that they have that capability – to transform how they behave, think, and identify themselves – is the moment when they recognise the distinction between self and identity. This distinction brings into being what Foucault describes as "the possibility of no longer being, doing, or thinking what we are, do, or think [and gives] new impetus . . . to the undefined work of freedom".[5] Thus, people are able to be flexible in their practices and production of identity, and they strengthen their senses of self.

To reiterate, individuals internalise the meta-narratives of their cultures, and of other regimes of power, and govern themselves in alignment with them. Freedom, according to Foucault and others, comes with questioning and explicitly recognising the sources of the beliefs and assumptions underlying those accepted truths. How far that questioning goes is critically important when it comes to considering the potential for change in human behaviour and experience. For any truly significant change to occur, the fundamental assumption that human being is flawed must be challenged.

Logically, if the self is flawed – *inadequate* for its purpose – then it is impossible for it to fulfil that purpose and no amount of blame, or punishment, or encouragement can transform it into what it is not. It follows that if human being *is* flawed then there is nothing much that can be done about human behaviour other than attempt to control ourselves and others. Foucault and others building on his work emphasise that the purpose of governing the self is not to liberate some better, original, or essential self; nor to transcend the self to become some better other. Rather, it is about knowing one's capability, and being responsible for doing what it takes to express that ethically, beautifully. To recognise the distinction between self and identity strengthens sense of self. However, to still hold the self as flawed is reductive and limits and weakens sense of self. By valuing the self as the process of being, and evaluating identity as the product of that process – the self's manifestation in many forms and expressions – people have the potential to improve their own actions, behaviours, and the quality of their experiences. Conduct of conduct, based on valuing oneself, might include doing what one knows to do, evaluating the results, discovering what conditions are needed for increased satisfaction or excellence, and finding ways to generate those conditions.

While belief in flawed human being goes unquestioned, it is relatively easy to ascribe inequitable conditions to assumed inadequacies in people, and only a step from there to have people seek to improve themselves rather than to challenge the conditions, especially if the alternative is to be marginalised. Such "games of truth" are reflected in what appears to be response from various technologies of governance, in part to foster consumerism, and of which Rose writes "we have been bound into relationship with new authorities, which are more profoundly subjectifying because they appear to emanate from our individual desires to fulfil ourselves in our everyday lives, to craft our personalities, to discover who we really are".[6]

Barbara Cruikshank writes that projects to build self-esteem and self-empowerment have been deliberately designed to shape the desires of, and secure the voluntary compliance of citizens through technologies of citizenship, in the United States and elsewhere.[7] To exemplify, she cites the California Task Force to Promote Self-Esteem and Personal and Social Responsibility, which was established in 1983 "to solve social problems – from crime and poverty to gender inequality – by waging a social revolution not against capitalism, racism, and inequality, but against the order of the self and the way we govern our selves".[8] Significantly, Cruikshank writes that assessment by social scientists failed to identify a lack of self-esteem as the cause of social problems, yet the program went ahead, in essence assigning responsibility for social problems to individuals.[9]

In the modern world there is a smorgasbord of *self-help* books, workshops, websites, and blogs offering ways to *improve, develop*, and *empower* the self in order to enhance the quality of the human condition, and relationship with place. Undoubtedly there is benefit in many of these, but they are of limited efficacy depending upon what is understood as *self.* Any self-esteem programme that does not recognise or question the underlying assumptions of self – and that does not distinguish between self, identity and behaviour – can deal only with management of experience and behaviour, and thus precludes transformative change.

Within a context of belief that human being is flawed, esteem of self is based on assessing as positive or negative aspects of personality, character, behaviour, achievements, and possessions. For instance, as Brené Brown puts it, we "*think* self-esteem.[10] Our self-esteem is based on how we see ourselves – our strengths and limitations – over time". Brown regards self-esteem as cognitive, not emotional, and of far less importance than shame, which she defines as "*the intensely painful feeling or experience of believing we are flawed and therefore unworthy of acceptance and belonging*".[11] But what people think of themselves generates much of what they feel, including shame. If people judge that there are more negatives than positives, they are likely to experience negative emotions, and even though the converse is also true, within a context of belief that human being is flawed, some part of the self must always be *wrong*. From Brown's research in the United States, she considers that disconnection from self and others is common, and primarily caused by shame.[12] In response, her programs teach "shame resilience". Brown writes that participants acknowledge great benefits from her programmes, but say they have to work to maintain them. How much greater might results be, if, instead of learning to be resilient *about* being ashamed, people learned to value rather than shame themselves, and to be healthy?

In this regard, Stuart Hill builds on a model that each of us has "an essential or core self [and] a range of adaptive, distressed, patterned selves (or expressions of self) that are what we have had to become at various times to survive".[13] Hill and Werner Sattman-Frese propose what they call holistic education, various therapies, and body–mind practices to clear adaptive patterns, support awareness of deeper connections, and promote autonomy, mutuality, and conscious caring.[14] Implicit in their understanding is a view of an essential, core self that is expected – when freed from adaptive, reactive selves – to behave wholesomely. In decades of praxis, I have probably seen some thousands of examples of positive results from work with people that could be taken as illustration and evidence of the premises summarised above. *However, such perspectives still do not come to grips with a clear conceptualisation of human being.*

To assume either that human being is flawed or that at some essential core human being is good still defines human being in terms of relative worth. If I follow Foucault's and others' notion that the purpose of governing the self is not to liberate some essential self, I recognise that – intrinsically – the self is neither flawed nor good and is, rather, a *process* that is capable of producing identity and behaviour that can be evaluated as *good* or *bad*. An understanding of the ambiguity (in the English language) of the word *value* can point to the problem I am teasing out here. *Value* refers both to the intrinsic meaning of something and to its relative worth. Intrinsically, something is what it is, and its relative worth is assessed in relation to desired or preferred outcomes. Thus, when self is conflated with identity and behaviour, if the identity and behaviour is evaluated as bad, this goes to prove that the self is flawed; conversely, positively evaluated identity and behaviour is taken as evidence that the self is good.

Earlier, I claimed that if people believe that being human is intrinsically wholesome, then they are likely to value themselves and their capability, and thus to develop strong senses of self. It might seem like splitting hairs, but that does not contradict what I have said above; the self is neither flawed nor good but, as people constitute themselves according to their beliefs, the difference in the consequences of selecting either belief is significant. What concerns me here is to distinguish between what might be described as a generic *goodness* and the infinite possibilities of meanings of *goodness*. Charles Taylor writes of "strong evaluations [and] moral intuitions which are uncommonly deep, powerful, and universal" and links these with human values such as dignity, well-being, integrity, what makes life worth living, and the flourishing of self and others.[15] He states that the self's "orientation to the good is not some optional extra, something we can engage in or abstain from at will, but a condition of our being selves with an identity".[16] Taylor is writing about what I posit as *fundamental good intent*. It is what I perceive to be a drive inherent in human being that moves towards fulfilment of values such as well-being and flourishing of self and others. As Taylor has it, concern with these values is not optional, nor restricted to one culture or another, but universal. What problematises this drive or concern is that human values, including *goodness*, receive variable shapes – that is, they take on a myriad of different meanings – in different cultures and narratives, from the meta- to the personal. Taylor's caution that there is "no guarantee that universally valid goods should be perfectly combinable, and certainly not in all situations" points to the predicaments of multiculturalism, and of people involved in migration.[17]

According to their own lights, people will do what they assume to be good and right. Problems, consternation, and conflict arise when people's understanding of what is good and right diverges from that of others. Deeper problems, such as inequalities and marginalisation of people based on racism, arise and are compounded when the differences in peoples' definitions of what is good and right are taken to mean that there is something inherently wrong, or flawed, in who the others *are*. Thus, I qualify that the claim I make for a strong sense of self – based on people believing that being human is intrinsically wholesome – requires both understanding and respect for the facts that everyone *has* an orientation to the good, every person's definition of what is right and good is unique, and thus, the shape or expression of goodness also varies.

SENSE OF SELF IN LIVED EXPERIENCE

The participants' narratives show some factors that have been significant in weakening or strengthening their senses of self. Sense of self is complex, affected by many things, and these examples neither simplify nor universalise it. Each person is distinctive, and these participants have developed their senses of self to varying degrees and in unique ways. Nevertheless, their narratives reveal patterns and provide insights that contribute to understanding how others might also strengthen their senses of self.

The participants felt that their senses of self were most weakened by shame, self-doubt, low self-esteem, fear of being unable to cope, rejection, lack of recognition and respect from others, and others' negative judgements of them. Paradoxically, events or circumstances that they experienced as being difficult or stressful stimulated them to strengthen their senses of self. In common, even in hard times, they mostly persisted in believing that they were capable of dealing with whatever challenges, or demands life presented, although sometimes they felt (and at times actually were) without agency to change external conditions. Difficulties confronted them with what they perceived as their strengths and weaknesses and gave them opportunities to become more aware of and to question assumptions and meanings underlying their experiences and responses to events. For instance, Carol's sense of self is embedded in fulfilling what she believes is her "duty to use what you have been given". Carol believes that she has "got brains", and says she uses them to challenge every assumption, every belief – including her own – and to challenge her honesty and motivations. Her approach to life is to "give it a full run, put everything into it, no bullshit!" As a result, she has developed a deep self-trust, and a trust in her ability to learn through her body and through her senses. Carol's sense of self is reflected in her summary: "You can count on everything going wrong, but what you can also count on is that you are creative enough to figure your way out".

Major challenges for Carola came with her choice to migrate to Australia. Until she was re-examined, she was not allowed to practice medicine. Carola soon completed the written exam but had to wait many months to do the clinical exam. She said it was very difficult because "it's like you have to do a driving test but you're not allowed to drive for a year". It deeply challenged her identity, "taking the ground out from under me – being a doctor, working with children – this is what I do". Then, having passed the clinical exam, the next step was supervised training. Rather than being assigned to work in paediatrics, which was her specialty, Carola was sent to a drug and alcohol ward and an AIDS unit. She says her sense of self strengthened when she stopped attaching it to her identity as one or another kind of doctor, accepted herself just as she was, and valued her capability to come through times of stress. At some stages in their lives, all the participants experienced that they strengthened their senses of self whenever they accepted themselves as they were, and valued their capabilities, even though there was a vast difference in the conditions with which, for example, regular and irregular migrants had to deal.

Significantly, their narratives show that when participants have contributed to others in some way, their senses of self have strengthened. In praxis, I have consistently found that when people feel they make no contribution to others, or their worlds, they may value their possessions or their achievements, but they do not place much value in themselves. There is not always a clear moment in time when it could be said that a participant's valuing and sense of self shifted, but, retrospectively, it is possible to see patterns. Carol's sense of self-worth grew through her work to establish Canada's first provincial day-care centre for unwed mothers. Yukari expanded her sense of self when she became involved in environmental activism and then when working with healing modalities. Julian's sense of self deepened and grounded during his years of community health work in India, and as a teacher. There are examples in the narratives of all participants. To me, the most poignant is in Shoukat's account.

Like Shoukat, most people who brave a boat journey in search of asylum do so in a desperate attempt to save their families from persecution, but in detention they can do nothing. As Amnesty International testifies, "Detention is proven to have significant impacts on people's mental health, in particular for those with torture and trauma experiences"; people who might otherwise recover from trauma and torture are further traumatised by long periods of detention.[18] There are high levels of distress – anguish, fear, depression, hopelessness – resulting in diminished ability to cope, self-harm, and suicide. There is no end date to this mandatory detention, nor boundary to the powerlessness people experience. Shoukat was relatively fortunate, because he was *only* in detention for one year, and, even though he still suffers, in some ways he felt his sense of self was strengthened by the fact that he had survived. As detailed earlier, within months of his release, Shoukat became a voluntary bicultural worker for Red Cross, and active in the Hazara community, as well as working part-time and studying to qualify for work in aged care. Shoukat feels that doing such things affirms his value as a human being.

Nene changed from being morbidly afraid to having a confident sense of self that continues to grow through her endeavours with other young humanitarian refugees to reduce racism, and professionally, as a social worker. And recall Kiros' story, which shows a sequence of contributions from when he was a boy, and walked from village to village to teach younger children. As an adult he taught at university, then worked with reclamation of community and land devastated by war, all of which built his sense of self prior to his becoming a refugee. In Kenya, Kiros had no rights and no support for his family. At that point, with loss of identity and status, he knew that in others' eyes he had become of no account. At first, he felt himself to be nothing, but the need to survive called on his belief in himself, and on the flexibility and capability he had already developed. He is clear that his sense of self strengthened further when work he found to do with refugee agencies also supported others.

The desire to contribute to community is typical of irregular migrants. I have heard comments that these people want to contribute because they are so grateful to have been granted asylum. As shown earlier in participants' examples, irregular migrants are certainly grateful, but their contribution also expresses cultural values that are centred in being part of and building community in the place where they now live. Critiquing changes in multicultural-ism in Australia, Val Colic-Peisker comments on possibilities of such cultural values contributing to society and writes that:

> There is an increasing disenchantment with competitive individualism that dominates English-speaking societies. Questions are increasingly asked about whether competitive individualism contributes to the common good, enriches the social capital, aligns with the preservation of the natural environment and advances the quality of life.[19]

Comparison of the narratives of participants from individualistic back-grounds with those from communal cultures reveals distinct differences: Those raised in societies dominated by competitive individualism, to one degree or another, struggled to discover and define who they are, and in growing their senses of self they found deep values, including contribution and community. Those raised in communal cultures did not seem to have a question about self in the same way – they knew who they were *because of* the group and culture within which they grew up as an integral and contributing part. Living in a Western society demands that they adopt an individualistic way of interacting, at least to some extent, and Nene, Khadga, and Kiros appear to have achieved that fairly comfortably. Jun and Yukari, from Japan, seem to have embodied something of both. In part, that could be attributed to their experience of living for considerable periods in Western countries. It might also reflect introduction of individualistic, Western nar-ratives to Japanese culture begun with occupation by the United States since the Second World War.

STRENGTHENING SENSE OF PLACE

Arguably, sense of place cannot exist without a sense of the self who is sensing the place – a concept that draws attention to the inextricable, relational nature of these senses. As Jeff Malpas explains, our primary ontological awareness is so enmeshed in a world of which we are part that at first there is no sense of being separate from it.[20] Subsequent awareness of ourselves as singular is essential to ordinary functioning, even while place remains the existential ground of our being. However, it is not necessary to so shut off awareness of place that we experience ourselves as separate from it. Awareness of the rhizomatic, relational nature of people and place is evident in many accounts of people's experience; it is present in reports of Indigenous knowledge and practice when people live in traditionally cultural ways, and in retelling of Indigenous life in the past.[21] Other people lose that relational awareness, come to feel themselves to be separate and even alienated from place, and in that process both their senses of self and of place weaken. As noted earlier, such loss can occur during the course of a person's life because of disruptive and dissociative effects of major changes to places, environmental disasters, and migration and other mobilities. Those, however, are not the only factors that weaken senses of place.

In a study of contemporary calls for *reconnection* of young people to nature [*sic*] and natural resources, Peter Kraftl and his colleagues write that "the guiding assumption for the majority of research about childhoods-natures is that connection with nature is a perceived 'good' for humans, but especially for children".[22] Sense of place is affected by the early relationships children have with place – which of course is part of nature – and the quality of nurturing and relationship they have with primary carers, who are also part of place for a child. If those early relationships are compromised by lack of care, as Andy Fisher explains, children begin to desensitise themselves to cope – "we lose bodily feeling and blot out our perception of a hurtful world".[23] It is a physical and psychological shutting off, or "freezing" of sensitivity. As Fisher writes:

> The meaning that children almost invariably make out of their abuse is therefore that they must be bad, inadequate, wrong, useless, unimportant, and so on for others to be so mistreating them. Their creative adjustment is to blame themselves.[24]
>
> The self exists to the extent that we respond to and maintain our own process of felt interaction with the world. Where our lives are frozen this process of experiencing is *missing* – and thus so are we. We feel alien to ourselves, disorganized, out of it; the center does not hold.[25]

Overt mistreatment of children is not the only form of *abuse* – as we might ordinarily define that word. There is abuse in the practices of any meta-narrative that assumes human being is flawed. Recall discussion above, that the deliberate cultivation of individualism and competition promotes extreme disengagement and alienation of people from themselves, others, and place. I see this disengagement and the desensitisation described as grounds to propose that for alienation of people from place to be addressed *first* we need to address alienation of people from themselves. Deborah Du Nann Winter endorses that notion when considering what might be needed for "healing the split between planet and self", and writes that "the basic principle to be drawn . . . is that our ordinary experience of ourselves as separate autonomous beings is incomplete and inaccurate. Recognizing our embedded role in the larger ecosphere will require a perceptual shift . . . and/or a shift in consciousness".[26]

In like vein, I contend that to be open to fully experience sense of place it is necessary to challenge ideas that the human and natural are binary categories. Interested in how an ecological worldview promotes personal change, Mitchell Thomashow designed methods to help people to connect experientially with sense of place: these include a sense of place meditation to cultivate awareness, "to slow down for a while and cherish the surroundings" and other experiential exercises exploring and mapping built places and landscapes.[27] Freya Mathews also writes about being present wherever we are – city or country, ugly place or beautiful – opening awareness of the relationality of being in place, and living in a way that is engaged with place, by "adapting oneself to the immediately available".[28] Significantly, for approaches to deepening or strengthening sense of place to be effective, people need to be able to *feel* – sensorially, emotionally, consciously.

SENSE OF PLACE IN LIVED EXPERIENCE

Although such modes of strengthening sense of place as noted above may be useful for immigrants at some point in time, they are not usually a priority. First, immigrants have to orient themselves. To recapitulate, each place embraces so much: there is terrain, the land itself and the way it is configured, its topography, its climate; the plants that grow there, trees and shrubs and flowers and foods; the animals and birds, domesticated and wild (see figure 10.1). There are cities and towns, large buildings and small, various forms of housing; services and amenities; transport. There are governing bodies and other institutions, hospitals, medical facilities, churches, post offices, prisons, police. There are shops and markets, food, clothing, and other commodities, restaurants, and hotels. There are civic features, monuments and parks, places of entertainment, and sports grounds. There are people of all ages and many descriptions, and all the networks and connections among them, and from them and the place to others in other places. There are local mores and customs; economic, political, and cultural geographies, rights and responsibilities; perhaps a plurality of cultures, religions, languages; forms of education, varieties of work and professions. Immigrants have to contend with all these factors, and more.

Even for migrants arriving from places of similar background, there are challenges of orientation, to find their way around, and begin to connect and relate. Fluency in the primary language is a huge advantage, although there still are differences in accent and vernacular expressions. People migrating from places that are vastly different can find the new place shocking, physically, emotionally, and morally. People from hot countries can suffer from the cold; in Hobart's winter, for instance, Nene is adjusting, but says her mother suffers badly, because her knees were injured in the years of homelessness. Coming from Canada, Carol found the heat in Sydney's summer appalling. Often there is deep loneliness, and sense of loss – of family, friends, identity – of all that is familiar, as in Shoukat's story, for example. Finding others of similar origin is important, places of worship, even familiar foods. Their initial experiences provide the base for immigrants' senses of the new place, and the meanings they begin to give to it. Availability of supportive services is important, and recognition by those resident in the new place, or lack of it, plays a significant role.

Most meaningful in participants' narratives are not peak experiences or side trips to places named as sacred – although both those are there – but the

Figure 10.1. A cultural worker caring for refugee children and introducing them to aspects of place in their new land.

everydayness of their senses of place, about which much has already been related in their accounts of migration and resettlement. Insights can be drawn from their practices and beliefs to underline what may be useful to others in transition and to reflect on the primary question: how, in conditions of migration, might we engender well-being, providing opportunity for both people and place to flourish?

As noted earlier, one of the ways participants describe how they strengthen sense of self is by accepting themselves as they are. Similarly, they begin to strengthen their sense of a new place when they accept not only that the new place is as it is, but that it *is where they are*. The narratives show different experiences if participants were forced to migrate, or chose to relocate. Early in the process of accepting where they were, commonly they compared the new places with their places of origin; then realised that wishing and imagining they were elsewhere did not help them to settle, but blocked awareness of the place they were in. Part of accepting being in a new place was to let go of hankering for someplace else. Several of the participants felt that being told by local people that they were "so lucky to be here" did not help. Neither was it helpful to be told that they "should love" some aspect or other of their new environment.

At a time of dealing with loss, being able to share fond memories of their places of origin was an important part of making the transition to settle in new places. The act of sharing meant that their memories of other places were *included* in their experience of the new place, thus lessening the feeling of loss. The transition to establish a new home sometimes involved trying to make the new place like the old one. Making a conscious choice to be in the new place, and to make it home, facilitated their ability to adjust and settle. For example, knowing that they had come to Tasmania by choice meant that Khadga and Kiros and their families arrived eager to learn about their new place and to establish their homes. What helped the irregular migrants most was coming to realise that they were safe, which – for people who have been very traumatised – takes time. These participants were strongly motivated to establish themselves and grateful for opportunities especially of education, employment, and for their families to flourish.

For some participants, strengthening sense of place occurs primarily through the relationships they build with people and social structures. Others grow their sense of place mostly through relating to features of the environment, and to other than human life. All the participants' narratives show that the most important factor was interacting with the new place. Whatever their differences, in common participants strengthened their sense of a new place by becoming familiar with it, normalising their interactions with it, finding individual ways to be comfortable. Some did that by exploring, locating their immediate surroundings in wider environs. Others needed to identify and establish boundaries. Carol says that when she first came to Australia she was disturbed because there was no boundary between inside and outside. Explaining how "elements of the landscape have an effect on our psyche", she says that in Canada the extreme cold of winter dictates a boundary between inside and outside:

> When we go outside we get ready for the elements, putting on our clothes and our boots and all those sorts of things. But we also get psychologically ready, and that is particularly for women. Most women in Canada put on full makeup always, before they go out the door – so your personality changes, you have your inside person and your outside person.

Carol found ways to settle by giving a positive meaning to what was unfamiliar, for instance by deciding that a lack of boundaries gave her the freedom to be herself wherever she is. She recognises in herself a proclivity to perceive or explain experience in a new place by reference to the old one – she explained this was like painters in early colonial Australia and Canada, who looked through eyes still attuned to English countryside and painted landscapes distorted by that perception. So, Carol consciously uses her acute curiosity to deepen her sense of place, intentionally opening her eyes and all her senses to know place through bodily awareness:

> You can't get to know a cockatoo by comparing it with another bird. You just have to really want to know, "What *is* a cockatoo?" *Look* at the colour of the sky, the light, embrace it on its own terms, and don't try to interpret it. I think it's just that if you spend long enough in a landscape, you begin to see, your body begins to see, and it begins to differentiate things. So, I think that's part of how we come to terms with it.

At the beginning of this book, I asked if sense of place can only occur in regard to particular places, or if is it possible to have an ontological sense of place – an awareness of place as a fundament of being. I wondered to what extent people are actually *aware* of an ontological sense of place and, if they are, what makes that awareness possible?

Reflecting on these questions, I find that several of the participants feel their sense of place is both more and other than the meanings they give to particular places, or their attachment to them. Yukari, Carola, Julian, and Carol all identify strongly with a sense of the whole Earth as *home*. Broadly, they see the planet as *our place*, not in any sense of ownership, but rather in accord with the original meaning of ecology – from *Oikos*, meaning home, and *humanus*, which literally means "earth dweller".[29] Their sense of *our place* links to Doreen Massey's "progressive sense of place", but goes beyond that to an ontological sense of place.[30] As Edward Relph notes, what Massey proposes is a version of what he has called "sense of places . . . characterised by breadth rather than depth of experience" and "to do with the appreciation of relationships and differences between many places".[31] However, following Malpas' argument, Relph also writes that an ontological sense of place "has to do with our grasp of being in the world".[32] Of the participants, Carola, Yukari, and Julian express that ontological sense of place most clearly. To them, it is an awareness that seems inextricable from their expanded senses of self, described earlier. As Yukari explains, "Expanding my area of living is a *feeling* of the Earth extending out" from wherever she is currently located. She describes it also as being at one point on a network of places and feeling connection with the whole network, and it is concomitant with her experience of growing her sense of self in new places. Carol feels aware of such an expanded sense of place occasionally; but, for her, an ontological sense of place appears to be more contingent. For example, Carol feels such connection in natural and "sacred" places, but loses touch with it, and feels oppressed in buildings of concrete and fluorescent light.

Again, there is similarity in how participants strengthen their senses of self and how they strengthen their senses of place by contributing to the places they are in – for instance, taking food to share at a school or sports event, responsibly disposing of waste, buying locally, getting to know the neighbours, and gardening. Gardening is particularly important to them, discovering what grows, and the timing of planting and harvest, attuning to climate and seasonal changes, growing fresh vegetables and herbs, eating what is in season. Commonly, the participants speak of mutuality between themselves and their places of living; for instance, Yukari considers that each place calls her to respond to it differently – from the highly technological environment of Tokyo to her small village house in Guatemala, where modern conveniences are almost completely absent. As well as learning to know the place, in that relating she becomes aware of new aspects of herself. Through that experience she expands her sense of self, her sense of particular places, and deepens her ontological sense of place. Yukari says she understands belonging as a feeling and quality of relating, and thus, for her belonging is not about transferring attachment from one place to another, but opening herself to interact and relate as fully as she can wherever she is.

Mostly, participants' narratives demonstrate practical methods for relating to *a* place, how to apply sense of place to become familiar with and settle somewhere new. But, also their narratives show that a more ontological sense of place underlies those practices, and some of the participants are more aware of it than others. Carola describes "a mutual taking care of"; *place* embraces her family home and its neighbourhood, the hospital where she works, the city and rural areas from which her patients come, the women's soccer team in which she plays, the school her son attends, her garden, and a community garden – and the land itself. Carola says that place – encompassing all those expressions – is the home that nurtures her.

> At the same time, I take care of it, and by doing that it becomes mine. So, I make a physical connection. If I didn't have a choice of where I would be, then, for me the place is part of the planet. It's almost like, then, you just go a lot deeper into the place, and it becomes irrelevant exactly where you are. I imagine roots down into the ground, making it deeper, right to the core if I need to; right into the earth, and then that for me is "I am here".

Overall, participants' narratives show just how important and processual sense of place and sense of self are to the well-being of people migrating and resettling in new places. The interaction and relationality of sense of self and sense of place is clear in their narratives, as is the difference in the quality of their experiences when these senses have been weak, and when they have been strong. All the narratives demonstrate that weakening one of those senses weakens the other, and strengthening one of them encourages strengthening of the other. They are not really separable. In regard to sense of place, this dynamic is most obvious in the stories of the irregular migrants: once they felt safe and sustained in new places, their confidence in themselves, and their senses of self strengthened.

It is evident in all the narratives that a strong sense of self has helped participants to come to terms with new places, to believe in their ability to handle the challenges, to interact and contribute, to develop and strengthen their sense of a new place – to feel that they have autonomy and to establish new belonging. In other words, strong senses of self helped them to develop regimes of practice conducive to settling well and minimising difficulties. Participants most undermined themselves and weakened their senses of self and place when they doubted themselves, felt they lacked worth, and held back from interaction with people and place. Conversely, they strengthened those senses when they stayed true to what is most important to them – to what they most value, which aligns with Taylor's assertion that we "are selves only in that certain issues matter for us. What I am is essentially defined by [what has] significance for me".[33] Values are those highly abstract, significant qualities or desired experiential states that motivate the participants' choices and behaviours. With all the range of meanings they give to those values, whatever their backgrounds, in common these people value family, community, humanity, participation, contribution, beauty, capability, flexibility, learning, respect, and self-worth. To illustrate just two of these, in regard to place, Carola advocates:

> Look for something beautiful, and it can be really small. It can be in the dirt. Really look in the environment for something beautiful and then you can be there, and there is always something there. You make it your home.

And in regard to self, Kiros believes:

> Everyone has a worth, whether we understand it that way, or not. People are people – they have value, they have purpose in life. They may not know their own purpose, or self-worth; their understanding of themselves could be different. But to consider that some people are useless, or that they don't have purpose – I can't do that. I respect people, so that's it.

NOTES

1. Rosenhek, 204.
2. Joseph Campbell, The Power of Myth: Interviews with Bill Moyers. Australian Broadcasting Commission, 1987.
3. Luyckz et al., 52.
4. Dean, 18.
5. Foucault, 'Enlightenment', 54.
6. Rose, 17.
7. Cruikshank, 4.
8. Ibid., 88.
9. Ibid., 92–93.
10. Brown, xxii.
11. Ibid., 5 [original emphasis].
12. Ibid., 241.
13. Hill, 183.
14. Hill and Sattman-Frese.
15. Taylor, Sources, 4.
16. Ibid., 68.
17. Ibid., 61.
18. Amnesty; Bhugra, Craig, and Bhui; Bhugra and Gupta; van der Kolk, *Traumatic Stress*.
19. Colic-Peisker, 583.
20. Malpas, Place, 52.
21. Abram; Bateson, *Ecology of Mind*; Campbell; *Four Arrows*; Koya and Alo; Some; Suzuki and Knudtson.
22. Kraftl et al., 301.
23. Fisher, 73.
24. Ibid., 74.
25. Ibid., 75.
26. Winter, 264.
27. Thomashow, 15.
28. Mathews, *Reinhabiting Reality*, 53.
29. Buttimer, 3, 219.
30. Massey, 'Global Sense'.
31. Relph, 'Environmental Challenges', 37–8.
32. Ibid., 38.
33. Taylor, Sources, 34.

Chapter 11

What Legacy Will We Leave?

Never doubt that a group of thoughtful committed people can change the world, it is the only thing that ever has.[1]

[It] seems to me that we need . . . not so much seek to destabilize the present by pointing to its contingency, but to destabilize the future by recognizing its openness. That is to say, in demonstrating that no single future is written in our present, it might fortify our abilities in part through thought itself, to intervene in that present, and so to shape something of the future that we might inhabit.[2]

The challenges of contemporary migration that I set out to address at the beginning of this book have grown exponentially in recent decades. The shift in tenor of public discourse is disquieting. It started before 9/11 and has escalated since from calls to unite against a graphically depicted "axis of evil" to broadcast accusations and warnings of terrorism in many guises, against which Western nations would need to defend. As the numbers of migrants escalated, countries they sought to enter – some welcoming at first – began to react to increase border controls and keep people out. Media ramped up the rhetoric, and the migrant crisis "ignited highly emotional political and public debates as to whether, how many and which refugees should be taken in".[3] Brexit Britain's moves to reclaim its borders are

supposedly not racist or xenophobic . . . [but] racism has come in through the back door as it has become legitimate to want to decide who comes in and who stays out and to talk openly of migrants as undesirable . . . to castigate the "outsider" who does not fully belong. Hence the exponential growth in hate crimes and racist incidents during this period in Britain.[4]

Racism has spiralled, governments have changed policies, and instrumentally deployed ethnic discrimination to exclude others.[5] States have acted to control populations within and without their borders, marginalising specific ethnic groups such as the Rohingya in Myanmar, Muslims in Denmark and other countries, the Roma in France, Mexicans – and many others – in the United States of America, and Uighur Muslims in China.

Governments – for example in the European Union and Australia – claim that humanitarian grounds validate the military actions they have taken to keep people out of their countries. An Australian Prime Minister keeps in his office a trophy made by a mate to mark his efforts to "stop the boats" when he was immigration minister – reports with photos of the trophy in the *New York Times* and other media note that Australia's "Operation Sovereign Borders has attracted international condemnation for the way it treats refugees, as well as praise from countries looking for similar ways to close their borders to refugees".[6]

A resurgence of extreme right-wing fundamentalism has encouraged populist fears and increasingly polarised with more liberal and left-wing views. Anti-Semitism has begun to flare again, but most strongly the extreme right has fuelled fears of people of Muslim faith, castigating them as terrorists. As Sarah Fine unequivocally states, the "equivalence between terrorism and refugees is a false one".[7] Nevertheless, fears of caricatured Muslims have led many people to countenance policies and border actions that might otherwise seem inconceivable. The pinnacle of reaction based on such fears shows up in acts of terror committed by white supremacists. It is appalling that the perpetrators of those acts attack people who are the actual victims of those the Western world identifies as terrorists. In March 2019, a young Australian man killed fifty people and wounded many more in an attack on Muslim worshippers at mosques in Christchurch, New Zealand. He – the radicalised, extreme right-wing, white supremacist – is the terrorist in this story, not the Muslim children, men, and women peacefully praying, who were his victims. Surely, it is time for us to wake up. The light in all of it, an extraordinary beacon of possibility, is the New Zealand Prime Minister, Jacinda Ardern, whose response was immediate, heartfelt, and calling upon people – especially leaders – worldwide, to let go of hate and *othering,* and to strive to create a different world.

Which brings me to the point – there are voices calling out the racist, ethnic, and other discriminatory policies, the atrocities, the crises, and the suffering of migrants in many circumstances, but at government levels most responses at best maintain the status quo. At least some members of the general public appear to be largely desensitised; taken over emotional thresholds consistently and often by politicised and sensational news stories, and equally evocative pleas for support of homeless and suffering refugees, people disengage.

Crimes against humanity are clearly still *thinkable* and we seem to be in an era remarkable for the *banality of terror*. Rather than calling the contemporary situation a global migration crisis, I believe it is indeed more accurate to name it a genuine *human emergency*.[8] I recognise this as a time of human emergency because on many fronts humanity is at risk, but there is also the other meaning, that humanity is potentially on the brink of *emerging* into an altogether new stage of existence.

Considering what legacy might be left from this time for future generations, some scientists, environmental groups, and others prophesy dystopian futures likely to result if climate change continues apace and produces far worse problems of migration. Others insist that such disasters, or at least the worst of them, can still be averted if we act now, and some envisage futures remarkable for the care and potential well-being of all people, not just a privileged few. One such is Tim Flannery, whose ideas for ways in which to build a viable future conclude with a lightly sketched vision of the world in 2050. Flannery thinks "we must leave room in our imaginings for a fundamentally different and much better future", and he writes primarily of cleaning up environmental nature and establishing healthy, ecologically sound practices.[9] Increasingly, people are recognising that self and place need to be addressed together if change is to happen; for instance, psychologists write that "Experiencing the self as separate from nature is the foundation of humanity's damaged relationship to planetary resources".[10] These authors believe that the only solution is to find ways to radically change people's mindsets to ecologically grounded worldviews and that it is urgent to find ways to accelerate that process – that the "future of humanity – and indeed all life on Earth – depends on it".[11]

A first step in making any creative change to the future is to realise, as Nikolas Rose confirms, that "no single future is written in our present".[12] It is also useful to reiterate Gregory Bateson's understanding that a person's "beliefs about what sort of world it is will determine how he sees it and acts within it, and his ways of perceiving and acting will determine his beliefs about its nature".[13] The future is not predetermined; we can take it as a blank canvas and paint it freshly as we wish, if we are willing to do the work of examining and questioning our current mindsets, the assumptions upon which our narratives are based, the beliefs that determine how we see the world and act in it.

In this book, I have taken contemporary migration as a context within which to explore how common assumptions, beliefs, narratives, and worldviews of individuals and communities produce and distribute power and how people's senses of self and of place contribute to the politics of everyday living and are significant in establishing the politics of well-being. I have shown that there is a correlation between the variations in people's capability, the

Figure 11.1.   Engaging with the wonder of life.

quality of their experience, and the strength or weakness of their senses of self and place (see figure 11.1). It is evident that the strength or weakness of those senses is directly linked to people's *sensibilities* – that is, the degree to which they are physically and psychologically open to experience or desensitised, dissociated, and alienated from self, others, and place. I have shown that the fundamental assumption that human being is flawed compromises physical and psychological openness. The participants' narratives and other examples illustrate these points. Sometimes the participants have questioned their beliefs and challenged conditions of truth governing their behaviours. Taking charge of their own lives when and where they felt they could, increasingly, they have come to accept and to value themselves, and to take responsibility for the quality of their experience. To varying extents, they are aware that they have agency, especially in regard to the conduct of their own conduct. Even those who have had a weak sense of self at some stage of their journey have shown agency in their construction of senses of self and of place.

The participants' narratives show that their journeys were instrumental in the development of their senses of self and place, mainly because changing conditions and experiences challenged them to question their certainties. Of course, events other than migration introduce such challenges during a person's lifetime. Unless we set about it intentionally, however, the process of recognising assumptions that we have held relatively unconsciously is largely inductive and can take a very long time. If we wait for events or other circumstances to wake us up, we may wait until experience becomes intolerable before looking to identify the underlying assumptions and changing them. Many people are troubled about contemporary global migration – voluntary, of necessity, or coerced – and suggest its challenges are a wake-up call the whole global human community should heed, not just individual people or separate states. And many more are seriously worried at the warning signs of escalating climate change – wildfires, floods, cyclonic and hurricane-force winds, eruptions, rising sea levels, and extinction of many species. How much more extreme does the message need to get before we are willing to take sufficient action?

Narrative interpretation is particularly relevant for recognising patterns over time. The participants' narratives illustrate that just as an assumption of a flawed human nature perpetuates suffering and dysfunction, an assumption of the nature of human being as valuable and wholesome enables an integrated and relational sense of self that generates wholesome behaviour. Further, a more relational sense of self makes healthy relationships with others and with place more likely, regardless of whether people are mobile or sedentary.

So, using narrative interpretation, as well as questioning the assumption that human being is flawed, I have challenged the sedentarist belief that people must stay in one place to achieve any kind of well-being and shown evidence to the contrary. Although it might be possible that many people would like to spend their lives in the place where they were born, clearly that is not necessary for well-being. Rather, the belief shows up as instrumentally supporting the sovereignty of nation-states and their assumed rights to determine boundaries and who may cross them, in or out. Fostering fears of different others also supports such exclusivity and control of citizens to maintain it. The more people's experience is examined, the more obvious it becomes that our worldviews presuppose our experience. How enabling would it be to change those two fundamental premises? It is clear that valuing the place that is our existential ground of being is essential if we are to have an environment that supports human life. Equally, it is essential to value humanity enough to bother. Conceivably, a privileged and extremely wealthy few could live on in futuristically engineered enviro-capsules, but it is probably beyond science to terraform the entire planet despite dystopian fantasies. Perhaps in such future imaginary, small groups of people would survive in odd protected pockets, but with such breakdown of technology and communication that it would be like a second Flood, with commensurate loss of knowledge and resurgence of a Dark Age.

If we question the underlying assumptions of the *conditions of truth* we have used to construct human–nature dualisms, it is possible to recognise that we have constructed an arbitrary split, and in the doing have created the alienation of ourselves from both self and place that has brought us to this point. We cannot change the past – so in that sense, there is nothing to fix. However, if we make no change to our beliefs and behaviours arising from them, as always, those assumptions will continue to be proven in our experience of ourselves, each other, and the way our world is. We can relate to ourselves, others, and all that is encompassed in the notion of place, ethically, and with respect if we *free* ourselves to do so. Mitchell Dean clarifies the process:

> By making explicit the forms of rationality and thought that inhere in regimes of practices, by demonstrating the fragility of the ways in which we know ourselves and are asked to know ourselves and how we govern and are governed, an analytics of government can remove the taken-for-granted character of these practices. The point of doing this is not to make the transformation of these practices appear inevitable or easier, but to open the space in which to think about how it is possible to do things in a different fashion, to highlight the points at which resistance and contestation bring an urgency to their transformation, and even to demonstrate the degree to which that transformation may prove difficult.[14]

It may indeed prove difficult to liberate ourselves from the narratives of our lives – from the personally, culturally, and socially assumed conditions of truth we have so taken for granted through generations. But if we are to halt what some call a stampede towards dystopia, we need at least to start to think about and question some of those underlying assumptions. To begin, how might we reconstruct the notion of human being as other than fundamentally flawed? As I see it, we can only succeed in such endeavour if we are rigorous in separating being from doing – remembering that people are not their behaviour – valuing the person, telling the truth about the behaviour and responding in ways that allow behaviour to become more and more wholesome. To be able to respond usefully, we need to deepen understanding of what actually motivates and causes human behaviour, and to discover what is present when people behave well; we need to identify what is missing when people behave harmfully, that if it were present might allow people to behave any differently. Then we need to consider how we might change conditions so that people have what they need to be *and* behave well:

> In ancient Hawaii, so legend has it, if people acted in a way that was harmful, they were not judged as bad, or wrong; rather, it was understood that they had lost their balance, and the community would join in supporting each person to recover their balance and restore harmony.[15]

The dynamic of conflating being with doing creates one of the greatest difficulties in conceiving of human being more positively. When a person's behaviour is judged as evil, the person is labelled as being evil, the crux of the issue, famously, in Hannah Arendt's distinction of the *banality of evil* – the ordinary, everydayness of it being *thinkable* for people to behave monstrously – and recognition that punishing individual perpetrators does nothing to change the system that produced and licensed them. If we do nothing to transform the conditions of truth – meta-narratives, the epistemes, the social systems and conduct of conduct that underlie current conditions – the messages that it is becoming urgent for us to change trajectory will continue to amplify. There really is no point in trying to save the children if we are unwilling to do anything about the conditions they will experience as they grow up and that will go a long way to determining how they will come to behave as adults. Just as *we* do now, as adults *they* will demonise and kill each other, force or be forced into escalating migrations, compete for wealth, experience ever-greater environmental disasters and ever-widening inequalities, lay blame elsewhere, and leave each other to drown.

Of course there are individuals now who do none of those things. It is obvious that many people deplore the current state of affairs, actively protest inequities and injustices, devote some part of their lives to care of the environment and other-than-human nature, contribute when and where they can to alleviate the suffering of others, and work to create a better world. The paradox is that society is made of individuals *and* it is the complex web of individual assumptions and beliefs that go to form the matrix of the conditions of truth that underlie our social, cultural, and personal narratives. Thus, for change to occur, we need to transform the matrix and that can only occur with liberation of individuals from the illusory certainty that conditions of truth that have been so, are so, and always will be so.

To change the assumption that human nature is flawed directly affects our relationship with people we view as different to ourselves. Rather than being afraid of people because they are different, changing that assumption opens opportunity to discern whether the diversity is harmful, or enriching. We might also realise that we have our humanity in common and it is only in expression that it is different. It is well-documented that migrants' feelings of belonging and well-being when relocating strongly hinge on their individual agency and initiative, and that they are also "very dependent on the host society: whether that society accepts them at legal, social, political and cultural levels and helps them to feel safe" or contests their presence.[16] Again, change to the social matrix of response to migrants begins with individuals:

> If refugees and asylum seekers are to be welcomed into any society, and shown
> a measure of hospitality, this will not be because the polity is welcoming but

because society is so. Hospitality is . . . a human relation rather than an institutional one. To the extent that we try to design institutions that perform a function that only people can, it seems unlikely that our efforts will meet with much success.[17]

Many factors of course determine the quality of any relationship. Sense of self and sense of place are the essence of respectful relating – if we do not respect ourselves it is very difficult to truly respect anyone or anything else. I have shown that if people are indifferent and desensitised, they are likely to be dissociated and alienated from themselves, others, and place. The more closed people are the more they relate to their ideas or *maps* rather than to who or what is actually present. In other words, they relate to their descriptions, beliefs, assumptions about or identifications of others, of places, or even of themselves. But people are able to develop and strengthen their senses of self and place, and thus to open themselves to relating freshly. Communication in one form or another most powerfully provides opportunity for people to learn enough about each other to change, or at least modify their fears and judgements of different others. Consistently, people sharing their stories humanises them in others' eyes, whether the speaker is a migrant or a member of a host community. When it comes to future imaginaries, I find myself agreeing with Bateson's view:

> I myself attach a great deal of value to the diversity of cultural patterns which variegate the world. They are beautiful things, and the fact of their diversity I feel to be beautiful. The problem, as I see it, will be one of ordering this diversity, not by eliminating all the patterns except one, but by devising patterns of communication which will transcend the differences.[18]

And to do such ordering of diversity, we may also need to rethink what we mean when we use the term *difference*. Some authors hold that if we do not rethink what we mean by that word, "we may re-inscribe an ontology of difference in which opposition, dominance, and hierarchy are naturalized in our very (non)thinking".[19] I think we need to take a meta-view of the process of being in life, and to set out – intentionally – to identify and change assumptions and beliefs that have outworn their "use by" date.

Such is the state of contemporary migration that many people from diverse disciplines are researching and writing about many aspects of it, from current conditions migrants experience, to policies and reactions of governments, and suggestions from disparate views for ways to better the situation. For example, rather than spending billions on offshore detention centres, the same money would provide infrastructure, health, and education, and migrants could be fully employed in building those. And rather than spending billions attacking over-filled and leaky people-smuggling vessels, it would take very much less to provide safe passage for people seeking asylum. And just think! Some of that money could be used to support stability in countries of origin, rather than aggression, so that it would be safe for people to stay there. Many people are investigating and suggesting such things because the messages are getting louder, and the challenges are great. I have referred to these matters enough to provide relevant context, but my focus has been on what it is that people already do – can do – and might do more of to change their own and others' experience from suffering to well-being in circumstances of migration. In the contemporary clime, I have the greatest respect for the resilience, intelligence, and deep love of life shown by people, and their persistence in face of suffering. I am grateful for the evidence they provide of the significance of sense of self and sense of place and how it is possible for people to strengthen them. As people demonstrate, these sensibilities are vital to engendering well-being and providing opportunity for both people and place to flourish.

How would it be if we were to envisage a quieter, slower world; one with a rich and marvellous diversity of people, and other than human life, and places; a world within which there is time to think, to laugh and to love; a place where people pause to "smell the daisies" more often and earlier – and there are still daisies.

NOTES

1. Usually attributed to Margaret Mead.
2. Rose, 4–5.
3. Davis et al., 1.
4. Anthias, 139.
5. Fine, Karolewski, and Rajaram.
6. Maureen Dowd, Trump Finally Makes a Friend, *New York Times*, September 15, 2018; accessed September 19, 2018, https://www.nytimes.com/2018/09/15/opinion/columnists/trump-finally-makes-a-friend.html.

I Stopped These, SBS News, September 19, 2018, accessed September 19, 2018, https://www.sbs.com.au/news/i-stopped-these-pm-s-boat-trophy-gains-international-notoriety.
7. Sarah Fine, 2018.
8. Kukashthas; Garelli, Sciurba, and Tazzioli.
9. Flannery, 161.
10. Amel et al.
11. Ibid., 5.
12. Rose, 4–5. In quote opening this chapter.

13. Bateson, 314.
14. Dean, 36.
15. Dugan.
16. Davis et al., 4.
17. Kukasthas, 266–67.
18. Bateson and Donaldson, 34.
19. Cockayne et al., 594.

Selected Bibliography

Abram, David. *The Spell of the Sensuous: Perception and Language in a More-Than-Human World*. New York: Pantheon Books, 1996.

Adey, Peter. *Mobility. Key Ideas in Geography*. Milton Park, Abingdon, Oxon: Routledge, 2010.

Albrecht, Glenn, Gina-Maree Sartore, Linda Connor, Nick Higginbotham, Sonia Freeman, Brian Kelly, Helen Stain, Anne Tonna, and Georgia Pollard. 'Solastalgia: The Distress Caused by Environmental Change'. *Australasian Psychiatry* 15 Supplement (2007): S95–S98.

Amel, Elise, Christie Manning, Britain Scott, and Susan Koger. 'Beyond the Roots of Human Inaction: Fostering Collective Effort toward Ecosystem Conservation'. *Science* 356, no. 6335 (2017): 275–79 [1–5].

Anthias, Floya. 'Identity and Belonging: Conceptualizations and Reframings through a Translocational Lens'. In *Contested Belonging: Spaces, Practices, Biographies*, edited by Kathy Davis, Halleh Ghorashi, Peer Smets, and Melanie Eijberts, 137–59. Bingley: Emerald Publishing Limited, 2018.

Arendt, Hannah. *The Human Condition*. Chicago, IL: University of Chicago Press, 1958.

———. 'The Perplexities of the Rights of Man'. In *The Portable Hannah Arendt*, edited by Peter R. Baehr, 31–45. New York: Penguin Books, 2003.

———. 'The Portable Hannah Arendt'. In *The Portable Hannah Arendt*, edited by P. R. Baehr, lxiii, 575 pp. New York: Penguin Books, 2003.

Arsenijevic, Jovana, Erin Schillberg, Aurelie Ponthieu, Lucio Malvisi, Waell A. Elrahman Ahmed, Stefano Argenziano, Federica Zamatto, et al. 'A Crisis of Protection and Safe Passage: Violence Experienced by Migrants/Refugees Travelling Along the Western Balkan Corridor to Northern Europe'. *Conflict and Health* 11, no. 6 (2017): 1–9.

Austin, Jon, ed. *Culture and Identity*. 2nd ed. Frenchs Forest, NSW: Pearson Education Australia, 2005.

———. 'Identity & Identity Formation'. In *Culture and Identity*, edited by Jon Austin, 7–15. Frenchs Forest, NSW: Pearson Education Australia, 2005.

————. 'Space, Place & Home'. In *Culture and Identity*, edited by Jon Austin, 107–16. Frenchs Forest, NSW: Pearson Education Australia, 2005.

Babacan, Alper, and Hurriyet Babacan. 'Multiculturalism in Australia'. *'İş,Güç' The Journal of Industrial Relations and Human Resources* 9, no. 3 (July 2007): 25–38.

Bates, Diane C. 'Environmental Refugees? Classifying Migrations Caused by Environmental Change'. *Population and Environment* 23, no. 5 (May 2002): 465–77.

Bateson, Gregory. *Steps to an Ecology of Mind*. London: Intertext, 1972.

————. *Mind and Nature: A Necessary Unity*. Paperback ed. London: Fontana Paperbacks, 1979.

Bauman, Zygmunt. *Liquid Times: Living in an Age of Uncertainty*. Cambridge: Polity, 2007.

Bawden, Richard. 'Epistemic Aspects of Social Ecological Conflict'. In *Social Ecology: Applying Ecological Understandings to Our Lives and Our Planet*, edited by David Wright, Catherine E. Camden-Pratt, and Stuart B. Hill, 52–63. Stroud, UK: Hawthorn, 2011.

Bendixsen, Synnøve K. N. 'Becoming Members in the Community of Value: Ethiopian Irregular Migrants Enacting Citizenship in Norway'. In *Migration Matters*, edited by Mahni Dugan and Arnon Edelstein, 3–22. Oxford: Inter-Disciplinary Press, 2013.

Bennett, Samuel. *Australian Discovery & Colonisation*. A Currawong facsimile classic ed. Vol. 1, Sydney: Currawong Press, 1981.

Bergmann, Sigurd, and Tore Sager. *The Ethics of Mobilities: Rethinking Place, Exclusion, Freedom and Environment*. Transport and Society. Burlington, VT: Ashgate, 2008.

Berman, Gabrielle, and Yin Paradies. 'Racism, Disadvantage and Multiculturalism: Towards Effective Anti-Racist Praxis'. *Ethnic and Racial Studies* 33, no. 2 (2010): 214–32.

Bhugra, Dinesh, Tom Craig, and Kamaldeep Bhui. 'Conclusions: What Next?' In *Mental Health of Refugees and Asylum Seekers*, edited by Dinesh Bhugra, Tom Craig and Kamaldeep Bhui, 299–301. Oxford: Oxford University Press, 2010.

Bhugra, Dinesh, Tom Craig, and Kamaldeep Bhui, eds. *Mental Health of Refugees and Asylum Seekers*. Oxford: Oxford University Press, 2010.

Bhugra, Dinesh, and Susham Gupta, eds. *Migration and Mental Health*. Cambridge, New York: Cambridge University Press, 2011.

————. 'Globalisation: Internal Borders and External Borders'. In *Migration and Mental Health*, edited by Dinesh Bhugra and Susham Gupta, 56–67, 2011.

Bissell, David. 'Thinking Habits for Uncertain Subjects: Movement, Stillness, Susceptibility'. *Environment and Planning A* 43 (2011): 2649–65.

————. *Transit Life: How Commuting Is Transforming Our Cities*. Urban and Industrial Environments, edited by Robert Gottlieb. Cambridge, MA: MIT Press, 2018.

Blainey, Geoffrey. *Triumph of the Nomads: A History of Ancient Australia*. Melbourne: Macmillan, 1975.

Brown, Brené. *I Thought It Was Just Me (but It Isn't): Telling the Truth about Perfectionism, Inadequacy, and Power*. First paperback ed. New York: Gotham Books, 2008.

Bruner, Jerome. *Acts of Meaning*. Cambridge MA: Harvard University Press, 1993.

Bruner, Jerome S. *Making Stories: Law, Literature, Life*. 1st Harvard University Press paperback ed. Cambridge, MA: Harvard University Press, 2003.

Buscaglia, Leo. *Bus 9 to Paradise: A Loving Voyage*. New York: Ballantine Books, 1986.

Buttimer, Anne. *Geography and the Human Spirit*. Baltimore. MD: Johns Hopkins University Press, 1993.

Buzzelli, Michael. 'Sense of Place, Quality of Life and Local Struggles for Environmental Justice'. In *Sense of Place, Health, and Quality of Life*, edited by John Eyles and Allison Williams, 169–84. Aldershot, UK: Ashgate, 2008.

Cabrera, Daniel, and Damian Roland. 'How Do We Structure Knowledge? . . . Enter the Rhizome'. *Medium*, 2014, accessed April 14, 2019. https://medium.com/@cabreraerdr/how-do-we-structure-knowledge-enter-the-rhizome-e80fdcef99a2.

Cameron, John. 'Introduction'. In *Changing Places: Re-Imagining Australia*, edited by John Cameron. Sydney: Longueville Books, 2003.

Campbell, Joseph. *The Hero with a Thousand Faces*. 2nd ed. Princeton, PA: Princeton University Press, 1968.

Capra, Fritjof. *The Turning Point, Science, Society and the Rising Culture*. 1983 ed. Toronto: Bantam Books.

Cardwell, Paul James. 'Tackling Europe's Migration "Crisis" through Law and "New Governance"'. *Global Policy* 9, no. 1 (February 2018): 67–75.

Carruthers, Ashley. 'National Multiculturalism, Transnational Identities'. *Journal of Intercultural Studies* 34, no. 2 (2013): 214–28.

Castree, Noel. *Nature. Key Ideas in Geography*. London: Routledge, 2005.

Chase, Susan E. 'Taking Narrative Seriously: Consequences for Method and Theory in Interview Studies'. In *Interpreting Experience*, edited by Ruthellen Josselson and Amia Lieblich. The Narrative Study of Lives. 1–26. Thousand Oaks, CA: Sage, 1995.

Clark, Mary E. *In Search of Human Nature*. London: Routledge, 2002.

Cobb, Nancy J., ed. *Adolescence: Continuity, Change, and Diversity*. 2nd ed. Mountain View, CA: Mayfield Publishing, 1995.

Cock, Peter. 'Blackwhite Senses of Country: Toward an Intermediate Sense for Australian Environmental Wellbeing'. In *Changing Places: Re-Imagining Australia*, edited by John Cameron, 90–97. Sydney: Longueville Books, 2003.

Cockayne, Daniel G., Derek Ruez, and Anna Secor. 'Between Ontology and Representation: Locating Gilles Deleuze's 'Difference-in-Itself' in and for Geographical Thought'. *Progress in Human Geography* 41, no. 5 (2017): 580–99.

Colic-Peisker, Val. 'A New Era in Australian Multiculturalism? From Working-Class "Ethnics" to a "Multicultural Middle-Class"'. *International Migration Review* 45, no. 3 (Fall 2011): 562–87.

Collins, Jock. 'Multiculturalism and Immigrant Integration in Australia'. *Canadian Ethnic Studies* 45, no. 3 (2013): 133–49.

———. 'Rethinking Australian Immigration and Immigrant Settlement Policy'. *Journal of Intercultural Studies* 34, no. 2 (2013): 160–77, accessed 10 May 2013. http://dx.doi.org/10.1080/07256868.2013.781981.

Cresswell, Tim. *On the Move: Mobility in the Modern Western World.* London and New York: Routledge, 2006.

———.'Towards a Politics of Mobility'. *Environment and Planning D: Society and Space* 28 (2010): 17–31.

Cronon, William, ed. *Uncommon Ground: Rethinking the Human Place in Nature.* New York: W.W. Norton & Co., 1996.

———. 'The Trouble with Wildernesss; or, Getting Back to the Wrong Nature'. In *Uncommon Ground: Rethinking the Human Place in Nature,* edited by William Cronon, 69–90. New York: W.W. Norton & Co, 1996.

Crossley, Michele L. 'Introducing Narrative Psychology'. *Narrative, Memory and Life Transitions* (2002): 1–13. Huddersfield, UK: University of Huddersfield.

Cruikshank, Barbara. *The Will to Empower: Democratic Citizens and Other Subjects.* Ithaca, NY: Cornell University Press, 1999.

Curthoys, Ann, Ann Genovese, and Alexander Reilly. *Rights and Redemption: History, Law and Indigenous People.* Sydney: University of New South Wales Press, 2008.

Dahlman, Carl, William H. Renwick, and Edward F. Bergman, eds. *Introduction to Geography: People, Places, and Environment.* 5th ed. Boston, MA: Prentice Hall, 2011.

Damasio, Antonio R. *Descartes' Error: Emotion, Reason and the Human Brain.* London: Picador, 1994.

———. *The Feeling of What Happens: Body and Emotion in the Making of Consciousness.* 1st ed. New York: Harcourt Brace, 1999.

———. *Self Comes to Mind: Constructing the Conscious Brain.* 1st Vintage ed. New York: Vintage Books, 2012.

Danaher, Geoff, Tony Schirato, and Jen Webb. *Understanding Foucault.* Cultural Studies, edited by Rachel Fensham, Terry Threadgold and John Tulloch. Sydney: Allen & Unwin, 2000.

Dannreuther, Roland. *International Security: The Contemporary Agenda.* Cambridge, U.K.: Polity Press, 2007.

Davis, Kathy, Halleh Ghorashi, Peer Smets, and Melanie Eijberts. 'Introduction'. In *Contested Belonging: Spaces, Practices, Biographies,* edited by Kathy Davis, Halleh Ghorashi, Peer Smets and Melanie Eijberts, 1–15. Bingley, UK: Emerald Publishing Limited, 2018.

Davison, Aidan. 'The Trouble with Nature: Ambivalence in the Lives of Urban Australian Environmentalists'. *Geoforum* 39 (2008): 1284–95.

Dean, Mitchell. *Governmentality: Power and Rule in Modern Society.* London and Thousand Oaks, CA: Sage, 1999.

DeMiglio, Lily, and Allison Williams. 'A Sense of Place, a Sense of Wellbeing'. In *Sense of Place, Health, and Quality of Life,* edited by John Eyles and Allison Williams, 15–30. Aldershot, UK: Ashgate, 2008.

de Montety, Felix. 'Michel Foucault on Refugees – Previously Untranslated Interview from 1979'. Progressive Geographies, accessed 29 May 2019. https://progressive geographies.com/2015/09/29/michel-foucault-on-refugees-a-previously-untrans lated-interview-from-1979/.

Di Masso, Andrés, Daniel R. Williams, Christopher M. Raymond, Matthias Buchecker, Barbara Degenhardt, Patrick Devinke-Wright, Alice Hertzog, et al. 'Between Fixities and Flows: Navigating Place Attachments in an Increasingly Mobile World'. *Journal of Environmental Psychology* 61, no. February (2019): 125–33.

Dimitrov, Vladimir. 'Complex Dynamics of Narratives'. Accessed 14 January 2014. http://www.zulenet.com/vladimirdimitrov/pages/home.html.

Doran, Peter. 'Care of the Self, Care of the Earth: A New Conversation for Rio+20?' *Review of European Community & International Environmental Law* 21, no. 1 (2012): 31–43.

Drengson, Alan, Bill Devall, and Mark. A. Schroll. 'The Deep Ecology Movement: Origins, Development, and Future Prospects (toward a Transpersonal Ecosophy)'. *International Journal of Transpersonal Studies* 30, no. 1–2 (2011): 101–17.

Dugan, Mahni. *The Integrity of Loving*. Sydney: Neuroads, 1991.

———. *The Rainbow Bridge*. 77. Sydney: Neuroads, 1997.

Dugan, Mahni, and Arnon Edelstein, eds. *Migration Matters*. Oxford: Inter-Disciplinary Press, 2013.

Dunn, K. M., A. Kamp, W. S. Shaw, J. Forrest, and Yin Paradies. 'Indigenous Australians' Attitudes Towards Multiculturalism, Cultural Diversity, 'Race' and Racism'. *Journal of Australian Indigenous Issues* 13, no. 4 (2010): 19–31.

Eccles, Jacquelynne. 'Who Am I and What Am I Going to Do with My Life? Personal and Collective Identities as Motivators of Action'. *Educational Psychologist* 44, no. 2 (2009): 78.

Edelstein, Arnon. 'Intimate Partner Femicide (IPF) among Ethiopian Women in Israel'. In *Migration Matters*, edited by Mahni Dugan and Arnon Edelstein, 141–65. Oxford: Inter-Disciplinary Press, 2013.

Elden, Stuart. 'Government, Calculation, Territory'. *Environment and Planning D: Society and Space* 25 (2007): 562–80.

———. 'A Conversation with Stuart Elden: Approaching Territory'. *Journal of Landscape Architecture* 24 (2016): 18–23.

———. 'Legal Terrain – the Political Materiality of Territory'. *London Review of International Law* 5, no. 2 (2017): 100–224.

———. 'The Uncollected Foucault'. *Foucault Studies* 20 (December 2015): 340–53.

Elliott, Anthony, and John Urry. *Mobile Lives*. International Library of Sociology. London: Routledge, 2010.

Erikson, Eric H. *Childhood and Society*. 2nd ed. New York: Norton, 1963.

Esipova, Neli, Julie Ray, and Anita Pugliese. 'The Demographics of Global Internal Migration'. *Migration Policy Practice Journal* III, no. 2 (April-May 2013): 3–5.

Evanoff, Richard. 'Bioregionalism and Cross-Cultural Dialogue on a Land Ethic'. *Ethics, Place & Environment: A Journal of Philosophy & Geography* 10, no. 2 (2007): 141–56.

Eyles, John. *Senses of Place*. Warrington, UK: Silverbrook Press, 1985.

Eyles, John, and Allison Williams, eds. *Sense of Place, Health, and Quality of Life*. Aldershot, UK: Ashgate, 2008.

Farbotko, Carol. 'Representing Climate Change Space: Islographs of Tuvalu'. (PhD thesis, University of Tasmania, 2008).

Farbotko, Carol, Elaine Stratford, Mark Jackson, and Suvendrini Perera. 'Review Forum. Reading Suvendrini Perera's Australia and the Insular Imagination'. *Political Geography* 30, no. 6 (2011): 329–38.

Farbotko, Carol, Elaine Stratford, and H. Lazrus. 'Climate Migrants and New Identities? The Geopolitics of Embracing or Rejecting Mobility'. *Social & Cultural Geography* 17, no. 4 (2016): 533–52.

Favell, Adrian. 'Migration, Mobility and Globaloney: Metaphors and Rhetoric in the Sociology of Globalization'. *Global Networks* 1, no. 4 (2001): 389–98.

Fell, Bruce. 'The Power and Influence of the Synthetic Cortex'. In *Social Ecology: Applying Ecological Understandings to Our Lives and Our Planet*, edited by David Wright, Catherine E. Camden-Pratt and Stuart B. Hill, 126–33. Stroud, UK: Hawthorn, 2011.

Fine, Sarah. 'Immigration and Discrimination'. In *Migration in Political Theory: The Ethics of Movement and Membership*, edited by Sarah Fine and Lea Ypi, 125–50. Oxford: Oxford University Press, 2016.

Fisher, Andy. *Radical Ecopsychology: Psychology in the Service of Life*. SUNY Series in Radical Social and Political Theory. Albany, NY: State University of New York Press, 2002.

Flannery, Tim. *Sunlight and Seaweed: An Argument for How to Feed, Power and Clean up the World*. Melbourne: Text Publishing, 2017.

Foucault, Michel. 'Truth and Power'. *In Power/Knowledge: Selected Interviews & Other Writings 1972–1977 by Michel Foucault*, edited by Colin Gordon, 107–33. New York: Pantheon Books, 1980.

———. 'Technologies of the Self'. In *Technologies of the Self: A Seminar with Michel Foucault*, edited by Luther H. Martin, Huck Gutman and Patrick H. Hutton, 16–49. Amherst: University of Massachusetts Press, 1988.

———. 'What Is Enlightenment?' Translated by Catherine Porter. In *The Essential Foucault: Selections from Essential Works of Foucault, 1954–1984*, edited by Paul Rabinow and Nikolas S. Rose, 43–57. New York: New Press, 2003.

———. 'So Is It Important to Think?' In *The Essential Foucault: Selections from Essential Works of Foucault, 1954–1984*, edited by Paul Rabinow and Nikolas S. Rose, 170–73. New York: New Press, 2003.

Foucault, Michel, H. Becker, R. Fornet-Betancourt, and A. Gomez-Müller. 'The Ethics of the Concern of the Self as a Practice of Freedom: An Interview with Michel Foucault'. Translated by P. Aranov and D. McGrawth. In *The Essential Foucault: Selections from Essential Works of Foucault, 1954–1984*, edited by Paul Rabinow and Nikolas S. Rose, 25–42. New York: New Press, 2003.

Four Arrows. 'The Missing Link: Neuroscience and Indigenous Wisdom'. *Noetic Now*, May 2012, no. 22, 1–3.

Fox, Peter D. 'International Asylum and Boat People: The Tampa Affair and Australia's "Pacific Solution"'. *Maryland Journal of International Law* 25, no. 1 (2010): 356–73.

Fozdar, Farida, and Brian Spittles. 'The Australian Citizenship Test: Process and Rhetoric'. *Australian Journal of Politics and History* 55, no. 4 (2009): 496–512.

Frankl, Viktor E. *Man's Search for Meaning: The Classic Tribute to Hope from the Holocaust*. Translated by Ilse Lasch and Gordon W. Allport. London: Rider, 2004.

Gallagher, Shaun, and Jonathan. Shear. 'Editors' Introduction'. In *Models of the Self,* edited by Shaun Gallagher and Jonathan. Shear, ix–xviii. Thorverton, UK: Imprint Academic, 1999.

Garelli, Glenda, Alessandra Sciurba, and Martina Tazzioli. 'Introduction: Mediterranean Movements and the Reconfiguration of the Military-Humanitarian Border in 2015'. *Antipode* 50, no. 3 (2018): 662–72.

Ghorashi, Halleh, Kathy Davis, and Peer Smets. 'Epilogue: Reflections on Belonging, Otherness and the Possibilities of Friendship'. In *Contested Belonging: Spaces, Practices, Biographies,* edited by Kathy Davis, Halleh Ghorashi, Peer Smets, and Melanie Eijberts, 379–89. Bingley UK: Emerald Publishing Limited, 2018.

Giddens, Anthony, and Philip W. Sutton. *Sociology.* 6th ed. Cambridge: Polity, 2009.

Gómez, Ángel, D. Conor Seyle, Carmen Huici, and William B. Swann, Jr. 'Can Self-Verification Strivings Fully Transcend the Self-Other Barrier? Seeking Verification of Ingroup Identities'. *Journal of Personality and Social Psychology* 97, no. 6 (2009): 1021.

Goodman, Grant K., Robert E. Ward, Martin Bronfenbrenner, Edward Norbeck, John M. Maki, and Harry Emerson Wildes. 'The American Occupation of Japan: A Retrospective View'. In *International Studies, East Asian Series*, edited by Grant K. Goodman. Kansas. MI: University of Kansas, 1968.

Goodson, Ivor F. *Developing Narrative Theory: Life Histories and Personal Representation.* London: Routledge, 2013.

Graham, Sonia, and John Connell. 'Nurturing Relationships: The Gardens of Greek and Vietnamese Migrants in Marrickville, Sydney'. *Australian Geographer* 37 (2006): 375–93.

Grandi, Filippo. 'Forced Displacement Today: Why Multilateralism Matters'. *Brown Journal of World Affairs* XXIV, no. 11 (2018): 179–89.

Grof, Stanislav. *Beyond the Brain: Birth, Death and Transcendence in Psychotherapy.* New York: State University of New York, 1985.

———. *Realms of the Human Unconscious: Observations from LSD Research.* New York: Viking Press, 1975.

———. *The Holotropic Mind: The Three Levels of Human Consciousness and How They Shape Our Lives.* First Harper Collins paperback ed. San Francisco, CA: Harper, 1993.

Hall, Joan Kelly. *Teaching and Researching: Language and Culture.* Applied Linguistics in Action. Edited by Christopher N. Candlin and David R. Hall. 2nd ed. New York: Routledge, 2013.

Hall, Stuart. 'New Cultures for Old'. In *A Place in the World? Places, Cultures and Globalization*, edited by Pat Jess and Doreen B. Massey. Oxford: Oxford University Press, 1995.

Hatton, Timothy J. 'Emigration from the UK, 1870–1913 and 1950–1998'. Research paper, University of Essex, 2003.

Havel, Václav. 'The Search for Meaning in a Global Civilisation'. In *The Truth about the Truth,* edited by W. T. Anderson, 232–38. New York: Tartcher/Putnam, 1995.

Head, Lesley M., Pat Muir, and Eva Hampel. 'Australian Backyard Gardens and the Journey of Migration'. *Geographical Review* 94 (2004): 326–47.

Hill, Stuart B. 'Autonomy, Mutualistic Relationships, Sense of Place and Conscious Caring: A Hopeful View of the Present and Future'. In *Changing Places: Re-Imagining Australia*, edited by John Cameron, 180–96. Sydney: Longueville, 2003.

Hillman, James. 'A Psyche the Size of the Earth: A Psychological Forward'. In *Ecopschology*, edited by T. Roszak, M. E. Gomes and A. J. Kanner. San Francisco: Sierra Club, 1995.

Hiruy, Kiros. 'Finding Home Far Away from Home: Place Attachment, Place-Identity, Belonging and Resettlement among African-Australians in Hobart'. Master's thesis, University of Tasmania. 2009.

Hopkins, Peter. 'Social Geography I: Intersectionality'. *Progress in Human Geography* XX, no. X (2017).

Horton, John, and Peter Kraftl. 'Rats, Assorted Shit and "Racist Groundwater": Towards Extra-Sectional Understandings of Childhoods and Social-Material Processes'. *Environment and Planning D: Society and Space* 36, no. 5 (2018): 926–48.

———. 'Three Playgrounds: Researching the Multiple Geographies of Children's Outdoor Play'. *Environment and Planning A: Economy and Space* 50, no. 1 (2018): 214–35.

Høstaker, Roar. 'The Rhizome, the Net and the Book'. *Empedocles: European Journal for the Philosophy of Communication* 8, no. 2 (2017): 151–65.

Hugo, Graeme. *Migration and Climate Change*. UK: Edward Elgar Publishing, 2013.

Hugo, Graeme, Helen Feist, and George Tan. 'Internal Migration and Regional Australia, 2006–11'. *Australian Population & Migration Research Centre Policy Brief* 1, no. 6 (June 2013): 1–6.

Isseri, Sanam, Nithi Muthukrishna, and Susan C. Phiilpott. 'Immigrant Children's Geographies of Schooling Experiences in South Africa'. *Educational Research for Social Change* 7, no. 2 (2018): 39–56.

Josselson, Ruthellen. 'The Hermeneutics of Faith and the Hermeneutics of Suspicion'. *Narrative Inquiry* 14, no. 1 (2004): 1–28.

Josselson, Ruthellen, and Amia Lieblich, eds. *The Narrative Study of Lives*, Narrative Study of Lives, vol. v 1. Newbury Park, CA: Sage, 1993.

Jupp, James. 'A Changing Identity'. *Australian Quarterly* 79, no. 3, *Australian Institute of Policy & Science 75th Year Commemorative Issue* (May-June 2007): 66–70.

Kamp, Alanna, Oishee Alam, Kathleen Blair, and Kevin Dunn. 'Australians' Views on Cultural Diversity, Nation and Migration, 2015–16'. *Cosmopolitan Civil Societies: an Interdisciplinary Journal* 9, no. 3 (2017): 61–84.

Kan, Chiemi, Mayumi Karasawa, and Shinob Kitayama. 'Minimalist in Style: Self, Identity, and Well-Being in Japan'. *Self and Identity* 8, no. 2 (2009): 300–17.

Kanahele, George Hu'eu Sanford. *Ku Kanaka Stand Tall: A Search for Hawaiian Values*. Honolulu, HI: University of Hawaii Press, 1986.

Karlsen, Elibritt. 'Australia's Offshore Processing of Asylum Seekers in Nauru and PNG: A Quick Guide to Statistics and Resources', edited by Parliamentary Services. Canberra: Department of Parliamentary Services, 2016.

Karolewski, Ireneusz Pawel, and Roland Benedikter. 'Europe's Refugee and Migrant Crisis: Economic and Political Ambivalences'. *Challenge* 60, no. 3 (2017): 294–320.

Keck, Charles S. 'Radical Educations in Subjectivity: The Convergence of Psychotherapy, Mysticism and Foucault's "Politics of Ourselves"'. *Ethics and Education* 14, no. 1 (2018): 102–15.

Keith, Michael, and Steve Pile, eds. *Place and the Politics of Identity*. London: Routledge, 1993.

Khorana, Sukhmani. 'The Problem with Empathy'. *Overland* (2015). Accessed October 16, 2018. https://overland.org.au/2015/10/the-problem-with-empathy/.

Knox, William. *Industrial Nation: Work, Culture and Society in Scotland, 1800–Present*. Edinburgh: Edinburgh University Press, 1999.

Kobayashi, Audrey, Valerie Preston, and Ann Marie Murnaghan. 'Place, Affect, and Transnationalism through the Voices of Hong Kong Immigrants to Canada'. *Social & Cultural Geography* 12, no. 8 (2011): 871–88.

Korzybski, Alfred. *Science and Sanity: An Introduction to Non-Aristotelian Systems and General Semantics*. 4th ed. Lakeville, MN: The International Non-Aristotelian Library Publishing Company, 1933. Sixth Printing 1980.

Kowal, Emma. 'The Politics of the Gap: Indigenous Australians, Liberal Multiculturalism, and the End of the Self-Determination Era'. *American Anthropologist* 110, no. 3 (2008): 338–48.

Koya, Cresantia F., and Allan A. Alo. 'Blood, Bones and Breath: The Human Body as a Cultural Site of Knowing; Exploring Multiple Notions of Trinity with Va Tapuia as the Basis of the Lived Samoan Experience'. In *Annual Samoa Conference, Samoa:* unpublished, 2011.

Kraftl, Peter, Jose Antonio Perrella Balastieri, Arminda Eugenia Marques Campos, Benjamin Coles, Sophie Hadfield-Hill, John Horton, Paulo Valladares Soares, et al. '(Re)Thinking (Re)Connection: Young People, "Natures" and the Water – Energy – Food Nexus in São Paulo State, Brazil'. *Transactions of the Institute of British Geographers* 44 (2018): 299–314.

Kukasthas, Chandran. 'Are Refugees Special?' *In Migration in Political Theory: The Ethics of Movement and Membership*, edited by Sarah Fine and Lea Ypi. Oxford: Oxford University Press, 2016.

Kymlicka, Will. *Multiculturalism: Success, Failure, and the Future. Report of Migration Policy Institute*. Brussels: Migration Policy Institute, 2012.

La Guardia, J. 'Developing Who I Am: A Self-Determination Theory Approach to the Establishment of Healthy Identities'. *Educational Psychologist* 44, no. 2 (2009): 90.

Levrau, François. 'Esteem and Respect in a Multicultural Society: A Critical Analysis of Axel Honneth's Recognition Theory'. In *Migration Matters*, edited by Mahni Dugan and Arnon Edelstein. Oxford: Inter-Disciplinary Press, 2013.

Lieblich, Amia. 'Looking at Change: Natasha, 21: New Immigrant from Russia to Israel'. In *Narrative Study of Lives*, edited by Ruthellen Josselson and Amia Lieblich. Narrative Study of Lives; V. 1, 92–129. Newbury Park CA: Sage, 1993.

Lieblich, Amia, Dan P. McAdams, and Ruthellen Josselson. *Healing Plots the Narrative Basis of Psychotherapy*. Washington: American Psychological Association, 2004.

Lopez, Mark. 'Reflections on the State of Australian Multiculturalism and the Emerging Multicultural Debate in Australia 2005'. *People and Place* 13, no. 3 (2005): 33–40.

Luyckx, Koen, Seth J. Schwartz, Bart Soenens, Maarten Vansteenkiste, and Luc Goossens. 'The Path from Identity Commitments to Adjustment: Motivational Underpinnings and Mediating Mechanisms'. *Journal of Counseling and Development* 88, no. 1 (2010): 52.

Macy, Joanna. 'Working through Environmental Despair'. In *Ecopsychology: Restoring the Earth, Healing the Mind,* edited by Theodore Roszak, Mary E. Gomes and Allen D. Kanner, 240–59. San Francisco: Sierra Club Books, 1995.

Madell, Geoffrey. *The Identity of the Self.* Edinburgh: Edinburgh University Press, 1981.

Maillet, Pauline, Alison Mountz, and Kira Williams. 'Exclusion through Imperio: Entanglements of Law and Geography in the Waiting Zone, Excised Territory and Search and Rescue Region'. *Social and Legal Studies* 27, no. 2 (2018): 142–63.

Malpas, Jeff. *Place and Experience: A Philosophical Topography.* Cambridge, UK: Cambridge University Press, 1999.

———.'Beginning in Wonder: Placing the Origin of Thinking'. In *Philosophical Romanticism,* edited by Nikolas Kompridis, 282–98. London: Routledge, 2006.

———. *Heidegger's Topology: Being, Place, World.* Cambridge: MIT Press, 2008.

Mann, Jatinder. 'The Introduction of Multiculturalism in Canada and Australia 19602–1970s'. *Nations and Nationalism* 18, no. 3 (2012): 483–503.

Manzo, Lynne C. 'The Experience of Displacement on Sense of Place and Well-Being'. In *Sense of Place, Health, and Quality of Life,* edited by John Eyles and Allison Williams, 87–104. Aldershot, UK: Ashgate, 2008.

Marano, Hara Estroff. *A Nation of Wimps: The High Cost of Invasive Parenting.* 1st ed. New York: Broadway Books, 2008.

Massey, Doreen B. 'A Global Sense of Place'. *In Space, Place, and Gender,* viii, 280 p. Minneapolis: University of Minnesota Press, 1994.

———. 'The Conceptualisation of Place'. In *A Place in the World? Places, Cultures and Globalization,* edited by Pat Jess, Doreen B. Massey and Open University. Oxford, New York: Oxford University Press, 1995.

Massey, Morris. *The People Puzzle: Understanding Yourself and Others.* Reston, VA: Publisher, 1979.

Massumi, Brian. 'Potential Politics and the Primacy of Preemption'. *Theory and Event* 10, no. 2 (2007). https://muse.jhu.edu/ Accessed 20 May 2019.

Mathews, Freya. 'Becoming Native to the City'. In *Changing Places: Re-Imagining Australia,* edited by John Cameron. Sydney: Longueville Books, 2003.

———. *Reinhabiting Reality: Towards a Recovery of Culture.* Sydney: University of New South Wales Press, 2005.

Maturana, H. R. 'Self-Consciousness: How? When? Where?' *Constructivist Foundations* 1, no. 3 (2006): 91–102.

Maturana, H. R., and F. J. Varela. *The Tree of Knowledge: The Biological Roots of Understanding.* Boston, MA: New Science Library, Shambala, 1987.

McAdams, Dan P., Ruthellen Josselson, and Amia Lieblich, eds. *Identity and Story: Creating Self in Narrative.* 1st ed, The Narrative Study of Lives. Washington, DC: American Psychological Association, 2006.

———. 'Introduction'. In *Identity and Story: Creating Self in Narrative,* edited by Dan P. McAdams, Ruthellen Josselson, and Amia Lieblich, 3–11. Washington, DC: American Psychological Association, 2006.

McLeod, John. 'The Significance of Narrative and Storytelling in Postpsychological Counseling and Psychotherapy'. In *Healing Plots: The Narrative Basis of Psychotherapy*, edited by Ruthellen Josselson, Amia Lieblich, and Dan P. McAdams, 11–27. Washington, DC: American Psychological Association, 2004.

McMaster, John, and Jon Austin. 'Race: A Powerful Axis of Identity'. In *Culture and Identity*, edited by Jon Austin, 49–72. Frenchs Forest, NSW: Pearson Education Australia, 2005.

Merchant, Carolyn. 'Reinventing Eden: Western Culture as a Recovery Narrative'. In *Uncommon Ground: Rethinking the Human Place in Nature*, edited by William Cronon, 132–70. New York: W.W. Norton & Co., 1996.

Metz, Isabel, Eddy S. Ng, Nelarine Cornelius, Jenny M. Hoobler, and Stella Nkomo. 'A Comparative Review of Multiculturalism in Australia, Canada, the United Kingdom, the United States and South Africa'. In *Research Handbook of International and Comparative Perspectives on Diversity Management*, edited by Alain Klarsfeld, Eddy S. Ng, Lize A. E. Booysen, Liza Castro Christiansen, and Bard Kuvaas, 131–70. Cheltenham, MA: Edward Elgar Publishing, 2016.

Metzner, Ralph. 'The Place and the Story: Ecopsychology and Bioregionalism'. *The Humanistic Psychologist* 26, no. 1–3 (1998): 35–49.

Mezirow, Jack. *Transformative Dimensions of Adult Learning*. The Jossey-Bass Higher and Adult Education Series. 1st ed. San Francisco, CA: Jossey-Bass, 1991.

Miller, Linn Maree. 'Being and Belonging'. PhD thesis, University of Tasmania, 2006.

Miramontez, Daniel R., Veronica Benet-Martinez, and Angela-Minhtu D. Nguyen. 'Bicultural Identity and Self/Group Personality Perceptions'. *Self and Identity* 7, no. 4 (2008): 430–45.

Modood, Tariq. *Multiculturalism: A Civic Idea*. 2nd ed. Cambridge: Polity, 2013.

Morley, David. *Home Territories: Media, Mobility and Identity*. Comedia. London: Routledge, 2000.

Mountz, Alison, Kate Coddington, R. Tina Catania, and Jenna M. Lloyd. 'Conceptualizing Detention: Mobility, Containment, Bordering, and Exclusion'. *Progress in Human Geography* 37, no. 4 (2012): 522–41.

Myers, Norman. 'Environmental Refugees: A Growing Phenomenon of the 21st Century'. *Philosophical Transactions of the Royal Society of London* (2001): 609–13.

Naess, Arne. 'Self-Realization: An Ecological Approach to Being in the World'. 4th Keith Roby Memorial Lecture in Community Science. Murdoch, WA: Murdoch University, 1986.

Noble, Greg. 'The Discomfort of Strangers: Racism, Incivility and Ontological Security in a Relaxed and Comfortable Nation'. *Journal of Intercultural Studies* 26, no. 1 (2005): 107–20.

Nolan, David, Karen Farquharson, Violeta Politoff, and Timothy Marjoribanks. 'Mediated Multiculturalism: Newspaper Representations of Sudanese Migrants in Australia'. *Journal of Intercultural Studies* 32, no. 6 (2011): 655–71.

Nynäs, Peter. 'From Sacred Place to an Existential Dimension of Mobility'. In *The Ethics of Mobilities: Rethinking Place, Exclusion, Freedom and Environment*, edited by Sigurd Bergmann and Tore Sager, 157–76. Burlington, VT: Ashgate, 2008.

Oberman, Kieran. 'Immigration as a Human Right'. In *Migration in Political Theory: The Ethics of Movement and Membership*, edited by Sarah Fine and Lea Ypi. Oxford: Oxford University Press, 2016.

Olsen, Jonathan. 'The Perils of Rootedness: On Bioregionalism and Right Wing Ecology in Germany'. *Landscape Journal*, March (2000): 73–83.

Pakulski, Jan. 'Confusions about Multiculturalism'. *Journal of Sociology* 50, no. 1 (2014): 23–36.

Pakulski, Jan, and Stefan Markowski. 'Globalisation, Immigration and Multiculturalism – the European and Australian Experiences'. *Journal of Sociology* 50, no. 1 (2014): 3–9.

Pallasmaa, Juhani. 'Existential Homelessness – Placelessness and Nostalgia in the Age of Mobility'. In *The Ethics of Mobilities: Rethinking Place, Exclusion, Freedom and Environment*, edited by Sigurd Bergmann and Tore Sager, 143–56. Burlington, VT: Ashgate, 2008.

Pardy, Maree, and Julian C. H. Lee. 'Using Buzzwords of Belonging: Everyday Multiculturalism and Social Capital in Australia'. *Journal of Australian Studies* 35, no. 3 (September 2011): 297–316.

Paterson, Helen M. 'Haptic Geographies: Ethnography, Haptic Knowledges and Sensuous Dispositions'. *Progress in Human Geography* 33, no. 6 (2009): 766–88.

Payne, Martin. *Narrative Therapy: An Introduction for Counsellors*. 2nd ed. London: Sage, 2006.

Pearce, Joseph Chilton. *Magical Child*. Harmondsworth, UK: Plume, 1992.

———. *The Death of Religion and the Rebirth of Spirit: A Return to the Intelligence of the Heart*. Rochester, VT: Park Street Press, 2007.

Perera, Suvendrini. *Australia and the Insular Imagination: Beaches, Borders, Boats, and Bodies*. 1st ed. New York: Palgrave Macmillan, 2009.

Perkins, Harvey C., and David C. Thorns. *Place, Identity and Everyday Life in a Globalizing World*. London, New York: Palgrave Macmillan, 2012.

Perkins, Rachel, and Marcia Langton, eds. *First Australians: An Illustrated History*. Melbourne: The Miegunyah Press, Melbourne University Publishing Ltd, 2008.

Piaget, Jean. *The Child's Conception of the World*. St. Albans, UK: Paladin, 1973.

Pile, Steve, and Nigel J. Thrift, eds. *Mapping the Subject: Geographies of Cultural Transformation*. London: Routledge, 1995.

———. 'Introduction'. In *Mapping the Subject*, 1–12.

———. 'Mapping the Subject'. In *Mapping the Subject*, 13–51.

Plumwood, Val. *Feminism and the Mastery of Nature*. Opening Out: Feminism for Today. London: Routledge, 1993.

———. 'Shadow Places and the Politics of Dwelling'. *Australian Humanities Review*, no. 44 (2008): 139–150.

Power, Paul. ' "Stopping the Boats": Australia's Appalling Example to the World'. (Paper presented at the Globalization of High Seas Interdiction: Sale's Legacy and Beyond, Yale Law School, New Haven, USA, 8 March 2014).

Rabinow, Paul, and Michel Foucault. 'Polemics, Politics, and Problematizations: An Interview with Michel Foucault'. In *The Essential Foucault: Selections from Essential Works of Foucault, 1954–1984*, edited by Paul Rabinow and Nikolas S. Rose, 18–24. New York: New Press, 2003.

Rajaram, Prem Kumar. 'Refugees as Surplus Population: Race, Migration and Capitalist Value Regimes'. *New Political Economy* 23, no. 5 (2018): 627–39.

Rapport, Nigel. 'Migrant Selves and Stereotypes: Personal Context in a Postmodern World'. *In Mapping the Subject: Geographies of Cultural Transformation,* edited by Steve Pile and Nigel J. Thrift, 267–88. London: Routledge, 1995.

———. 'Introduction'. *In Human Nature as Capacity: Transcending Discourse and Classification*, edited by Nigel Rapport. New York: Berghahn Books, 2010.

RCA, Refugee Council of Australia. 'Offshore Processing Statistics'. Sydney, 2019.

Read, Peter. *Returning to Nothing: The Meaning of Lost Places*. Cambridge, UK: Cambridge University Press, 1996.

———. *Belonging: Australians, Place and Aboriginal Ownership*. Cambridge, UK: Cambridge University Press, 2000.

Reith, Gerda. 'Consumption and Its Discontents: Addiction, Identity and the Problems of Freedom'. *British Journal of Sociology* 55, no. 2 (2004): 283–300.

Relph, Edward C. *Place and Placelessness*. Research in Planning and Design. London: Pion, 1976.

———. 'Senses of Place and Emerging Environmental Challenges'. In *Sense of Place, Health, and Quality of Life*, edited by John Eyles and Allison Williams, 31–44. Aldershot, UK: Ashgate, 2008.

Reuveny, Rafael. 'Climate Change-Induced Migration and Violent Conflict'. *Political Geography* 26, no. 6 (2007): 656–73.

Riviere, Peter. 'Shamanism and the Unconfined Soul'. In *From Soul to Self,* edited by M. James C. Crabbe, 70–88. London: Routledge, 1999.

Rodaway, Paul. 'Exploring the Subject in Hyper-Reality'. In *Mapping the Subject: Geographies of Cultural Transformation*, edited by Nigel J. Thrift and Steve Pile, 241–66. London: Routledge, 1995.

Roof, David. 'The Ethical Domains of Individualism: Nietsche and Emerson's Pedagogic Vision'. *Philosophical Studies in Education* 45 (2014): 168–78.

Rose, Nikolas. *Inventing Our Selves: Psychology, Power, and Personhood*. Cambridge Studies in the History of Psychology. Cambridge, UK: Cambridge University Press, 1996.

———. *The Politics of Life Itself: Biomedicine, Power, and Subjectivity in the Twenty-First Century*. Information Series. Princeton, NJ: Princeton University Press, 2007.

Rosenhek, Ruth. 'Earth Community'. In *Stories of Belonging: Finding Where Your True Self Lives,* edited by Kali Wendorf. Sydney: Finch, 2009.

Roszak, Theodore. *Unfinished Animal*. New York: Harper & Row, 1977.

———. *The Voice of the Earth. An Exploration of Ecopsychology*. Grand Rapids, MI: Phanes Press, 2001.

Rouse, Roger. 'Questions of Identity'. *Critique of Anthropology* 15, no. 4 (1995): 351–80.

Russell, Peter. *The Awakening Earth: The Global Brain*. London: Ark, 1982.

———. *Waking up in Time: Finding Inner Peace in Times of Accelerating Change*. Revised edition of The White Hole in Time 1992 ed. Novato, CA: Origin Press, 1998.

Ryback, David. 'Humanistic Psychology's Impact and Accomplishments'. *Journal of Humanistic Psychology* 51, no. 4 (2011): 413–18.

Sale, Kirkpatrick. 'There's No Place Like Home'. *The Ecologist* 31, no. 2 (March 2001): 40–43.

Sandercock, Leonie. *Towards Cosmopolis: Planning for Multicultural Cities*. Chichester, UK: J. Wiley, 1998.

———. 'When Strangers Become Neighbours: Managing Cities of Difference'. *Planning Theory & Practice* 1, no. 1 (2000): 13–30.

Sattmann-Frese, Werner J., and Stuart B. Hill. *Learning for Sustainable Living, Psychology of Ecological Transformation*. Morrisville, NC: Lulu, 2008.

Schiff, Brian. 'The Function of Narrative: Toward a Narrative Psychology of Meaning'. *Narrative Works: Issues, Investigations, & Interventions* 2, no. 1 (2012): 33–47.

Sciurba, Alessandra, and Filippo Furri. 'Human Rights Beyond Humanitarianism: The Radical Challenge to the Right to Asylum in the Mediterranean Zone'. *Antipode* 50, no. 3 (2018): 763–82.

Seed, John. *Thinking Like a Mountain: Towards a Council of All Beings*. Philadelphia, PA: New Society Publishers, 1988.

Seigel, Jerrold E. *The Idea of the Self: Thought and Experience in Western Europe since the Seventeenth Century*. New York: Cambridge University Press, 2005.

Seligman, Martin E. P. *Learned Optimism: How to Change Your Mind and Your Life*. 1st Vintage Books ed. New York: Vintage Press, 2006.

Serov, Banafsheh. 'Jasmine Petals'. In *Stories of Belonging: Finding Where Your True Self Lives*, edited by Kali Wendorf, 10–29. Sydney: Finch, 2009.

Sheldrake, Rupert. *The Rebirth of Nature: The Greening of Science and God*. London: Rider, 1991.

Sheller, Mimi. 'Mobility, Freedom and Public Space'. In *The Ethics of Mobilities: Rethinking Place, Exclusion, Freedom and Environment*, edited by Sigurd Bergmann and Tore Sager, 25–38. Burlington, VT: Ashgate, 2008.

Sheller, Mimi, and John Urry. 'The New Mobilities Paradigm'. *Environment and Planning A* 38 (2006): 207–226.

Slavkova, Magdalena. 'Negotiating "Bulgarianness" by Bulgarians and Gypsies Abroad'. In *Migration Matters*, edited by Mahni Dugan and Arnon Edelstein, 65–86. Oxford: Inter-Disciplinary Press, 2013.

Slominski, Peter, and Florian Trauner. 'How Do Member States Return Unwanted Migrants? The Strategic (Non-)Use of "Europe" during the Migration Crisis'. *Journal of Common Market Studies* 56, no. 1 (2018): 101–18.

Some, Sobonfu. 'A Place to Call Home'. In *Stories of Belonging: Finding Where Your True Self Lives*, edited by Kali Wendorf. Sydney: Finch, 2009.

Stalker, Peter. 'Stalker's Guide to International Migration'. http://www.pstalker.com/migration/index.php.

Stratford, Elaine. 'Belonging as a Resource: The Case of Ralphs Bay, Tasmania, and the Local Politics of Place'. *Environment and Planning A* 41, no. 4 (2009): 796–810.

———. *Geographies, Mobilities, and Rhythms over the Life Course: Adventures in the Interval*. New York: Routledge, 2015.

Stratford, Elaine, Elizabeth McMahon, Mark Jackson, Carol Farbotko, and Suvendrini Perera. 'Reading Suvendrini Perera's Australia and the Insular Imagination'. *Political Geography* 30, no. 6 (2011): 329–38.

Strawson, Galen. 'The Self'. In *Models of the Self*, edited by Shaun Gallagher and Jonathan. Shear, 1–24. Thorverton, UK: Imprint Academic, 1999.

Sui, Daniel, and Dydia DeLyser. 'Crossing the Qualitative- Quantitative Chasm I: Hybrid Geographies, the Spatial Turn, and Volunteered Geographic Information (VGI)'. *Progress in Human Geography* 36, no. 1 (2012): 111–24.

Suzuki, David T., and Peter Knudtson. *Wisdom of the Elders: Honoring Sacred Native Visions of Nature*. New York: Bantam Books, 1992.

Tarnas, Richard. *The Passion of the Western Mind: Understanding the Ideas That Have Shaped Our World View*. New York: Ballantine Books, 1991.

Taylor, Charles. *Sources of the Self: The Making of the Modern Identity*. Cambridge, MA: Harvard University Press, 1989. 7th Printing 1994.

———. *The Ethics of Authenticity*. Cambridge, MA: Harvard University Press, 1992.

Thomashow, Mitchell. *Ecological Identity: Becoming a Reflective Environmentalist*. Cambridge, MA: MIT Press, 1995.

Trilling, Daniel. *Lights in the Distance: Exile and Refuge at the Borders of Europe*. London: Picador, 2018.

Tuan, Yi-Fu. *Space and Place: The Perspective of Experience*. Minneapolis, MI: University of Minnesota Press, 1977.

Tucci, Sabrina. 'Libyan Cooperation on Migration within the Context of Fortress Europe: North/South Relations During the Last Decade of the Gaddafi Era'. In *Migration Matters*, edited by Mahni Dugan and Arnon Edelstein. Oxford: Inter-Disciplinary Press, 2013.

Urry, John. *Sociology Beyond Societies: Mobilities for the Twenty-First Century*. London: Routledge, 2000.

———. *Mobilities*. Cambridge, UK: Polity, 2007.

van der Kolk, Bessel A. 'Clinical Implications of Neuroscience Research in PTSD'. *Annals of the New York Academy of Sciences* 1071, no. 1 (2006): 277–93.

van der Kolk, Bessel A., A. McFarlane, and Lars Weisaeth, eds. *Traumatic Stress: The Effects of Overwhelming Experience on Mind, Body, and Society*. Paperback ed. New York: Guilford Press, 2007.

Walsh, Kate. *The Changing Face of Australia: A Century of Immigration 1901–2000*. Sydney: Allen & Unwin, 2001.

Webber, Kimberley, and Andrea Fernandes. 'Australia's Migration History'. NSW Migration Heritage Centre, http://www.migrationheritage.nsw.gov.au/belongings-home/about-belongings/australias-migration-history/.

Wendorf, Kali, ed. *Stories of Belonging: Finding Where Your True Self Lives*. Sydney: Finch, 2009.

Weston, Anthony. *The Incomplete Eco-Philosopher: Essays from the Edges of Environmental Ethics*. SUNY Series in Environmental Philosophy and Ethics. Albany, NY: SUNY Press, 2009.

Wheeler, Annie. 'Working Together for a Change'. Independent Study, University of Western Sydney, 2004.

Widdershoven, Guy A. M. 'The Story of Life: Hermeneutic Perspectives on the Relationship between Narrative and Life History'. In *The Narrative Study of Lives*, edited by Ruthellen Josselson and Amia Lieblich, 1–19. Newbury Park, CA: Sage, 1993.

Wihtol de Wenden, Catherine. 'Migration, Citizenship and the Global Refugee Crisis'. *Journal of Intercultural Studies* 39, no. 2 (2018): 224–37.

Winter, Deborah Du Nann. *Ecological Psychology: Healing the Split between Planet and Self*. Mahwah, NJ: Lawrence Erlbaum Associates, 2003.

Wise, Amanda. 'Sensuous Multiculturalism: Emotional Landscapes of Inter-Ethnic Living in Australian Suburbia'. *Journal of Ethnic and Migration Studies* 36, no. 6 (2010): 917–37.

Woodsmall, Wyatt. *INLPTA Trainer's Training*. 249, A1–15. Munich: International Neuro-Linguistic Programming Trainer's Association, 1994.

Zibung, Jessica. 'The Hypocrisy of Hybridity'. *Overland: Progressive Culture Since 1954*. 232, no. Spring (2018): 39–44.

Index

About the Author

Mahni Dugan is Adjunct University Associate within the Institute for Study of Social Change at the University of Tasmania, Australia. An educator, counsellor, and consultant with more than forty years of experience in the field of professional and personal development, Mahni has worked internationally with people from many and diverse backgrounds, cultures, and age groups. Her research interest is multidisciplinary and focuses on social change and well-being of people and place.

www.ingramcontent.com/pod-product-compliance
Lightning Source LLC
Chambersburg PA
CBHW021811270326
41932CB00007B/142